*indie *porn

A CAMERA OBSCURA BOOK

indie *porn*

Revolution, Regulation, and Resistance

ZAHRA STARDUST

Duke University Press   *Durham and London*   2024

© 2024 Duke University Press. All rights reserved
Printed in the United States of America on acid-free paper ∞
Project Editor: Liz Smith
Designed by Courtney Leigh Richardson
Typeset in Whitman and Real Head by Westchester Publishing Services

Library of Congress Cataloging-in-Publication Data
Names: Stardust, Zahra, [date] author.
Title: Indie porn : revolution, regulation, and resistance / Zahra Stardust.
Other titles: Camera obscura book.
Description: Durham : Duke University Press, 2024. | Series: A camera
obscura book | Includes bibliographical references and index.
Identifiers: LCCN 2024007308 (print)
LCCN 2024007309 (ebook)
ISBN 9781478031062 (paperback)
ISBN 9781478026815 (hardcover)
ISBN 9781478060048 (ebook)
Subjects: LCSH: Pornography—Law and legislation. | Pornography—
Government policy. | Pornography—Censorship. | Pornography—Social
aspects. | Pornography—Economic aspects. | Capitalism. | BISAC: SOCIAL
SCIENCE / Gender Studies | SOCIAL SCIENCE / Media Studies
Classification: LCC HQ471 .S737 2024 (print) | LCC HQ471 (ebook) |
DDC 306.77/1—dc23/eng/20240422
LC record available at https://lccn.loc.gov/2024007308
LC ebook record available at https://lccn.loc.gov/2024007309

For Stormy

Contents

Part III. The Hustle

Part IV. Tensions

This book was written on the lands of the Gadigal, Bedegal, Turrbal, Yaggera, Yugambeh, and Wangeriburra peoples, land which was stolen and, over 230 years after invasion, has never been ceded.

As the oldest living culture on earth, Aboriginal and Torres Strait Islander peoples continue to resist ongoing colonization, theft, and genocide. Every day I learn from the strength, power, wisdom, and sovereignty of First Nations people and their continuing connections to land, water, and culture. I commit to the fight for treaty, truth telling, and land back.

Always was, Always will be, Aboriginal Land.

Acknowledgments

No piece of work can ever be attributed to one person alone. This book found its way together from many late-night tête-à-têtes over herbal tea, deliberations over vegan dinners, and conversations on porn sets. It was written from windowsills, strip clubs, changing rooms, mountain cottages, Ute trays, and airplanes; from fragments of thoughts and scribbles on Post-it notes that accumulated in desk drawers and the bottom of bags over many years.

It formulated and gestated across continents and stewed in circular rumination before it found any articulate form on paper. The semblance of thoughts finally came together in my rainbow home over endless cups of chai surrounded by a library of open books.

My attempt has been to capture a movement that is vibrant and shifting, and subjects whose ideas, lives, and experiences continue beyond its pages. My challenge has been to offer a critique of its complexity and contradictions, knowing we are all part of it together, acknowledging that such an account is always curated and incomplete.

I owe so much gratitude to the participants who shared their insights, expertise, and critical minds with me. Knowledge is not discovered—this text draws from the collective wisdom, writing, organizing, autobiography, and art-making of sex workers who came before me.

To all the ex-lovers who made porn with me, the perverts who funded me, the friends who collaborated with me, the queers who have held me—it's been wild.

Thank you to Jiz Lee for being such a source of knowledge, integrity, and kindness; to Constance Penley for your hospitality, storytelling, and championing; and to Lynn Comella for your direction and mentorship.

Thank you to Kath Albury, for your pep talks and encouragement; Daniel Joyce, for your handwritten notes and generosity; Ramaswami Harindranath, for your expertise and guidance; and Ben Golder, for renewing my love of critical legal theory.

Thank you to Scarlet Alliance for your consultation on my methods and drafts, especially to Jules Kim, Janelle Fawkes, and Gala Vanting. Thank you to Elizabeth Ault and Benjamin Kossak at Duke University Press for holding me in good hands.

To Lorelei Lee, Danielle Blunt, and Gabriella Garcia for the writing-turned-therapy sessions which allowed us to grieve and birth so many things; Kendra Albert for being a facilitator of new friendships; Chibundo Egwuatu and Mireille Miller-Young for your brilliant thinking and open-ended chats; Nic Suzor for cultivating such a warm intellectual culture.

To Ash for the pivotal Tarot readings; Teresa for the old-school film equipment; Caitlin Hamilton, Emilie Auton, and Kavitha Suthanthiraraj for your PhD peer support; Nick Apoifis for asking me the hard questions; Hilary Caldwell for your offers of writing retreats; Kerryn Drysdale for your expert eye and pot plants; Ivan Crozier for recounting BDSM history over backyard tea.

To all the rescue pups that have accompanied me: my hot water bottle Ichigo, my study buddy Sabretooth, my lady of leisure Beverley, and my panty thief Sparky.

To the spaces that have nourished me: Golden Lotus for the phở; Khamsa Café for the black sesame donuts; Ruby Lonesome for the Buddha bowls.

And my family: to my brother-in-love Drift for the home-cooked meals; my heartthrob River, who forever challenges and inspires me; and my magical, iridescent, miracle Stormy—you changed my life.

Finally, to all the sex workers walking the halls of academia before me, alongside me, and after me: Solidarity to you (you know who you are).

Cinematic Intimacies

Toronto

It's 2 a.m., and I am filming a threesome scene in a hotel suite in downtown Toronto in front of a BBC news journalist. The hotel is abuzz with an influx of professional purveyors of pornography from around the world—performers, producers, pioneers—all in town for the ninth annual Feminist Porn Awards. This is the last of three shoots I've done to take advantage of the unusual scenario of having a wealth of performers and producers all in one central location. I still have welts from a spanking scene I filmed with UK kink connoisseur Blake for Australian "smart porn" site Bright Desire and Blake's Dreams of Spanking, but they seem to heal in time for my shoot with red-haired beauty April Flores for my own subscription website, Explicit Diary of an Exhibitionist Femme.

The Feminist Porn Awards themselves are a spectacle: chandeliers, champagne, evening gowns, burlesque shows, pole dancers, a VIP party, and even a hair-and-makeup artist offered to nominees. One could be forgiven for thinking we were at the Oscars, only the names of the categories are somewhat sassier (including the Golden Beaver Award, Smutty School Teacher Award, Hottest Dyke Film, and Best Boygasm) and the trophies are shaped like various types of butt plugs. I am awarded Heart Throb of the Year and, to celebrate, am shooting a film with James Darling and Wolf Hudson, porn icons from San Francisco and Los Angeles. James and Wolf are on either side of me, each with one of my feet in their mouths, and indie porn pioneer Courtney Trouble is holding the camera, zooming in on the saliva. The BBC journalist sits in the corner, studiously taking notes. He is so quiet I forget he is there until I am editing the footage later and catch a glimpse of his feet.

I have traveled approximately thirty hours from Gadigal Country (so-called Sydney, Australia) to get here. A few days earlier I lined up in six-degree

Feminist Porn Awards 2014, Capitol Theatre, Toronto. Image by K. Boyce.

temperatures outside a local cinema in a queue that seemed to go for miles to attend a screening of *Public Provocative Porn: The Year's Best in Feminist Film 2014*. I showed a short called *The One on the Bottom*, filmed and edited with a former lover, that critiqued Australia's queerphobic approach to classification and censorship. Coming from a country with criminal penalties for the public screenings of explicit material, it was surreal to experience a public screening of pornography at an established cinema, like a trip back to the seventies "golden era" of porn. There was tiered seating, a mezzanine level, surround sound, a giant screen—even popcorn. Our piece was shot old school—on a miniDV—but most were shot with digital cameras, and one was recorded entirely on an iPhone.

The awards, screenings, and workshops are happening alongside the second annual Feminist Porn Conference at the University of Toronto. For me, it's the highlight of the week. The space is teeming with performers, directors, producers, academics, tech geeks, and sponsors coming together for industry talk. The foyer is bursting with vibrant flyers for feminist, queer, and indie content: Madison Young is selling her framed anus prints; performer Siouxsie Q conducts interviews for her Whorecast podcast. There are practical workshops on self-care and allyship for sex workers; business track sessions on website development and affiliate programs; panels on sexual racism and labor; and informative sessions on the archiving of feminist pornography as part of special historical collections.

I am booked to speak on a panel entitled "Feminist/Porn Battlegrounds," and the title itself is telling. At the heart of the conference are ongoing conversations about the politics of pornography. When we market our content as real and authentic, does this work obscure the sexual labor behind its production? How might a focus on visibility and inclusion operate to financially reward tech platforms instead of performers? Can porn really be marketed as feminist if the workers report poor experiences on set? These issues continue to thread through the feminist porn movement in years to come, prompting new approaches to labor practices and production ethics, and demanding a restructuring of the technological, economic, and legal environment in which pornography is regulated.

Berlin

A year later, it is opening night of the Berlin Porn Film Festival 2015. The walls are plastered with flyers, graffiti, and ticket stubs, and in my peripheral vision I catch María Bala's bright yellow stickers, "Support Your Local Pornographers." The festival boasts seven days of content running from 10 a.m. to 2 a.m. with concurrent workshops, panels, lectures, and exhibitions, including an opening midnight screening of *The Rocky Horror Picture Show*. Running since 2006, PFF is an alternative, independent film festival in Kreuzberg at the oldest cinema in Germany, Moviemento. Amateurs and artists around the world are invited to submit, and each year the festival screens an average of one hundred films to around eight thousand viewers, 50 percent of whom are international visitors.

The program, in German and English, features a mix of categories, including fetish porn, gay porn, lesbian porn, queer and trans porn, as well as sex work shorts, political porn, and experimental porn. One of the most entertaining categories is "fun porn," which includes fisting porn with sock puppets, a musical-horror-drama centered on philosopher Georges Bataille's *Story of the Eye*, and a pious interpretation of the Bible, *Fuck Me in the Ass 'Cause I Love Jesus*. The films are irreverent and playful, but also tender and moving.

The breadth and diversity of content is spectacular, from short films to feature films to documentaries. There are biographical films charting the lives of such key figures as Peter de Rome, the "grandfather of gay porn," historical films documenting the development of the queer flagging hanky code, and subversive takes on old fairy tales—in Wes Hurley's *Zolushka*, a gay adaptation of *Cinderella* meets *Tom of Finland*, the protagonist loses his boot and potential suitors line up to offer him rim jobs. This year the festival has a focus on sex and disability, featuring such films as Antonio Centeno and Raúl de la Morena's *Yes, We Fuck!* and AJ Dirtystein's *Don't Pray for Us*, challenging stereotypes of infantilization and portraying people with functional diversity as desirous and desiring.

I have been invited to be on the jury for the kurzfilmwettbewerb, the short film competition. We nominate Blake for *Houseboy*, a film about a queer submissive in a kinky household. Notably, Blake has just had their website Dreams of Spanking shut down by the British Authority for Television on Demand (ATVOD) pursuant to new Audiovisual Media Services (AVMS) Regulations. The regulations prohibit the depiction of BDSM activities in online video-on-demand services, and Blake has been fighting a public battle to have it reinstated. Many of the films are community collaborations, and a genre called *docuporn* explores the lives and stories of queer communities in urban centers in Germany, Sweden, and the United States. Australian producers are also represented: Morgana Muses's film *It's My Birthday and I'll Fly If I Want To* sees her elevated in rope bondage for her fiftieth birthday; Gala Vanting's film *Chrysalis* features a rebirth experience by the sea as Magnolia is sewn with needles and feathers; Ms Naughty's *Perversion for (Feminist Fun and) Profit* offers a humorous take on anti-porn morality.

Much of this work is festival release only: Porn film festivals like this offer rare opportunities to see experimental, low-budget films with aesthetics, bodies, and practices that otherwise may not be sold or screened on commercial platforms. The atmospheric pleasure of the cinema is far removed from the supposedly isolated experiences of porn viewership in the home or by the couple: All around me I can hear gasps, laughs, groans, murmurs, heckling, and affectionate giggles, and viewers ask critical questions of the filmmakers in the Q and A that follows each session. It's a far cry from the regulatory imaginary that fears what pornography is purportedly teaching its supposedly innocent audiences. Loud, interesting, and exuberant conversations continue in the hallways, bar, stairwell, pavement, and the queue for the gender-neutral bathrooms.

Amsterdam

As I travel across Europe, I have the opportunity to undertake an intensive Summer Institute on Sexuality, Culture and Society program at the University of Amsterdam. It is official Pride month, and the city is alive for summer. Amsterdam is often referred to as the Venice of the North, and legs dangle from houseboats that line the city's 165 canals. I cycle past the Homomonument, three pink triangles of granite, a memorial to commemorate the persecution of queers during the Holocaust. I visit the iconic bronze statue of Belle, in the Oudekerksplein (the Old Church's Square), erected in honor of sex workers, and drop in for tea with Mariska Majoor, founder of the Prostitute Information Centre, an educational center open to students, visitors, and sex workers that houses a mini museum of sex work. And, of course, I can't help but find time to squeeze in some porn projects—which, thanks to sexuality activist and educator Marije Janssen, have been funded by the city's Pride committee.

Our first event is educational. Erotic imaginist Gala Vanting and I are presenting a squirting workshop called "Get a Handjob" in leather bar The Eagle, and it's the first time this men-only leather bar has been opened up to women, trans, nonbinary, and gender-diverse patrons. Gala has gathered medical diagrams, porn scenes, and supplies ready for me to hop up into the sling for our live squirting demo and Q and A with our participants, who now include a couple of my university classmates. In the evening, I screen six of my films at the independent Filmhuis Cavia cinema for a sold-out session called "Queer Sex Down Under." Filmhuis Cavia has been running nonprofit special films for more than thirty years at the old Princess Beatrix Schippersinternaat and was founded in 1983 by a squatters' movement from the Staatsliedenbuurt. The cinema sports only thirty-nine seats, a number that has stayed historically low so that it could technically operate as a sex cinema and screen nonclassified hardcore films. Although it screens films wherever possible on 16mm and 35mm reels, Filmhuis Cavia is the first cinema in the Netherlands where you can pay for drinks and tickets using Bitcoin.

Despite media narratives about the Netherlands' progressive, enlightened approach to sex, while we are there, sex workers in Amsterdam are protesting gentrification, the closure of red-light windows, and a sex work licensing system that requires mandatory registration and criminalizes undocumented migrants. In the city, a queer collective is staging a protest against official Pride by paddling among the floats in small dinghies to object to the corporatization of Pride in light of the Netherlands' anti-immigration policies and right-wing Islamophobic vitriol. At the weekly queer night at the Vrankrijk, an autonomous political café, the collective has painted a mural appropriating corporate Pride. Instead of reading "Canal Pride," it reads "Anal Pride" with a painting of a giant mohawked dyke standing in the middle of the canals, holding up a miniature man in a suit, and wiping her arse with the letter C.

Introduction

Democratizing Pornography

This book is about the relationships between law, social movements, and political strategy. It does three key things. First, it demonstrates why indie porn is valuable. It documents its liberatory promises, its aspirations to democratize the kind of content we see, visions to pioneer more ethical production practices, and desires to change our relationships not only to sex but also to media, society, and capitalism. Second, it argues that in order to build just and equitable sexual cultures we need to overhaul the international regulatory infrastructure that governs sex and create enabling economic, technological, and legal environments. For independent sexual media to thrive, we require a reassessment of how classifiers understand risk, how platforms conceptualize harm, how businesses extract labor, and how governments value pleasure. Third, it examines the creative strategies of the indie porn movement to resist dominant structures, generate alternative cultures, and build liberatory futures. Because indie pornographies both resist and are shaped by their regulatory environments, they offer lessons about stigma, respectability, and co-optation. In the pages to come, I argue that watching, listening, and paying attention to indie pornographies tells us at once about the dangerous functions of neoliberal regulatory systems but also about the creative tactics and strategies of social movements that deliberately (and provocatively) butt up against them.

Revolutionary Promises

Since the early 2000s, a vibrant international movement has flourished across the world, pioneering online pornography that has been variously labeled as DIY, indie, feminist, ethical, queer, alt, and, more recently, fair trade, artisanal, cruelty-free, and even organic. International porn film festival circuits have emerged in Chile, Argentina, Mexico, Colombia, Brazil, Germany, France, Australia, Denmark, the Netherlands, the United States, Canada, and the United Kingdom, to name a few. Queer, feminist, and indie porn films are being produced throughout Asia, with a thriving porn movement in South and Central America. Chinese artists, such as Fan Popo (whose film series *The Hutong Vibe* was billed as Beijing's first queer feminist porn), have relocated to Berlin to produce and screen their work. As technologies are becoming increasingly affordable and intuitive, producers are taking up the charge of various feminist pornographers. Candida Royalle, who established Femme Productions in the 1980s, insisted that women must take control of the reins of production (Comella 2016, 96). Annie Sprinkle, who pioneered post-porn-modernism mixing sex, art, and activism, famously asserted, "The answer to bad porn isn't no porn. It's better porn" (Sprinkle and Leigh 2002). In 2016 feminist pornographer Madison Young released the DIY *Porn Handbook: A How-to Guide to Documenting Our Own Sexual Revolution*, which provides hands-on advice for shooting, editing, distributing, and "guerrilla marketing" films and encourages audiences to "make the porn you want to see!"

For many producers, indie porn production is being heralded as a mechanism for social change. Feminist pornographies are being described as both "a genre and a political vision" (Taormino et al. 2013, 18), DIY pornographies are being heralded as a "socio-political movement" (Young 2016, 11), and others are being described as "interventionist pornography" that can "queer capitalism through alternative economic practices" (Saunders 2020, 275). Indie porn projects themselves make claim to a revolutionary politics, from Courtney Trouble's site Indie Porn Revolution ("subversive smut made by ladies, artists and queers") to films like Chelsea Poe's *Fucking against Fascism*, the profits from which are donated to Trans Lifeline and Black Lives Matter. Australian producers Sensate Films even coined the designation "Slow Porn Revolution," rejecting the capitalist production of "fast porn" and aligning themselves with movements for slow food and slow fashion by focusing on ethically aware, local, and sustainable productions. The Abya Yala shorts at the 2020 San Francisco PornFilmFestival, curated by Érica Sarmet, demonstrate how pornography can be a medium for "a collective subaltern resistance movement" to deconstruct the relationships between sex and colonization. Films in their curated program spoke to the relationships between bodies, sexualities, geographies, colonization, forced Christianization, epistemicide, military dictatorships, and Indigenous and Black genocide. In these iterations, indie pornographies are centering new voices, visions, and standpoints for what pornography can be and for whom.

DIY pornographies herald a promise to not only diversify but also *democratize* pornography. They are concerned not simply with the final product, but with the overarching *process*. As performers move behind the camera, self-funding and self-publishing their work, they are no longer models appearing in someone else's project, but authors of their own fantasies, curating their own images. As porn production moves away from major studios and into homes and bedrooms, accelerated by the global COVID-19 pandemic, individuals can film, edit, and sell their own content, thereby increasing the range of visible bodies, genders, aesthetics, and sexual practices, with the potential to dilute dominant representations and to change viewers' relationships to sex. Production is no longer confined to California's so-called Porn Valley. Instead, pornography can now be filmed on one's smartphone, in one's home, and by one's friend—instigating the new genre of iPornography (Pink Label 2014).

Indie porn, as I argue in the pages ahead, is making waves in production values by challenging traditional production ethics. Because so many indie producers have ventured away from working for porn companies to create and star in their own content, they have brought an increased focus on the rights of performers, collaborative decision-making, and transparency. Porn performers are strategizing to create systems of mutual aid, resource exchange, and skill sharing. They are active in adult and youth sex education, leading discussions on consent culture and sexual health. Some are rejecting extractive labor practices by insisting on joint ownership of the final media project or profit-sharing arrangements that value collective cooperation. In these moments, independent pornographies are working to decentralize the industry in ways that go further than simply diversifying content—they seek to redistribute power, labor, and wealth in global media production.

The liberatory promises of indie porn, then, are not simply about the content. They are about our relationship to work. Indie pornographies aim to revolutionize conventional relations of worker/producer and labor/profit by reducing reliance on intermediaries and offering solo and community producers greater control. As platforms enable the sale of custom clips and direct-to-consumer forms of distribution, new technologies have been celebrated as having the capacity to "destroy the careers of professionals," acting as a social and economic equalizer (Coopersmith 2008, 49). The dwindling reliance on being hired for studio shoots means that performers are now increasingly in positions to speak out against unjust and unethical practices in the industry. Whether threatening to destroy the industry or simply to reshape it, these avenues to participate have been conceptualized as a form of *sabotage*. Access to production technologies offer individuals and communities the potential to disrupt or intercept the wealth of multinational conglomerates (Preciado 2013, 38). At least, this has been the theory.

Regulatory Fantasies

However, it is here that indie pornographies hit major hurdles, tensions that this book is concerned about. In practice, the promises of indie porn sit against a backdrop of erotophobic regulatory paranoia. User-generated porn is frequently produced in environments in which the production, sale, screening, and/or advertising of pornography is criminalized through a complex web of classification and criminal and broadcasting laws. Prohibitions on content disproportionately impact queer sexual practices and women's body fluids and permit narrow representations of sex and sexuality. The sexist, queerphobic, ableist, and racist legal frameworks that govern pornography are based on simplistic narratives about the value and effects of sexual representations and do little to protect the well-being of performers. They are based on regulatory *fantasies* of what porn is and does. These fantasies are ultimately counterproductive: They foreclose the kinds of initiatives that could directly improve the experiences of both performers and consumers. Indeed, public debates about risk and danger consistently ignore the issues performers repeatedly raise—privacy, stigma, data security, industrial rights, compensation, workplace health and safety, unionization, discrimination, and access to justice. The experiences of indie performers and producers challenge the underlying logics of regulators, who appear completely divorced from the realities of porn production.

But it is not only the legal context that poses a problem. Independent producers are working within a saturated market and global gig economy that demands high volumes of material and expects it for free. They are navigating an increasingly privatized online space with blanket bans on sexual media, communication, expression, and advertising through restrictive terms of use and narrow community standards. The ability to use pornography as a medium to effect social and political change is constrained by the sweeping sanitization, gentrification, and rigorous policing of sex in online space. While social media platforms obsess about nipples (building classifiers to identify nudity), hosting services and streaming platforms ban the depiction of body fluids (including menstrual blood, breast milk, and urine) and non-procreative sexual practices (such as fisting, pegging, and G-spot ejaculation). Sex workers, sex educators, and sexual subcultures are maliciously flagged, suspended, demoted, demonetized, and deplatformed, treated simply as collateral damage. Algorithmic tagging and ranking systems benefit white performers and afford lower visibility and earning potential to Black performers, Indigenous performers, and people of color, thereby perpetuating racial stratification in the industry.

These conditions are not conducive to radical content. All of this provides an incentive for indie producers to create content that is safe, sanitized, and risk-averse and clips that are likable, clickable, and geared to eliciting search engine results. It maintains an environment in which tube sites (the new corporate giants of pornography) monopolize the market by pirating independent content or requesting it for free in turn for exposure or traffic. Meanwhile, tube sites like Pornhub and Brazzers (both formally owned by the company MindGeek, now acquired by private equity firm Ethical Capital Partners and rebranded as Aylo) sustain their business through massive advertising revenue. They dominate search engine optimization (SEO) to outrank smaller websites in Google search results, regardless of whether they actually have the content (a Google search for "Crashpad porn," for example, indicates hits for Pornhub even though Pornhub does not host any of Pink and White Production's original and iconic queer Crash Pad Series). By financial necessity, small or solo producers often flock to companies with the highest percentage of payouts, leaving small hosting and streaming companies struggling for volume and traffic.

This is hardly the redistribution of wealth and power that indie producers hoped for. With multiple disparate income streams, performer payouts can be convoluted and heavily diluted by the few payment processors that allow adult content. The largest profits from the online porn market end up in the hands of tech companies, consumers come to expect porn for free, and selling porn becomes unviable for independent producers, resulting in the erasure of vibrant sexual cultures from online space. The precarious positioning of porn workers in a global marketplace dominated by multinational corporations is sustained by neoliberal policies that leave marginalized workers without protection to fend for themselves. Just when indie porn is poised for maximum impact—to democratize, deprofessionalize, and redistribute—it is stymied by a unique convergence of capitalist and regulatory forces. Porn regulation has historically been predictable and heavy-handed, struggling to keep pace with technological developments. But now, in addition to the tired practices of prohibition, we are witnessing reinvigorated forms of regulation ripple across the industry through commercial practices of extraction, assimilation, co-optation, and intermediary power that quash and dilute the potential of indie pornographies.

Resistance Politics

Following on from the promises and limitations of indie porn movements, this book focuses on the various strategies indie porn producers deploy for political currency, economic survival, and legal recognition in the context of regulatory overkill and economic downturn. As I outline in the chapters ahead, indie producers are savvy. They have campaigned for consumers to pay for their porn, launched affiliate programs to incentivize referrals, diversified their income streams, and found innovative methods of distribution. In some cases, they have turned offline to retro forms of distribution, such as print, art, and festivals. In other cases, they have found workarounds to sell personalized content direct to consumers or digitally minted non-fungible tokens (NFTS) as a way to mitigate the effects of piracy. Against the legacy of centralized production in mainstream studios, indie producers have pitched their work as documentary, authentic, fair trade, and artisanal and themselves as creators of unique and custom content. Trans performers in particular have become what Sophie Pezzutto (2020) calls "porntrepreneurs," workers in an increasingly precarious gig economy where "even hustlers need side hustles." Individuals are finding new ways to differentiate their products and capture a market niche in the context of eroding welfare states, proliferating piracy, and discrimination against adult businesses.

This is where indie porn holds lessons for other social movements. In their more neoliberal iterations, indie pornographies present an appeal for diversity and inclusion, toward a pluralistic vision of participation. They differentiate themselves from so-called mainstream porn by positioning themselves as a more progressive alternative. This, I argue, is less of a revolutionary move and more of a marketplace intervention, with producers invested in creating a greater variety of viable alternatives for consumers. But in their more politicized and radical iterations, indie pornographies go beyond representational critique and issue a more destabilizing challenge that deconstructs how and why we categorize, produce, and regulate sexual material at all. In these moments, indie pornographies offer a "post-pornographic" interrogation that contests the category of pornography altogether. They critique the processes through which value is placed on particular practices or bodies and question why sexually explicit media is sequestered from other forms of art and culture.

There are numerous pitfalls that come with social movement work. At present there are proposals to codify, certify, and label *ethical porn*, with some seeking to professionalize the industry by granting stamps of approval to guide consumers. While these interventions are sparking important ethical debates, the criteria used for determining which porn is *good* have sometimes relied on class-based ideas of taste or conflated ethics with legality. The risks in creating bounded categories of *ethical porn* are that they can simply be co-opted by tube sites wanting their corporate brand to appear to be diverse and inclusive (without changing their operating structures); that so-called *good porn* might be codified narrowly by governments, leaving everything at the fringes still (or further) criminalized; or that the self-congratulatory audiences who only consume bourgeois, fair trade pornography produce further hierarchies of stigma that marginalize workers who do not have access to industry certification. There are serious challenges ahead to ensure that these initiatives are not simply read as substitutes for decriminalization, destigmatization, decarceration, or decolonization, which require a fundamental reimaging of how our societies situate sexual labor.

Similarly, advocating for indie porn can have inadvertent consequences. Now that there is widespread cultural investment in authenticity, documentation, and representations of *real* sex, indie porn risks producing formulaic and conventionalized tropes of what constitutes *real* sex, *real* bodies, or *real* orgasms in ways that audiences will recognize as authentic. The imperative to emphasize the identitarian, confessional, and personally fulfilling aspects of this work (amateur exhibitionists doing what they love) has led to dubious commercial practices among porn companies (such as staff at one Australian erotica site being expected to identify and remove what they interpreted as *fake* orgasms). Further, it has been a means by which producers can extract even more labor from performers (by expecting them to perform without remuneration) and produce greater entitlement among audiences for free content. These patterns have not emerged in a vacuum; rather they are a product of late capitalism, where the boundaries between work and identity are rapidly dissolving.

Looking to indie porn debates is therefore instructive for social movements because it allows us to move beyond regulators' preoccupations with risk and access and instead delve deeper into the politics of respectability, diversity, and reform. Listening to performers changes the political demands. For example, if we seek only better porn or rubber stamps, we are selling ourselves short. We cannot simply "add women and stir" and expect that pornography will be democratized. Tech will not save us. Indie pornographies are about more than just *good porn*. While industry-labeling mechanisms are useful for transparency, they are no substitute for workers' rights. In turn, workers' rights do not reduce the need to resist the glorification of work altogether. While diverse content is a laudable goal, it does not address the fact that content creators may be low-income individuals from marginalized communities producing content for multinational corporate platforms. The geographical dispersal of content creators from Los Angeles hubs to bedrooms throughout Romania and Colombia raises new issues about national income disparity and international trade. Because indie porn has been a means through which individuals—particularly those who have been locked out of other forms of labor—have sought to participate in a global economy, content creation can be a means of survival and mobility in a context of widespread unemployment, housing insecurity, and racialized capitalism. What is at stake, therefore, is more than simply visibility on film; it is also a reevaluation of the ways in which we stratify sex, organize labor, and distribute resources.

Whores in the Academy

I came into the world of porn at a time when Australia was experiencing unprecedented recognition of pornographic artists on the international festival circuit. In 2009 I was performing at Sexpo, the adult industry convention, alongside special guest porn stars Monica Mayhem and Sasha Grey at a special erotica film festival to fundraise for the Australian Sex Party. I was to be the party's first ever parliamentary candidate, campaigning for comprehensive sex education, a national classification scheme, and decriminalization of sex work. That same night I was approached by Feck, an alternative erotica company, and asked if I wanted to shoot for their site, Beautiful Agony, which depicted people masturbating but only captured their faces. Indie porn in Australia was buzzing—by 2015 a *Vice* magazine headline read: "Australia's Thriving Art-Porn Industry Is Run by Women" (Morgans 2015). Australian producers and performers were winning international awards, being featured in film festivals, contributing to literature, advocating through national media, and I was joined by Christian Vega and (now multiple award-winning AVN and XBIZ star) Angela White in running for parliament as *out* porn stars.

And yet Australia was renowned for a draconian regulatory model with classification and criminal prohibitions on the production, possession, sale, and screening of explicit content. As a performer, I was interested in how the movement was prefiguring its own politics and values. I was traveling to festivals and sets across Europe, the United Kingdom, and North America, so my home country provided a unique departure point through which to compare the practices of these regions. But as a policy advisor and law graduate, I was interested in how the concerns of regulators were completely detached from these porn cultures and ethical conversations. In grasping to control something that clearly resisted regulation, regulators themselves were responding to a projected *fantasy* of how pornography is produced and consumed, one that had little to do with the realities of our lives.

The majority of books about pornography are written by people who do not make, watch, or create pornography. This need to distance oneself from pornography can be seen in the opening chapters of many popular books on the sex industry, wherein the author deliberately divorces themselves from the topic in order to appear neutral. Constance Penley (2015b) refers to this kind of tactic as the "elitist manoeuvre" used to avoid tainting one's reputation. Porn consumers are frequently Othered in debates about pornography (McKee 2017). Legislators proclaim they do not watch pornography and are expected to resign if they do. Studying sex is often considered "dirty work" (Attwood 2010a, 178): The study of it, the doing of it, and the teaching of it attract institutional and professional risks, especially for those who deign to teach content analysis or porn literacy (McNair 2009). Some suggest that "it might be inadvisable to teach porn without tenure" (Attwood and Hunter 2009). If they're unlucky, academics can even have their porn studies course outlines subpoenaed, as Constance Penley did during the obscenity trial *U.S. v. Stagliano* (693 F. Supp. 2d 25 [D.D.C. 2010]; see Penley 2015a).

Sex workers in academia are often seen as being too close to the subject, or biased, or are expected to identify as former or ex–sex workers in order to be heard. In her interviews with sex workers, Jennifer Heineman (2016) found that those in academia who consciously separate their erotic and intellectual work do so as a "conscious tool of navigation and survival" (5). Porn performers have spoken at universities to share their experiences of adult industry work (for example, see Maxxine and Hidalgo 2015, 279), though in some cases their events have been canceled or protested against, or faced backlash (Comella 2015, 283; Lee 2015d, 272). While the academy needs sex worker voices, the institutional structure of publishing and teaching brings rewards for academics (career benefits, employment opportunities) but can risk and even jeopardize income and safety for sex workers (Lee and Sullivan 2016).

During the course of my research, there was an emotional toll to being a sex worker in the academy (Stardust 2020). Colleagues informed me that they had watched my porn, I shared hallways with academics who wanted my work criminalized, and one article claimed the subject of my research was "putrid" and "the promotion of a degrading subculture" that should never have received funding (Moynihan 2016). A student's father complained to the dean of the law faculty that a porn star was teaching criminology, emailing screenshots from my personal Facebook page and prompting the university to seek legal advice on whether they could hire an *out* sex worker. But not all of my experiences were negative. The fact that I was a porn worker studying other porn workers was viewed by some as meriting recognition. My face appeared on an enlarged poster in a portrait series as part of a university campaign to display diverse thought leaders tackling inequality. An artwork of me painted by sex worker artist Nada DeCat was displayed as part of a Pride exhibition hosted in partnership by a multinational law firm and an investment banking company. On these occasions, our work was discussed alongside hors d'oeuvres and champagne and speeches about workplace diversity strategies and inclusivity benchmarks. These instances represented a different kind of risk—one of co-optation.

My candidacy—like my experience as a porn performer—was shaped by my white, cisgender, tertiary-educated, and middle-class privilege, which afforded me access to platforms and opportunities. As Robert L. Reece (2015) has argued, the "Duke University Porn Star" Belle Knox, who was outed as a porn actress while at university, was able to leverage her story, largely protected by "white, upwardly mobile feminine respectability" to become a "media darling," but she is unlikely to have received the same reception if she was a Black woman working in porn to fund her college tuition. We ought to be suspicious that such instances are signs of danger rather than progress, where sex—but only some privileged iterations of it—becomes institutionalized. At the same time, sexual assault on campus is a national crisis; such professions as psychology, teaching, medicine, and law are excluding sex workers from admission; and course curricula (particularly in social work) often pathologize and stigmatize sex work, making it difficult for sex worker students to participate.

Among other things, then, this book seeks to expand upon the politically astute and sophisticated conversations that porn performers are already having within the industry about queer, trans, feminist, race, disability, and resistance politics, what I refer to as the "epistemology of whores"—a unique lens through which sex workers know about the world. This is in the spirit of Jill Nagle's edited volume *Whores and Other Feminists* (1997), in which she argues that "incorporating sex worker feminisms results in richer analyses of gender oppression" (1). In doing so I sit within a tradition of feminist inquiry that makes space for partial perspectives and situated knowledges (Haraway 2003), and I foreground the experiential knowledge of porn performers as the point of departure from which to understand broader trends in pornography regulation. My work draws from the collective knowledge and broader ongoing dialogues within porn cultures, building on sex worker research, writing, autobiography, and advocacy over the past four decades. It forms part of a new wave of sex-working researchers challenging the conventions and institutions of academia.

Porn Studies

The field of porn studies has blossomed since Linda Williams published *Hard Core: Power, Pleasure, and the "Frenzy of the Visible"* (1989). Williams followed decades of political and cultural debates about sexual cultures, feminist representation and censorship, which heightened during the 1970s and peaked in the 1980s "sex wars" (Duggan and Hunter 2006). Throughout the 1990s, porn performers and scholars united to write about queer and feminist sexual cultures represented in hard copy magazines, cinema, and VCR porn (Gibson and Gibson 1993) and to critique the Christian right and second-wave feminists' attempts to control women through crackdowns on the civil liberties of gay men, lesbians, and sex workers. In the late 1990s and early 2000s, internet pornography brought new publication, distribution, and regulation frameworks, prompting a new focus on "netporn" (Albury 2004), which examined classification systems, labor markets, and taste cultures. More recently, porn studies scholars are asking what it means to decolonize pornography in settler colonial states (Mackay and Mackay 2020; Gregory 2017). Acceleration in the use of automation to generate, detect, and regulate pornography brings new opportunities for porn studies to explore the intersections of machine learning and sexually explicit media.

Popular culture texts about the dangers of pornography position porn as big industry and producers as a capitalistic monolith. Such "broad diagnoses of contemporary culture as pornified" (Paasonen 2011, 2) dismiss alternative pornographies as too marginal to warrant serious engagement. Their overwhelming lack of engagement with alternative and independent pornographies has been a frequent critique, given that they "constitute a sizeable share of the market" (Weitzer 2011, 671). In anti-pornography feminisms, heterosexuality is assumed and ubiquitous: "It provides the basic framework for all pornography, even that which is produced by and for queers" (Thompson 2015, 750–51). By collapsing disparate pornographies into one monolithic category, these approaches eclipse more nuanced understandings of sexual cultures and media engagement. Instead, in this book I follow Linda Williams's reflection that we ought to "map the remarkable decentring effects of proliferating sexual representations" (Williams 2004b, 171).

This book is thus situated within a burgeoning literature on independent pornographies. This body of work ranges from the emergence of a women's market and consumer base (Smith 2007) to the transnationalism of feminist pornographies (Sabo 2012), the blending of sexual literacy, feminist consciousness-raising, and health promotion (Comella 2017), and the popularity of gay male pornography among women audiences (Neville 2018). Research into queer porn has emphasized its important role in eroticizing safer sex (Strub 2015) and its value in affirming and validating queer audiences who are marginalized by mainstream production (Ryberg 2015; Smith, Barker, and Attwood 2015). However, while research often focuses on the effects of porn content on consumers, less attention has been given to the specifics of production and distribution in a globalized marketplace or the strategies of independent producers.

A new generation of researchers are examining the political economy of pornography. Rachael A. Liberman's (2015) qualitative interviews with US-based directors and performers of feminist pornography have elicited important data about labor conditions, income streams, and workplace trends. Heather Berg's book *Porn Work* (2021) uses pornography as a vehicle to unpack the problems of work under capitalism, while Maggie MacDonald explores the organizational tactics of such free porn sites as Pornhub. In her fieldwork in Los Angeles and Las Vegas, Sophie Pezzutto (2019) documents how trans porn performers have navigated and survived changes in the industry by developing "a carefully curated personal brand" (30). Paul Ryan (2019) documents how male sex workers use Amazon Wish Lists to receive gifts for online content on Instagram, and Dan Laurin (2019) has explored how direct-to-consumer platforms, such as OnlyFans, despite being hailed as saviors in a dwindling industry, actually require new forms of "subscription intimacy" and emotional labor. Conversations have now turned to whether OnlyFans—like other sharing economy moguls, such as Uber—could be categorized as an employer, enabling sexual content creators to claim entitlements and protections (Marston 2020).

This book does not situate pornography as an inherently radical practice. It is not an uncritical celebration of sex. There are plenty of texts that cause us to reflect on the limitations of independent pornographies, mostly from scholar-activists of color, disabled people, and trans and gender-diverse folk for whom white feminist, cis-centric, and ableist visions of sexual-liberation-through-orgasm have fallen awfully short. If focused only on individual desire, preference, and choice, a pleasure agenda in and of itself will not be sufficient to destabilize the kyriarchy. However, pleasure (and pornography in particular) is a site at which we see multiple systems of domination and oppression intersect. It is, therefore, a site on which we see powerful acts of resistance. In *A Taste for Brown Sugar: Black Women in Pornography* (2014), Mireille Miller-Young documents how Black performers continue to fiercely fight back against poorer working conditions, lesser pay, and devaluation of their bodies. Siobhan Brooks (2010) has shown that spaces of sexual commerce—including purportedly feminist ones—often remain racially stratified. Kink spaces that profess sex-positivity can still act to reproduce racialized inequality (Weiss 2011), and performers of color are often hypersexualized and racialized as "repetitive caricatures" (Shimizu and Lee 2004, 1386). Despite this, the Black Sexual Economies Collective (Davis et al. 2019) notes that "the forces of commodification, exploitation and appropriation that render black sexualities both desirable and deviant also provide the spaces, networks, and relationships that have allowed black people to revise, recuperate, and rearticulate their sexual identities, erotic capital, and gender and sexual expressions and relations" (6). Black women navigate their role as protagonists in film by finding agency, pleasure, and desire in performance (Nash 2014), negotiating a space for power and playfulness (Cruz 2016), establishing Black-owned businesses, and pioneering better production values that could have ripple effects throughout film and media industries. Regulatory, technological, and economic environments, therefore, ought to support, build, and enhance the agency, autonomy, and power of communities of color over their own content and working environments.

A focus on diversity and inclusion alone will not necessarily lead to material changes in the conditions and lives of marginalized content creators. Trans performers have critiqued the slow inclusion of trans women into feminist pornographies (Hill-Meyer 2013), what Drew Deveaux coined the "cotton ceiling" facing trans women in lesbian pornography (Steinbock 2014), as well as the cisnormative "aesthetic-erotic hierarchy" that rewards passing and can clash with a performer's own gender affirmation process (Pezzutto 2019, 40). As Cherie Seise (2010) argues, to posit representation as the forefront of queer politics without discussion of material inequalities promotes a narrow concept of a liberated queer sexuality. Trans porn performers have been at the forefront of changing the language of pornographic marketing, renegotiating what performers are expected to do on set, and challenging cisnormative and cissexist expectations over how performers relate to their bodies, genders, and bodily functions. The voices of trans performers must be amplified and centered to achieve meaningful industry change.

Similarly, the emphasis on visibility in independent pornographies may also have a different significance for performers with disabilities who historically have been fetishized or depicted as "freakish" (Shakespeare, Gillespie-Sales, and Davies 1996; Mollow and McRuer 2012, 1). Loree Erickson's work on queercrip pornography describes how some performers (femmes and people with chronic illness, learning disabilities, or mental health disabilities) are erased and rendered invisible, while other performers live with "hypervisibility" because of their fatness, Blackness, or adaptive devices (Erickson 2015, 113). People with disabilities working in pornography continue to fight for transformation of production infrastructure to enable access and participation and against stereotypes of tragedy, curiosity, fetishization, and undesirability. For Loree, the end goal is not incorporation or even mainstreaming, but rather "transforming the way marginalized people and communities see themselves and think about themselves in order to mobilize folks to make structural and systemic change" (Erickson 2020b). There is a wealth of knowledge to be learned from queer disabled porn collectives, such as those Loree is part of, not only in terms of making pornography itself more accessible (such as with captioning and audio descriptions) but also in terms of building regulatory, technical, and economic environments that enable access to and participation in pornography on people's own terms by offering collective care and support.

As a result, this book approaches claims of revolution and democratization with caution. Despite their claimed opposition, so-called alternative pornographies sometimes have substantial overlap and entanglement with mainstream pornographic aesthetics and practices (Biasin, Maina, and Zecca 2014, 15). The borders between commercial and noncommercial are, in fact, "increasingly elastic" (Paasonen 2010, 1300). With performers and producers cutting across genres and industries, working in both independent and corporate productions, the divide between mainstream and alternative is ambiguous to say the least. A wealth of scholarship from internet studies also cautions us to be critical about claims of techno-utopianism. Digital content creators are now engaged in new forms of affective, relational, and aspirational labor in the hope of being paid (Baym 2018; Duffy 2017). The architecture of social media requires people to edit themselves into safe-for-work, apolitical, un-opinionated, inoffensive versions of themselves (Marwick 2013, 163). Production of the "self" involves the generation of celebrity branding where intimacy is performed through "confessional culture," memoir, and "reality" genres (Senft 2008). These economic, technical, and regulatory structures continue to fashion practices, identities, and representations of sex. As a result, as Katrien Jacobs (2014) argues, "the generic web architecture of indie pornography creates a flattening of alternative sexuality instead of fostering the potential for creative rebellion" (127). In this book I argue that we ought to think about democratization of pornography not only in terms of the decentralization of production and distribution but also in terms of the redistribution of material wealth, ownership of infrastructure, and access to decision-making power.

Made up of four parts, *Indie Porn* moves through the aspirations, strategies, and tensions of the movement as it interacts with legal, economic, and technical obstacles. Part I, "Porn Cultures," documents the pioneering interventions and provocations of this social movement as it moves beyond inclusion and diversity and toward demands for collective ownership, labor rights, and distributed wealth. Part II, "Regulatory Fantasies," charts the frameworks of risk, harm, and offensiveness that have made their way from historical obscenity legislation into classification laws and through to new forms of online content moderation. Part III, "The Hustle," documents the tactics and strategies of indie porn to survive this climate, including the mobilization of authenticity narratives and building a base of ethical consumers. Part IV, "Tensions," draws out the risks of employing respectability politics, the problematic distinction between good and bad pornography, and the pitfalls of engaging in porn law reform. Finally, the book concludes by gesturing to the role of carceral surveillance in regulating pornographies and offering a glimpse of the innovative, world-building, and artistic projects sex workers are leading in the tech field. It calls for a coalitional politics between social movements for lasting social change.

Auto-pornographic Ethnography

I began research for this book in 2012. At the time, I was part of a documentary titled *Independent Pornography in Australia* by Sensate Films, which showcased key issues affecting Australian indie porn producers. I used themes from this documentary—including infrastructure, criminalization, isolation, and ethics—as a starting point to develop a methodology to further explore how porn regulation affected my communities. In consultation with Scarlet Alliance, Australian Sex Workers Association (the national peak body representing sex workers), Eros Association (the national body representing adult businesses), and speakers on the 2013 feminist porn panel at the Perv Queerotic Film Festival, I developed research questions that would elicit knowledge useful to both producers and performers. While much research on pornography is concerned with consumption, I chose to focus on labor. I took a four-pronged approach involving qualitative interviews with Australian porn performers, producers, and stakeholders to speak back to legal and policy frameworks: auto-ethnography (performing in and producing pornography) to enrich the interviews; a legislative and case law review to understand the overarching regulatory climate; and archival research to provide the historical context. Throughout the project I engaged in consultation with Scarlet Alliance and my participants, from designing questions and methodology to coding, analysis, and reporting.

In 2015–16 I conducted sixty-to-ninety-minute qualitative interviews with thirty-five porn producers, performers, classification stakeholders, community organizers, and academics. Twenty of the interviews were with porn producers of various sizes and scales, sixteen of whom (80 percent) were also performers, appearing either in film, photography, or print. Of the sixteen performer-producers, eleven operated as solo producers, four operated in a two-person partnership, and one was a feature director for a company. Most of the sole-trader, performer-producers running their own sites and projects were cisgender queer women, nonbinary people, trans men, and queer men. They were eligible to participate if they identified themselves and/or their work as queer, feminist, ethical, alternative, or kinky. Because my project was framed as being about pornography rather than online sex work, many of the participants who self-selected were represented on the international porn film festival circuit and had sufficient class and white privilege to be publicly out. In solidarity with sex worker guidelines on ethical research, I paid porn performers an honorarium of $150 for their involvement to value their time, knowledge, and expertise. The costs were partially funded by a faculty grant and partially self-funded by my own sex work.

In addition to producers, I interviewed spokespeople from four organizational bodies: Scarlet Alliance, Eros Association, Electronic Frontiers Australia (a nonprofit digital rights organization), and the Australian Queer Archives (the biggest repository of historical materials about LGBTIQ+SB experience in Australia). These bodies offered historical contexts on political strategies for sex worker rights, lobbying campaigns to legalize the sale of adult films, government attempts to filter and regulate the internet, and print/performance cultures of queer sexual representation.

I further interviewed six classification stakeholders: ACON's (formerly the AIDS Council of NSW) sexual health project for kinky and sexually adventurous women, which ran from 2012 to 2018 and used sexual imagery for health promotion; *Archer* magazine, a print publication about sexuality, gender, and identity established in 2013 (its second issue was removed from newsagent shelves because it was deemed "inappropriate for sale"); *Dirty Queer*, a queer print magazine featuring photographs and articles between 2010 and 2016; Melbourne Queer Film Festival, the largest and oldest queer film festival in Australia; Tilde, the Melbourne Trans and Gender Diverse Film Festival, which launched in 2014; and an anonymous queer porn film festival established in 2009 that screened sexually themed films alongside panels and workshops. These stakeholders all used sexual content for the purposes of community building, health promotion, and subcultural formation and were subject to classification and criminal laws. Finally, in order to explore different conceptual approaches to sex, pleasure, and regulation, I interviewed five Australian academics with expertise in pornography, classification, and media.

While my insider positionality allowed for access, it did not follow that the experience of porn production in Australia was identical. My participants and I shared some common experiences of stigma and discrimination by virtue of producing in a criminal environment that necessitated being attuned to risks of identification from law enforcement, all resulting in anxiety and uncertainty. However, people's risks and abilities to comply differed depending on the size of their business, amount of capital, citizenship status, gender, class, ethnicity, and HIV status. As such, in *Indie Porn* I take a peer approach in the spirit of "nothing about us without us" but with the caveat that "us" is actually a heterogeneous alliance, often characterized by divergent experiences, investments, and stakes. I see indie porn producers not as a homogenous, collapsible group, but as folks who have come together in the spirit of finding affinities and solidarities for the purpose of political struggle.

I was interested in building community through the research. During the project, participants often wrote to me asking for clarification about the legal framework, for academic references for articles they were writing, or to proofread their work. I assisted one participant in writing her first individual submission to a senate inquiry on porn law reform. I took a feminist approach in approaching interviews as a two-way conversation rather than as a data-extraction exercise, offering my own experiences in an effort to share something personal and inviting feedback on my interpretations. Because of the risk of incrimination, participants could opt to be identified by pseudonyms, to edit their transcripts, and to review draft chapters for accuracy, confidentiality, and context. However, some made the political choice to be identifiable—Angela White, for example, deliberately uses her legal name in pornography to reject shame and stigma. In the write-up, I took an affirmative action approach that prioritized the voices and experiences of performers over producers in order to lessen the potential for the research to become a marketing or public relations exercise and to give performers a chance to speak back about their on-set experiences.

I supplemented this interview data with a legal and archival review, sitting in my kitchen wading through folders of state and federal classification and criminal legislation and case law to understand systems of content regulation and how they had been used to prosecute both producers and retailers. I flew to Flinders University in Adelaide to visit the Eros Foundation Archives and trawled through decades of correspondence, campaigns, parliamentary records, explanatory memoranda, bills, and Hansard to understand the political milieu in which these laws originally developed. I rummaged through flyers, magazines, and gay newspapers at the Australian Queer Archives in Melbourne, where I found local community porn projects and periodicals dating back to the 1970s. I traveled to Canberra, home of Australia's Parliament and known as the country's capital of porn and pyrotechnics, to visit the *X-Rated: Sex Industry in the ACT* exhibition at the Canberra Museum and Gallery, which featured newspaper clippings, posters, lobbying letters, vintage model releases, and home-made amateur porn from the 1980s. These materials allowed me to understand the regulatory clashes, media environment, and distribution challenges of indie pornographers in historical context.

Because I conducted my interviews before the widespread proliferation of platformed sex work (and the market dominance of OnlyFans) and before the onset of the COVID-19 pandemic, this book offers insights into how the gig economy has transformed the indie porn landscape. I compare my participants' experiences with data from my recent projects and collaborations. These include quotes from the multi-stakeholder workshop "Gendered Online Harm," which I ran with colleagues at the Australian Research Council Centre of Excellence for Automated Decision-Making in 2021; findings from a qualitative project I undertook on platform cooperatives and alternative governance models for sexual content moderation in 2023; and collaborative research I undertook with colleagues at the New York–based activist collectives Hacking// Hustling and Decoding Stigma between 2020 and 2022, during and following my fellowship at the Berkman Klein Center for Internet and Society. As a result, the book moves through several significant industry and technological moments over the past decade. Sadly, but perhaps unsurprisingly, many of the core issues facing indie performers remain the same.

Porn was not abstract for me—I was *in* it. Over the course of my career, I performed with erotica companies, independent producers, and individual sex workers. We created products that were sold on platforms and DVDs, licensed to overseas sites, and screened at film festivals. I performed both in Australia and internationally, including shooting scenes with performers from Sydney, Melbourne, Canberra, San Francisco, Los Angeles, and London. I won awards for both porn performance and production and screened films at festivals across North America, the United Kingdom, and Europe. During this time, I collaborated on art projects related to pornography, including photo essays for queer women's health promotion (top ten tips for G-spot ejaculation!), a durational window display (to protest the gentrification of sex industry spaces), artist panels, and live demonstration sex education workshops in Toronto, Amsterdam, and Berlin. I wrote for industry journals, adult magazines, anthologies, sex advice columns, parliamentary inquiries, and legal working groups; hosted international porn performers and directors when they came to Australia; shared advice, skills, and tips with other producers; and had hundreds of informal, on-the-job, behind-the-scenes conversations about porn, work, and the future.

In *Indie Porn* I speak as someone intimately involved in indie, queer, feminist, and ethical porn movements, not only as a writer and academic but primarily as a queer femme, producer, and sex worker. My foray into the industry began as a stripper in the "red light" district of Kings Cross in Sydney. For around fifteen years I worked across clubs, hotels, garages, stages, expos, magazines, brothels, dungeons, and people's living rooms, performing a range of services from blow jobs, massages, lap dances, stage shows, centerfolds, and BDSM to what some customers called "adult Cirque du Soleil." As such, I am part of this movement, beyond the confines of the research, and share responsibility for how we have navigated regulation, marketed our work, presented our stories, and used space we were afforded along with the gaps we have inevitably left and mistakes we have made. Rather than being a detached or neutral observer, auto-ethnography allowed me to situate my personal, individual, and local experiences within broader cultural, social, and structural frameworks.

I call my approach *auto-pornographic ethnography*. In doing so, I draw upon Jennifer Heineman's (2016) approach of using ethnography to build a "more holistic, fleshy, and compelling examination" (38) and Kristen C. Blinne's

FIGURE I.1. The author's former subscription website. Flyer by Luna Trash. Original photographs by Ryan Ambrose, Adam Jay, and Richard Arthur.

(2012) "auto-erotic ethnography" of masturbation, the latter inspired by Ken Plummer's (1995) work on the power of telling sexual stories and Audre Lorde's ([1978] 1997) work on the erotic potential. Because my writing is less about sexual pleasure and more about sexual labor, I extend Blinne's concept with reference to Paul Preciado's (2013) concept of the "autopornographic body" (38), a term he uses to describe individuals who produce their sexual selves in an online commercial sex market. For me, auto-pornographic ethnography involves the process of how we fashion and produce ourselves for sexual commerce. Offering up excerpts from behind-the-scenes is my attempt to deconstruct a naturalized sexuality and explore how the pornographic self is manufactured. In this sense, pornography is not so different from other forms of social media production. The practice for me was, in fact, quite ordinary, and my intention was to bring readers beyond the hype to engage with pornography in a more quotidian manner. My "field notes" are scattered throughout as a series of vignettes, small peepholes into my life on set, at festivals, in forums, and behind-the-scenes, spanning a period of over ten years. I offer these first-person stories in the spirit of connection, to invite you into the pornographic set so that you can experience it *with* me, with the hope that it will lead to new ways of understanding the bodily labors of pornography.

Part I

porn
cultures

Pornocamp

I had zero experience in film when I started making DIY porn. Everything I learned was by observation, skill-sharing, and trial and error. Of the two main companies I'd shot with, one was thereafter prosecuted and relocated to Amsterdam. I didn't have a camera, audio equipment, or editing software but knew some people who did. DIY porn became a community exercise: I asked my friend to film me masturbating with a Sony handycam in my ex's garage. We borrowed a fucking machine from a couple I met at a rope workshop. I insisted my then-girlfriend break into an abandoned warehouse before it was bulldozed to film me fucking myself in the toilet cubicles. A pole dancing friend donated two boxes of Barbie dolls for a photo set using Barbie as a dildo. I spent hours at home devising the best angle to film myself squirting, editing around blurry footage, and searching for the cords to convert film to digital. It was old-school DIY porn.

Because necessity fuels innovation, I was surrounded by tech-savvy and resourceful sex workers. We shared tips on what size to export films for quicker buffering, how to export content for a big festival screen, how to use affiliate programs, and how to keep ourselves safe in a legal environment that was gray at best. Producing in Australia brought numerous restrictions. We couldn't host our content lawfully on Australian servers, so we needed to run subscription sites using overseas hosts or license our content to international platforms. We had meetings about how to sell our products via sites like Queer Porn TV, PinkLabel.tv, and Indie Porn Revolution. We had conversations about licensing conditions, the kind of content we could shoot (and its restrictions: children and scat), who owned the copyright, how the income would be distributed, and whether we would provide trailers, showreels, or partial scenes for advertising.

In 2013 we held an informal meeting of independent feminist pornographers in Melbourne and called it "Pornocamp." Adult entertainment expos, which charge high fees for booth rental, were often inaccessible for indie producers. People were doing such disparate projects, and we wanted to share tips, skills, and resources. Everyone seemed to be on their own, making it up as they went along. We sat on the floor of an inner-city apartment eating snacks and showing each other excerpts of our work on laptops. There were political decisions to make during editing: what to leave in, what to remove, what to emphasize. Some found it important to show performers putting on condoms, using dams, reapplying lube, and asserting boundaries—moments that might otherwise end up on the cutting-room floor. What other producers considered unnecessary or unsexy—moments of mishap or "failure" or miscommunication—could be crucial for depicting a vocabulary for how to negotiate risks, limits, safety, and pleasures.

Only a couple of producers I knew could live on their income from porn. I certainly couldn't rely on the income from my subscription website, in part because the only billing company available for Australian businesses at the time, Zombaio, was going broke and had stopped paying people out. I had payments trickling in—including royalties from DVDs or clip sites. Porn work was sporadic, available only every few months. Most of my income was made up of the bread-and-butter work of stripping, teaching pole dancing, and various kinds of sex work. Among independent producers we traded content to sell on our individual sites and worked out ways to cross-promote. "Diversify your income stream" was advice we all heeded.

Over the next ten years, the technologies changed significantly. I went from producing porn scenes for DVD to making custom golden shower videos for OnlyFans subscribers to creating freshly minted lactation photographs for Mint Stars to sell as non-fungible tokens (NFTs). In that decade I could chart my entire fertility journey through porn: filming solo masturbation clips in between IVF embryo transfers, shooting a threesome in my friend's KinkBnB while six months pregnant, and finally, ten weeks post-partum, pumping out breastmilk to make into lotions and lattes. Luckily, a few sites permitted the depiction of lactation, though I could not include scenes of my chihuahua lapping up the leftovers.

During that period, a recurring issue became where to host, screen, and share our material. As subscription sites were dying, producers moved to video-on-demand. As tube sites flooded the internet, some moved to patronage and crowdfunding. But rapidly these options were foreclosed—Patreon began prohibiting pornographic content. Even *Playboy*—at least for a time—

stopped printing nudes. Performers found other pools of income in ancillary activities—dancing, webcamming, escorting, selling dirty knickers, or running workshops. As websites began preemptively removing sexual content, many of us were reassessing the commercial viability of pornography. Sex was increasingly being removed from public space. It left us wondering what the future held—for porn in particular and for sexual media more generally.

1

Guerrilla Porn

Motivations and Interventions

"I started by accident," Morgana Muses tells me of her foray into pornography. Born in the small rural town of Coober Pedy in central South Australia, Morgana began producing and starring in her own porn following her divorce and a twelve-year period of celibacy. She hit the international stage when she won a Petra Joy award for first-time filmmakers, for a film she made about hiring a male escort. Seeking to contest the representation of older women on screen, Morgana now runs her own production business Permission for Pleasure. "I'm fifty years of age and trying to tackle ageism in porn in a more genuine and respectful depiction," she tells me. "Less clichéd and caricature-like than what appears to be the norm in porn." In addition to being a role model for many emerging filmmakers and suburban housewives, Morgana features in the documentary *Morgana* (2019, directed by Isabel Peppard and Josie Hess), which charts her journey through love, sex, and community.

Morgana's story sheds light on the motivations behind why people create indie porn—from entrepreneurial self-actualization to survival under late capitalism. In her book *Porn Work: Sex, Labor, and Late Capitalism* (2021), Heather

FIGURE 1.1. Morgana Muses (*right*) tackles ageism in her eponymous, award-winning feature documentary directed by Isabel Peppard (*left*) and Josie Hess (*middle*) and funded via a Kickstarter campaign. The film premiered at the Melbourne International Film Festival in 2019. Image by Zan Wimberley.

Berg describes how pornography occupies a liminal space between work and pleasure, existing "at the intersection of life and work, pleasure and tedium, entrepreneurial hustles and waged labour" (1). Many individuals turn to pornography because they are dissatisfied with straight work or what David Graeber (2018) called "bullshit jobs"—"pointless jobs just for the sake of keeping us all working" (xvi). For people with caretaker responsibilities, chronic illness, or disability, porn can occupy a status of what moses moon (2021) calls "nonwork" or "antiwork"—a flexible way to get money while resisting the cult of work.

Over the past five decades, the kinds of people producing pornography have become increasingly diverse. Although the screening of porn in cinemas during the 1970s, the industry's so-called golden era, did create porn stars, the disintegration of DVD and advent of the internet changed the phenomenon of stardom. With intuitive technologies reducing barriers to entry (anyone with a smartphone can take nudes), performers no longer need to be screen actors: Changing modes of production and decentralized sets mean that everyone is a potential pornographer. Increased channels to audiences facilitated newcomers' entry to the industry, accelerated by the COVID-19 pandemic: As Gwyn Easterbrook-Smith (2022) writes, sites like OnlyFans appealed to demographics such as un/under-employed women with "increased caregiving responsibilities" during lockdowns (252). People sought work to navigate the cost of living, the shortage of rental properties, access to medication, and exorbitant student fees. A recent study among OnlyFans creators in the United States found that new content creators were motivated by flexibility, autonomy, and control (Hamilton et al. 2022, 14).

The confluence of people making sexual content—from influencers to fitness models to animators to cosplayers—has complicated how regulators think about pornography itself. It has also complicated solidarity work, with some creators eschewing identities as porn performers or sex workers, resulting in boundary work to differentiate between the overlapping practices of online sex work, porn production, sexting, and camming. Porn performers now navigate platforms flooded with "sex workers who previously relied on in-person work, newly unemployed straight workers trying their hand at sexual labor, and non-sex worker 'tourists' looking to dabble in it" (Berg 2021, 17–18). Some have critiqued whether wealthy celebrities should even be permitted on sites like OnlyFans, which can credit its success and notoriety to sex workers (Sanchez 2022). And yet, unlike the resulting media, the work itself can be ephemeral. Over the course of my research some of my participants retired from the industry and new actors emerged, reflecting the transient nature of porn work.

Agency and Expression

Independent production can be appealing for many reasons. The performers I interviewed—a mix of industry veterans and newcomers—all had different pathways to producing. Some had worked in the sex industry for over a decade prior to embarking on porn. Some, like Angela White, began working in pornography when they turned eighteen. Others had started in porn to supplement their income following long periods working as BDSM practitioners, escorts, masseuses, nude models, and webcammers. For performers like Morgana, their career pivot began later in life, spurred by personal expression and exploration. Creating porn was often a mix of personal and professional pursuits: Producers were hobbyists, small businesses, and sole traders working in cooperatives with partners, colleagues, and friends. Those I spoke with were making a mix of feature films, DVDs, print magazines, subscription content, video-on-demand scenes, and custom clips.

Like sex workers who feel stifled by management and turn to independent work, porn performers turn to indie production for increased agency and flexibility. Sometimes the catalyst arose from poor on-set experiences and a desire for better working conditions. One of my interviewees, Luna Trash, began an alt-glam site called Trash Dolls with her friend Dolly because they were both unhappy with the exploitative business practices they had experienced at SuicideGirls and sought to create an indie alternative. Independence allowed performers to have greater control over the content. Sindy Skin, a solo performer-producer and "cheeky femme fatale" who originally created kink porn for her own subscription site, said, "I still have the absolute ability to take it down whenever I want," something that performers are rarely afforded when working for larger companies.

Others sought avenues to represent themselves in ways that were not possible working for big businesses. Angela White, who had worked with numerous Australian girl-next-door erotica companies, said she made the shift to solo production because she wanted to make content that was outside their ambits: "Because I produce my own content, I've been able to create a safe environment for me to explore things that I wouldn't have necessarily felt comfortable doing under another producer or director." Working for other companies often requires performers to adhere to specific body types, while being independent afforded Angela her own creative license to take a more body-positive approach.

Performers turn to indie production to avoid typical practices of gatekeeping and hiring discrimination—on the basis of age, race, sexuality, gender, size, and ability—that characterize traditional porn companies. Historically (and still today) companies assume that marginalized performers need to be siloed into niche markets or separate websites to appeal to consumers, and yet this assumption is not reflective of audience desire: As Sophie Pezzutto (2019, 34) points out, searches for trans pornography on Pornhub quadrupled between 2014 and 2017. New opportunities to describe oneself and determine one's own rates can also be a means for marginalized individuals (who have been seen as spectacle or entertainment) to financially benefit from forms of fetishization and voyeurism they are already subjected to. In her research among Aboriginal sex workers in Australia, Corrinne Sullivan (2022) describes how sex work can be a means of capitalizing on racial fetishism.

For performer-producers like Morgana, a turn to independent production represented an opportunity for self-actualization and self-expression. Many performers I spoke to described porn as a medium for personal self-exploration and for experiencing "firsts." In 2016 Dick Savvy, a gay male producer

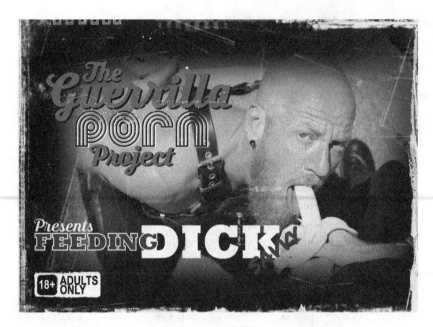

FIGURE 1.2. Known for his infamous hairdressing business, the Naked Barber, former Sydney Mister Leather Dick Savvy established the Guerrilla Porn Project to showcase Sydney's underground fetish scene through community, "no-budget" porn. Image courtesy of Dick Savvy.

also known as the Naked Barber for his nude hairdressing and grooming business, created the Guerrilla Porn Project, a group of kinksters making queer, art-house erotic films. "In my thirties I did a few amateur porn things, and I kind of was never happy with them, not that proud I guess of the way they filmed it. So I wanted to make porn that I was happy and proud to show off," Dick told me. "I also wanted to experiment in front of the camera doing things I've never done before but have been fantasies or thoughts of mine, to have that first experience in front of the camera and also break my boundaries." In such instances, user-generated production brings opportunities for authorship, agency, and pleasure.

What Is Indie Porn?

What does it mean to describe porn as independent? In this book, I use *indie porn* as both an umbrella term and a relative term. The concept of independence arises from a relationship, so iterations of independent pornography are inevitably about independence *from* hegemonic values and processes. Like indie film more generally, indie porn producers often aspire to be autonomous and free from reliance upon or influence by corporations. They may use their own resources rather than being affiliated with major studios, screen content to local audiences via their own networks, work as freelancers without contracted loyalty to particular companies, crowdfund their projects, use alternative distribution channels, or refuse to cooperate with global, monopolistic, or corporate partners. Independent porn production—again, like other genres of indie film—relates to both structure (often solo operations, small partnerships, or collectives) as well as to funding, budget, and practice (including the producer's relationships to capital, investment, and distribution). As discussed below, indie producers also conceptualize independence as being philosophical in the sense that they seek to preserve the integrity of their artistic vision regardless of marketability. Indie porn producers are therefore unified by the impetus to imagine and create independent relationships to representation, production, distribution, and consumption of sexually explicit content outside those that currently exist in mainstream models.

However, as I argue throughout the book, despite its fantasy of independence, indie porn is in fact deeply reliant upon interpersonal and community relationships. As disability activists have long argued, independence is a myth. Oftentimes, the collaborations my participants describe could best be understood as "community porn." Partnerships and collectives characterize the genre: Participants rely upon one another, and the survival of each is bound up together. Indie porn is therefore inherently interdependent, both in the relationships that sustain it and in the ecosystems that disseminate it.

Building on this, I use *indie porn* as an overarching category to describe a collection of movements, people, and projects. Under this umbrella may be DIY pornographies that encompass decentralized and independent production using new technologies (Coopersmith 2008), amateur pornographies that are "self-produced in a non-professional way" (Zecca 2014, 321), feminist pornographies that foreground women's agentic desires and subjectivity (Liberman 2015, 174), queer pornographies that are "unbounded by gender binaries and sexual essentialism" (Lipton 2012, 205), and ethical pornographies that emphasize fair payment and workplace conditions (Mondin 2014). On some occasions, independent pornographies overlap with the movement for post-pornography wherein they blend art, porn, and politics to contest regimes of sexual representation altogether and to destabilize the meaning of what constitutes pornography (Stüttgen 2009). On other occasions, they remain firmly grounded and invested in pornography as a category and industry itself.

Because indie porn comprises such diverse and distinct projects, in this book I use pornograph*ies* in its plural form to emphasize that pornography is not one homogenous, unified thing. Sometimes there is considerable overlap between producers' identities and stakes. However, others are distinct and require disclaimers. In other words, not all ethical porn is necessarily independent; not all independent porn is necessarily amateur; and not all queer porn is necessarily ethical. Unsurprisingly, many of these terms have now been co-opted for mainstream use. For example, following the popularity of "pro-am" porn, the term *amateur* porn has become a generic signifier for corporate industry co-optation and imitation of amateur aesthetics (Zecca 2014, 331). *Alternative* porn has also been taken up to describe a popularized genre of *alt-porn*, iconic for its punk, goth, and raver aesthetics and highly commercialized in its operations. Because of this, it helps to come back to the concept of *relationships* to representation, production, distribution, and consumption when thinking about indie porn.

But can pornography really be independent in an environment that is so imbricated in networked technologies? As a response to studio production, indie porn has come to signify a utopian promise to democratize, diversify, and decentralize media landscapes. However, one might argue that in the context of platformization, independent content production is neither novel nor revolutionary. Rather, outsourced labor is now *the* business model of global tech companies in a sharing economy. Just as companies like Uber and Airbnb outsource drivers and accommodations, platforms like Pornhub and OnlyFans outsource sexual content production to geographically dispersed individuals. Consequently, in order to earn an income, indie producers are incentivized to build their brand as micro celebrities, acquire sophisticated marketing skills, juggle multiple social media accounts, establish sponsored partnerships, and "embody a model neoliberal subjectivity with an ethos of networking, self-branding, self-reliance, and process optimisation" (Pezzutto 2019, 52). In this context, the pornographic scenes themselves become "just a marketing tool" for other income streams (Berg 2016, 160). Independent production has therefore become a hallmark of mainstream distribution.

This tension is not new; indie porn producers wrestled with their relationships to mainstream distributors in the eras of cinema and home video. However, the gig economy and the platformization of sex have made independence even more elusive and political organizing more necessary. As opportunities for studio contracts have declined and scene rates have dropped (Tarrant 2016), porn work is "tempered with heightened financial precarity" (Easterbrook-Smith 2022, 252). Porn workers are increasingly dispersed and exhausted; "the

FIGURE 1.3.
The Toytool Commit-
tee, an independent
production house
in Valencia, Spain,
prints "Support Your
Local Pornographers"
stickers. The film by
the same name was
voted best short film
by the audience at the
Perv Queerotic Film
Festival in Australia in
2015. The committee
calls for visibility and
respect for small, indie,
low-budget, and sex-
positive filmmakers.

same atomization that made at-home production both accessible and pandemic-safe also made it hard to build collective power" (Berg 2021, 18). Because of this spread, indie porn comprises diverse cohorts with different investments, sta-tuses, stakes, and strategies. The lack of viable avenues for formal organizing (due to criminalization, stigma, isolation, and exclusion) means that the infor-mal interventions of indie producers are increasingly important.

We can see the movement for indie porn in diverse political projects of varying scale. The existence of indie festivals (like the Berlin Porn Film Fes-tival), awards ceremonies (such as the Feminist Porn Awards), public cam-paigns (for example, "Pay for Your Porn"), social enterprises (including the Ethical Porn Partnership), and alternative platforms (such as Pink Label) in-dicate that there is a distinct groundswell of energy geared toward creating al-ternative porn cultures and practices. Alongside this, the advocacy of performer collectives (such as the Adult Performer Advocacy Committee in California), the generation of campaigns (such as the Toytool Committee's "Support Your Local Pornographers" project originating in Valencia, Spain), the staging of protests (including a face sit-in protest in London), the sharing of mutual aid initiatives (like the BIPOC Adult Industry Collective in the United States), and the teaching of sex education (such as the Sex School platform in Berlin) demonstrate how indie porn operates as a site of political resistance. As Berg (2021) argues, we ought to pay attention to informal struggles and individual interventions because it is through these "daily acts of refusal" and political imaginings that performers can make cracks in and push back against the status quo (7). As this chapter illustrates, performers are proactive in generating alternative ways of negotiating sex, valuing performers, curating content, and sharing profits—interventions that can be understood as world-making (and web-making) practices.

Home Video to Tube Sites

Indie pornographies have been facilitated through technological advancements, from the advent of print media to home video and the internet. When independent production accelerated with the advent of home video during the 1980s, queer and feminist pornographies were at the forefront, creating new kinds of representations and conventions. Feminists in the United States had been participating in sexual consciousness-raising groups, community education, and resource-sharing since the 1970s, including Betty Dodson's iconic workshops where she invited women to orgasm together using a Hitachi Magic Wand. In the 1980s, for example, Deborah Sundahl produced videos instructing women in G-spot ejaculation, and Susie Bright cofounded and edited *On Our Backs*, a magazine featuring lesbian erotica. Arthur J. Bressan Jr., who produced the 1978 documentary *Gay USA*, was producing gay porn films that have now been digitally restored. Throughout the 1980s and 1990s, Nina Hartley released series of explicit sex education videos; Carol Queen starred in *Bend Over Boyfriend*, instructing audiences in the practice of pegging; and Annie Sprinkle merged visual art, film, education, and performance by inviting people to view her cervix through a speculum. She also produced the first porn film involving a trans man with phalloplasty. Asian-American trans filmmaker Christopher Lee produced work on VHS throughout the late 1990s/early 2000s and later founded the San Francisco International Transgender Film Festival. Sinnamon Love, who launched her first website in 1999, is now archiving her work as an industry trailblazer as part of the Archiving the Black Web Research Group.

An early internet wave of queer porn creators helped foster an environment in which digital films could take off, including by Fatale Media, $PREAD,

ButchBoi.com, Debbie Sundahl, SIR Productions' Jack Strano and Shar Rednour, the CyberDyke online network, and Sex Positive Productions. In the early 2000s, online queer porn websites, such as Shine Louise Houston's Crash Pad Series and Courtney Trouble's Indie Porn Revolution, sought to include trans sexuality, size positivity, and self-deterministic representations of people of color. Independent sites, such as Furry Girl and Erotic Red, depicted amateur, menstruating, and hairy bodies aimed at countering hegemonic stereotypes of women, while trans performers, such as Tobi Hill-Meyer, James Darling, Drew Deveaux, and Chelsea Poe, led the way in authoring new iterations of trans porn that rejected and redefined how trans bodies and selves could be portrayed and desired.

The movement also evolved transnationally, with feminist porn flourishing in Denmark, Sweden, the Netherlands, and the United Kingdom (Sabo 2012) and a "new women's pornography" emerging (Smith 2007). Petra Joy from Germany gave awards to first-time female filmmakers, French performer and director Ovidie produced both feature films and porn documentaries, and from Spain, Erika Lust produced her series X Confessions, inviting individuals from around the world to submit fantasies to be made into pornographic films (Sabo 2012). Performers also found intersections with social and ecological justice movements. Annie Sprinkle began producing eco-sexual porn embracing sexuality and fertility in nature, and encouraging people to find their "e-spot," and in Europe, the group Fuck for Forests began to make and sell porn to fundraise for environmental projects, including seed exchange, permaculture, and rainforest preservation (Măntescu 2016).

Australia's own independent porn culture developed from a vibrant history of print magazines, live-sex performances, and DIY productions. In the "golden era" of the 1970s (Calder 2016), gay porn was featured in magazines and newspapers, and during the 1980s, individuals and couples produced amateur and homemade videos. Throughout the 1990s and early 2000s, women and queers on the East Coast performed irreverent, iconoclastic striptease at queer strip clubs, such as Wicked Women and Gurlesque, paving the way for an erotic print culture with *Slit* magazine and *Dirty Queer* magazine (see Crowley 2008; Henderson 2013; Drysdale 2019). Meanwhile, as the nineties internet boom facilitated the development of online porn, women began to buy and sell content on sites like Ms Naughty's Pure Cunnilingus and For the Girls. In the early 2000s, performers who had worked for the male-run companies Abby Winters and Feck moved on to build their own websites. As film festivals began to proliferate, indie producers began creating short screeners for festival circuits.

When they emerged, tube sites reportedly cut worldwide pornography industry revenue by three-quarters (Pinkser 2016), scraping and aggregating clips then streaming them for free. One company, MindGeek (established as Manwin in 2007), embarked on a strategy of both horizontal and vertical integration, acquiring porn production studios in addition to other tube sites, swallowing up their competitors and becoming a monopolistic owner of both production and distribution. MindGeek (which owned Pornhub until 2023) achieved market dominance through piracy, money laundering, and data harvesting (Ovidie 2017). To survive in this era, indie performers moved toward patronage, affiliate streams, and direct-to-consumer content, developing workarounds to declining pay rates in the gig economy.

Do-It-Yourself Culture

Contrary to representations of the pornography industry as a homogenous global entity, tech monopolies and criminal laws work to incentivize small-scale and local production. In Australia, for example, a large part of the industry is performer-led. A survey by Eros Association found that 79 percent of producers were women, 50 percent identified as LGBTIQ, and a third of all participants switched between performer, producer, and directing responsibilities (Eros Association 2018). On the one hand, this environment, marked by resource-sharing, community-building, skill-sharing, and collaboration, encourages do-it-yourself culture. At the center of DIY culture is "the idea that you can do for yourself the activities normally reserved for the realm of capitalist production" (Holtzman, Hughes, and Van Meter 2007, 44). On the other hand, as I discuss in chapter 5, DIY production also involves higher overheads (for makeup, travel, testing, hosting, etc.), effectively transferring the material costs of production onto performers. DIY production therefore becomes a double-edged sword, with the resourcefulness of communities becoming an opportunity for further extraction.

Among my interviewees it was common for performer-producers to learn skills in front of the camera that they could apply behind the camera. People reported borrowing equipment, software, sets, and costumes and swapping things of value. In some cases, funding for printing, sound, lighting, or fees would be raised through community crowdfunding. One of my participants, Aeryn Walker, who runs her own geek porn site Naughty Nerdy, reported doing everything herself, from filming, performing, editing, coding, and marketing. Others, like Angela White (who was still working from Australia at the time of our interview but has since gone on to achieve mainstream success with her own production company in LA), had established a company over-seas and hired contractors to assist with filming, editing, and web develop-ment. Others, like Michelle Flynn of Light Southern, would collaborate with performers and license content to overseas websites. Sometimes a group of friends would trade makeup, editing, or set design among such diverse loca-tions as people's homes, warehouses, outdoor spaces, and studios.

Indie pornographers have different definitions of what constitutes inde-pendence. For some it was about autonomous funding, being self-sufficient, and not relying on a corporate budget. For others, the size of their business and their relationships with commercial parties were relevant factors. Some-times, participants used "independent" in the sense that one person did every-thing, operating as a kind of "one-person show." For others, independence was about self-funding to ensure that commercial incentives did not interfere with the integrity of their political vision. While they refused corporate advertising, some queer projects still made space for not-for-profit community groups to place ads for free. Producers who accepted some financial support maintained a distinction between financing and content so that investors did not impact their creative direction. To avoid reliance on outside parties, it was common for performers to use money from their other sex work activities, such as strip-ping or escorting, to fund porn production.

However, producer iterations of independence were also shaped by the larger global landscape of media production and distribution. Even where porn is pro-duced on a local scale, it may be distributed and sold and licensed via interna-tional networks. Some solo operators had established a company in the United States simply to be able to access billing services or registered their business in Europe in order to avoid criminal laws. Increasingly, queer and feminist per-formers were collaborating with and crossing over into mainstream environ-ments, and, in turn, mainstream companies were purchasing indie content.

Class-based factors are involved in who can afford to be independent. Among my interviewees, those with straight jobs outside the industry could rely less on mainstream distribution networks, whereas full-time performer-producers from minority groups often needed to hustle for visibility and opportunity. The costs of participating can also be higher when performers are expected to ad-here to white, cisgender beauty standards—as Pezzutto (2019, 39) documents, many trans performers acquire costs for surgeries and procedures or have en-tered the industry in order to fund their gender affirmation, especially when medical insurance is unavailable.

Engaging with mainstream distribution entails a tension for indie produc-ers. It offers the power and financial resources to move content via circuits and expose one's work to broader audiences. In this sense it can be appealing to producers who seek to mainstream their content. But working with global distributors can also threaten to commoditize a political intervention and compromise the integrity of a project. At the Perv Queerotic Film Festival in Sydney in 2013, Courtney Trouble spoke about the tension of releasing the film *Lesbian Curves* through the California company Girlfriends Films. The decision was influenced by a desire to share queer sexual cultures with a broader audience; however, a number of the performers were nonbinary and did not identify as lesbian. Mistress Tokyo, a professional dominatrix working from her own dungeon, pointed out in our interview that ethics "can become diluted as you get a larger and larger production scale." Whether and how to engage in international distribution mechanisms presents a real challenge—one I explore further in the "Diversity Washing" vignette.

Gala Vanting, a performer who produced short films with her colleague Aven Frey, questioned the possibility of maintaining integrity when working with commercial distributors, investors, or companies. Having left Australian erotica company Feck to produce her own material, in our interview she wondered "whether that [feminist and pleasure-positive message] stays intact when there is a corporate interest at hand." For her partnership, Sensate Films, such "threats" provided an incentive to "stay in the corner and [have] less visibility." Sensate Films made a political decision not to produce in volume and instead to keep their business small, local, and community-connected. In fact, they had deliberately coined their own mode of production, "slow porn," akin to slow fashion and slow food, that rejects the mantra of *more, faster!* and instead intentionally slows down in order to pay attention to the experience of media creation with presence. These tensions between visibility, ethics, scale, and pace are at the heart of indie porn.

Community Archives and "Docuporn"

Indie porn challenges assumptions about who porn is for. For many, producing indie pornography is more than simply a business venture, exporting alternative content to straight audiences. Queer producers in particular describe a desire to document the wide variety of sexual practices and cultures they are immersed in as an archive for their own communities. The era of "real porn" saw a shift toward describing performers less as actresses or actors and increasingly as sex documentarians. Helen Corday, who ran her own subscription site, described in our interview the effects of increasingly available technologies in capturing more diverse sexual connections. Technology, she said, is democratizing the whole process, and it does mean that you see some amazing films coming through short film festivals that have been shot on iPhones that are really high quality, and that's happening with porn as well, and I actually think that's fantastic. I think user-based porn is going to transform this conversation about porn's impact on human sexuality into one that's much more positive because it is going to be a reflection of what we're really doing and wanting and desiring less so than a very small group of people producing a vast amount of content.

Producers I interviewed spoke about creating a new genre called "docu-porn," which seeks to build an archive of recordings of the sexual cultures, politics, and practices within their communities. Sensate Films produced what they called a "docu-portrait" referencing portraiture about BDSM and intimacy. Instead of fetishizing kink or capitalizing on its taboo, they present kink as an ordinary part of people's lives. On their website, Gala Vanting and Aven Frey write: "In its inquiry into the loves and lives of 5 subjects, it presents unique, articulate, and thoughtful perspectives on how kink can function in our lives—as a practice of art or intimacy, as a mode of expression or release, as an iteration or obliteration of self, as a way to play, a way to fuck, a way to love, a way to be ordinary."

In this sense, documentary porn emerged as a reaction to the nineties era of blockbusters and mass consumption. A regular photographer of community fetish events like Gurlesque and Hellfire, and producer of erotica website Shot with Desire, Cat O'Nine Tails described how her explicit work was informed by subcultures of queer performance: "There was so much amazing underground things happening in Sydney in the noughties; it was kind of like a documentary thing, as well as capturing the expression of people's sexuality in an alternative way." Similarly, for *Slit* magazine, the project was in part "inspired to produce" and to re-create in the tradition of past iconic dyke magazine *Wicked Women*. Coeditor of *Slit*, Meredith discussed how the magazine was an attempt at archiving the vibrant sexual performance scene in the wake of Gurlesque, which had run in Sydney for a decade.

> [My] thing was always about creating cultural spaces for us to kind of be nourished by. . . . It was a pretty amazing time; we were part of a sexual community that performed for each other. . . . Gurlesque really succeeded in creating and contributing to a sex and body positive community as well as creating and stimulating an amazing physical sexual performance culture unique to Sydney. . . . I suppose for me being an amateur historian I just thought "All this stuff is going to disappear. No

one's going to know it ever happened." So for us, for me, I thought a lot of it was about archiving these queer subcultures that will just vanish.

Such indie porn initiatives are not only about *documenting*; they are also about *creating* culture and community. With the magazines and films come festivals, food, conversations, and collaborations. When I asked my interviewees about their production motivations, some women reported a desire to create content that they personally liked and found attractive and that centered on personal choice and taste. By comparison, queer producers often reported a desire to produce something *by* and *for* the community. Although these goals no doubt overlap, and the curation of community content also involves individual artistic license and depends on connection to particular social scenes, queer producers described their production in ways that were less about individual pursuits and more about community relationships. Aorta Films, whose tagline is "lusty, opulent, ethical fuckery," call their queer indie porn platform Community Hardcore. Although *community* is often elusive and imagined, queer producers I spoke to felt a level of accountability to ensure that their work was bigger than the individual—serving a collective interest rather than just promoting individuals, stars, or careerism. Speaking at a time before start-up culture necessitated self-branding, Xavier Marz, cofounder of the photography print magazine *Dirty Queer*, remarked to me, "I don't want it to just be a fucking self-promotion." While self-promotion and community building may not be mutually opposed, Xavier reiterated his desire to serve and speak to community. Domino, from *Slit* magazine, reflected on this process of capturing, documenting, and archiving as a powerful driver: "When we first talked about it in that first issue, we talked about it as a history of the present, a photographic and text-based personal album for the community to retain for themselves about the extremely special things that were happening, that people were sharing with their bodies and their imaginations."

Slit magazine is now archived at the Australian Queer Archives, and both *Slit* and *Dirty Queer* are held at the National Library of Australia. While print media has different value, audiences, and circuits than digital content, this is part of a wider international trend, with projects to archive and digitize feminist porn taking place at various academic institutions. This process of porn-as-documentation aims to contribute something toward community memory—to participate in, create, and preserve a queer countercultural history. Nic Holas, a queer porn performer who had worked with such gay porn companies as Treasure Island Media, remarked: "We need a pornography that

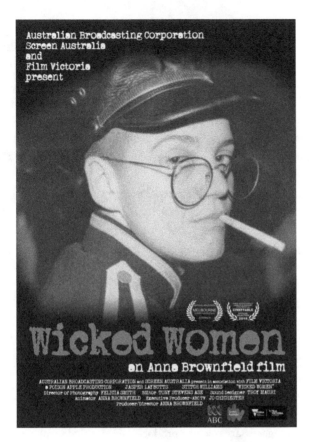

Australian Broadcasting Corporation
Screen Australia
and
Film Victoria
present

Wicked Women
an Anna Brownfield film

AUSTRALIAN BROADCASTING CORPORATION and SCREEN AUSTRALIA present in association with FILM VICTORIA
a POISON APPLE PRODUCTION   JASPER LAYBUTTS   STITCH WILLIAMS   "WICKED WOMEN"
Director of Photography FELICIA SMITH   Editor TONY STEVENS ASE   Sound Designer TROY MAURI
Animator ANNA BROWNFIELD   Executive Producer–ABC TV   JO CHICHESTER
Producer/Director ANNA BROWNFIELD

FIGURE 1.4. Jasper Laybutt and his partner Lisa Salmon produced *Wicked Women*, a lesbian erotica magazine, from 1988 until 1996. The magazine began on the kitchen table of their Redfern (a Sydney suburb) sharehouse, using a typewriter with a broken "W." The film of the same name was produced by feminist filmmaker Anna Brownfield with resources from the Australian Queer Archives.

reflects the kind of sex that we're having. . . . [Bareback porn] is an authentic representation of the type of sex that gay men are already having. It is not an instruction manual, and it's certainly not an aspirational guide. It's a reflection of what's already happening. It's a mirror, not a prediction."

Pornographies can tell us about the preoccupations of sexual subcultures, but they also play a role in *creating* as well as *reflecting* them. In the process of selecting meaningful content, producers offer up alternative accounts of sex to preserve cultural experiences. Of course, archives are not a definitive record of history; nor is a documentary necessarily an exposé of truth: They are partisan and incomplete impressions, selected and *curated* within a process of mediation and storytelling. But the imperative to collect and record this culture—as well as to screen it back to one's peers—reflects a desire to create counterpublic spaces, overshadowed knowledges outside those that are recorded and remembered as part of official histories.

Collaboration

By bringing their experiences in front of the camera to their role as producers, many performers are aspiring to improve production standards by putting performer needs at the core. A performer-centered approach avoids making assumptions about a performer's bodily capacity, sexual preferences, descriptors, or pronouns by paying attention to their access needs and providing space for their own decisions and boundary setting. Not making assumptions about how a person might use their body or experience pleasure was considered a task for a producer's self-reflection. Liz Alexander, former director of Tilde, Melbourne's Trans and Gender Diverse Film Festival, which launched in 2014, said in our interview, "I think there has been a particular history of who gets fucked, who fucks, what does this particular body part actually mean in the context of porn." Trans women, for example, often face stereotyped expectations, such as that they will maintain an erection, ejaculate, or simply present in ways that do not reflect their identity, desires, or practices. As Tobi Hill-Meyer (2013) writes of one set, "I'm a butch dyke and my sex life never focused much on penetration, but for the shoot I had to shave myself, put on stockings and heels, and hold my balance while leaning over and spreading my ass cheeks" (155–56). Trans masculine and nonbinary sex workers have described leaving camming because of cissexism and racism, including the cis-centric structure of tagging on platforms (Jones 2021).

Adjusting one's expectations and undoing assumptions about how individuals experience pleasure is a necessary role of a producer. As disabled sexologist Shanna Katz (2016) describes in her "disability inclusive DIY porn tips," this requires designing accessible sets for crip sex, asking all performers (not just those who are visibly disabled) about their needs and accommodations, and being proactive in offering information about how sets look and feel. As Katz details, access could include providing extra seating for sign language interpreters, making available pillows or wedges for modifying positions, setting aside quiet rooms for decompression, offering mobility-accessible bathrooms, and avoiding flashing lights, fumes, or noise that could trigger PTSD, epilepsy, or migraine. Part of this approach, writes Katz, involves producers being "ready to fuck up" (158) and being prepared to acknowledge, apologize, and be accountable instead of defensive when they make a mistake. Indeed, many disabled artists prefer to work in peer spaces where they find what Mia Mingus calls "access intimacy" (Mingus 2011; Erickson 2020a), an organic intimacy generated when working with other disabled folks who have a deep, shared or lived understanding of one's access needs and experiences of ableism. In particular, Katz notes how disabled folks frequently come up with "scrappy and creative" sex hacks: "Can't hold on to this sex toy because she lacks muscle control in her hand? Watch her figure out how to use another body part, or even duct tape it to body. . . . Can't see his submissive because he is blind? Experience his submissive wearing a bell on his collar so his dominant knows exactly where he is every time he moves" (2016, 157).

One of the key interventions of feminist pornographies is a shift away from hierarchical, top-down models of direction toward horizontality and collaboration. A collaborative approach between producer and performer effectively devolves some of the power traditionally exercised by directors. While projects might have a central person responsible for the organization, administration, and logistics, often their role is to act in the best interests of performers. Feminist porn production has trended toward treating performers as directors of the scene, whereas formal directors take on the role of facilitator.

In her film *Blonde*, Madison Missina describes performers as "co-directors" with one another in the sense that they direct their own scenes. In our interview, Madison said this arose because "I didn't like so much having very choreographed sex scenes where I'm told what I'm meant to find sexy or when I'm meant to come." She had experienced male directors offering unsolicited suggestions about what they thought was sexy regardless of whether it appealed to the performers, thoughts often based on gendered stereotypes of lesbian sex. Having a say over how her sexuality was depicted rather than mimicking producer fantasies was important to her. Similarly, Nic Holas described the director's role more as "bearing witness." While this still involved some degree of participation, he said, "It's so much more about the performers delivering an authentic experience, and you as the director just bearing witness to that, and, if anything, being more of a cheerleader than a dictator." In these projects, performers are playing an active role in the conception and creation of the product. Domino said of *Slit* magazine, "It's hard to even refer to the persons in these shoots as models because often they were participants creating the images themselves."

Sensate Films goes further, actually listing performers as directors or writers in their film credits to formally recognize their contributions as well as tweaking their model releases so that performers have more options for ownership. Gala Vanting described Sensate Films' model release as having a "choose-your-own-adventure" style, meaning that performers have options under each clause to make decisions about each aspect of distribution.

> We've broken the release now into different options, such as revenue share, in which over time a certain percentage is split between the performer

FIGURE 1.5. *Amor com a cidade* (Loving the city) is a record of sexual experimentation within the cities of São Paulo and Porto Alegre in Brazil. Made with "many hands and no sponsorship," the film explores urban space, architecture, and public pornography. Image by Pornô Clown, courtesy of Juliana Dorneles and the San Francisco PornFilmFestival.

and Sensate Films. There's also an outright model fee option . . . [or] the performer can also choose to simply release the image to us for use. And then there are a whole bunch of options as to how you want to be used for promotion, whether you need your face to be out of promotional things, and what level of exposure is comfortable for you. . . . There is this built-in structure for the performer to think about and make decisions about their level of exposure, the worth of their labor, and how they want to see the thing together—how much control they want over that.

In these cases, the end product may be jointly owned, with decisions made together about where the film is submitted, licensed, or distributed. It may be shared with performers (as part of a trade content-share agreement) to use or sell themselves. There may be a profit-sharing or royalty system whereby profits are divided between contributors or royalties are proportionate to the clicks they receive. Performer-producers also participate in affiliate systems whereby they can share and promote each other's work and receive certain percentages of sign-up fees. These initiatives recognize the central importance of performers and also seek to generate wealth more equitably among workers and producers.

Beyond Fair Pay

So what about the pay? Democratized production and an expanding performer pool means that studio rates per scene have rapidly diminished, while platforms reap commissions from their creators. In late January of 2021, the *New York Times* ran an article titled "Jobless, Selling Nudes Online and Still Struggling," describing women turning to OnlyFans to pay medical bills, childcare, and rent only to find a saturated market and little reward (Friedman 2021). Sophie Pezzutto (2019, 38) describes the trans porn performers she spoke with as having experienced homelessness, unemployment, discrimination, and poor remuneration—the majority did not own property and had no medical insurance or substantial savings. Chanelle Gallant, one of the founders of the Feminist Porn Awards, wrote in her reflections ten years later that in her efforts to make feminist content more visible and celebrated, the criteria of the awards focused too much on representation. In doing so, Gallant (2017) writes, they missed an opportunity to incorporate some of the critical insights of "sex worker feminism 101[:] . . . pay women well for work that is feminized, undervalued and often precarious." Against this backdrop, indie porn has the potential to re-vision the value of sexual labor and reinscribe systems of performer worth.

The performers I interviewed had a strong sense of what their labor power was worth. Gala Vanting described performers as "the person on whose back this piece of media is made." When she became a producer, the performer experience became "the paramount question." In an industry where the common stereotype is that anyone can get rich quick, prioritizing the performer experience could put the brakes on capitalistic exploitation for maximum profit. Taking a performer-centered approach could mean slower processes, increased collaboration, longer approval times, further negotiation, and conscious approaches to distribution. As Gala said, it "really does affect the way that we can produce, and how fast, and where we distribute and what our release looks like; it affects every level of the business." Ethical labor practices were not quick tick boxes that could allow producers to continue with business as usual; rather, attention to ethical production could disrupt conventional patterns of doing business.

A staple part of ethical production for performers is appropriate financial consideration in return for their labor. Performer-producers were adamant that fair pay should be incorporated into business costs as a baseline factor, above profit or viability, and that performers should be paid even if the product had not yielded a monetary return. Some practices of building in a royalties or profit-share system recognized the accruing value of the media product once it left the hands of the producers. Reflecting on her own experience as a performer, Lucie Bee, a pansexual nonbinary geek sex worker, believed that good pay was reflective of "the respect they have for me as an artist." Performers saw adequate compensation as indicative that a producer's politics was, as Helen Corday put it, "not just in the intent" but also in practice. Michelle Flynn, who licensed her content to sites in the United States, started her bargaining price with a minimum of what performers had to get paid: "If I can't pay the performers what I think is reasonable, then I won't do it." Even one local queer film festival I spoke to whose project was financially unsustainable, and whose directors were not paid to run the event, still made sure they paid performers, filmmakers, panelists, presenters, and hosts.

There was no consensus among my interviewees about what constituted adequate financial consideration, or whether rates of pay should be standardized, negotiable, or set by performers. In her blog on ethical porn, Michelle Flynn discloses average pay rates in order to encourage transparency, consistency, and a reference point for negotiation. Angela White described the aim as being to ensure that "everybody who's involved in that collaboration is satisfied," with both the content and the compensation. However, some interviewees interrogated the ways in which value was placed on particular bodies or practices in the marketplace. Standard practice among mainstream companies is to set particular rates for sexual activities. For example, companies may pay different amounts for solo masturbation scenes, girl/girl (G/G) scenes, boy/girl (B/G) scenes, or anal scenes. One Australian company paid an extra $50 per additional orgasm. In one sense, paying more for "extras" is a common practice that allows a worker to demarcate their boundaries in a transparent way. However, the different value afforded to these acts tells us about whose bodies and which practices are valued. A B/G scene pays more than a G/G scene because it involves a penis and hence is considered "real sex." Anal pays more because of societal taboos associated with the anus, because fewer performers are willing to do it, or, as Angela White pointed out, because of the labor involved in preparation. The lower pay offered to women of color and the higher pay for white performers who do interracial scenes reflect the racial stratification of sexual labor and racist devaluing of Black performers.

Some producers I interviewed did not wish to exploit or capitalize on these racial and sexual hierarchies, choosing instead to compensate performers for their time rather than a particular sexual output. Instead of determining a performer's worth with reference to heteronormativity, sexual racism, or commercial value, indie producers I talked to wanted to value performers for whatever they brought to the scene (their experiences, desires, expression), regardless of its potential for monetization. Helen Corday, for example, as part of a broader shift away from orgasm-centric scenes and a reassessment of orgasm as the central pinnacle moment of sexual encounters, paid a flat fee to performers with no expectation for orgasm. Her approach does not reduce sexuality to a set of predetermined positions, routines, or bodily outputs, and it rejects explicit sex as somehow more special, vulnerable, or personal than other intimacies. In the United States, performers such as Daisy Ducati, Ana Foxxx, and King Noire have spoken out about pay disparities and interracial pornography (McGowan 2020). The BIPOC Adult Industry Collective has formed a mutual aid fund, in part to compensate performers for declining work from companies that continue to participate in interracial rate discrepancies or racist marketing. These shifts represent a reassessment among indie producers of how bodies and practices ought to be valued.

Similarly, the work of Sensate Films interrogates why the level of explicitness ought to make content more valuable. Their films include power exchanges and play piercing and are screened at porn film festivals as erotically charged, sexually themed films but often without any sexually explicit content. While there are rarely close-up shots of genitals, Sara Janssen (2016) writes that Sensate's work is "as hard core as they can get" (17). Gala Vanting described how her work complicates classification categories.

> If you were from the Classification Board sitting and looking at our work I think you would have a hard time figuring out what to call this. Often our films don't feature explicit sex, but sometimes they do. But that's not imperative to us. We're more interested in a philosophical and aesthetic engagement with sexuality as a whole, not necessarily sex as an act. So we are interested in exploring identity and fantasy, and sometimes we even delve into deeper philosophical and political questions, and people watch a film like that and ask, "How is that porn?"

In displacing sex, these films reflect a broader context in which explicit sex is widely available (and has lost economic value), along with a queer approach that situates eroticism beyond particular body parts or sexual practices. Such iterations resemble "post-pornography," made famous by Annie Sprinkle in her live performance and book *Post-porn Modernist* (1991). Instead of naturalizing or reifying sexual practices, post-pornographies blend sexually explicit material with performance art and provide a space in which to reflect, resist, and reconfigure how we imagine sex. In doing so, post-porn can deconstruct naturalizing regimes of sexual representation and challenge the ways that bodies are categorized and valued.

Collective Ownership

Indie porn producers want much more than just fair pay: The new generation of producers are looking to redistribute wealth and to use their medium to support essential services. When producing her film *Fucking against Fascism*, Chelsea Poe (n.d.) wrote that it "was conceptualised as a way to make something on a small enough budget that we could use it to raise money for life-saving charities." While anti-pornography advocates paint pornography producers as motivated primarily by profit, my interviews demonstrate that independent producers have much more complex relationships with capitalism, often finding creative ways to resist and repurpose it, funneling cash flow to communities in need.

Producers' different relationships with capital affect how they produce and what their content looks like. While a few producers I interviewed were able to operate full-time, each spoke about the difficulty of making a viable living. Some were full-time sex workers who used porn to supplement their income, diversify their skills, or attract business for in-person sessions. Some producers were just breaking even. For some, capital value of the product was important if only so that they could afford to pay the workers appropriately and cover costs. Many projects were not considered to be financially viable but continued nonetheless because they were considered politically valuable. No one involved with porn had grandiose expectations of wealth. As Gala Vanting said, "For me it was definitely politics first, then maybe capitalism. Money wasn't my primary motivator at the time I started making porn. I make things that I want to make before I make things I know I can sell."

Some projects were deliberately anti-capitalist in their intentions. In the editorial to their fifteenth issue of *Slit*, Domino and Meredith maintain that while no one is paid to contribute, no one earns income from the product, and the focus is on "creating sex culture with the ambitious aim of trying to carve out some possibilities for a non-commodified sexuality." They refer to *Slit* as sitting outside of a paradigm of consumption and instead as "a symbiotic relationship between voyeurs and exhibitionists, not buyers and sellers" (*Slit* 2012, 3). In our interview, Domino recalled that they and Meredith were

> thinking about this idea of, you know, the economy of desire, seeing the potential for the magazine to consider the possibilities of creating a dialogue

of sex and sexuality which is non-commodified, a space for sharing bodies, desires, creativities. So, a space where that kind of capital exchange is less relevant. And also one where our role as producers and editors did not create an employment-style relationship; rather what we wanted from the start was a collaboration, where all contributors (which included ourselves) were (literally) in it together.

In its anti-capitalist approach *Slit* demonstrates the value of indie porn, not only in creating a culture that doesn't rely on professionals, corporate infrastructure, or expensive equipment but also in expanding the *use* rather than the *exchange* value of porn. This project illustrates that indie porn is *useful* beyond the monetary value for which it sells—it promotes community building, supports local skill-sharing, has worth, and *does* political work. Although they may exist in a capitalist economy, indie pornographies have value beyond the market. Porn film festivals, panels, workshops, and exhibitions continue to be important spaces for dialogue, connection, interaction, and feedback. Contrary to regulatory assumptions that treat pornography as existing outside of culture and without having any redeeming value (an issue we encounter in chapter 3), many of these projects persist despite the lack of financial incentives and in the face of criminalization because they are politically, culturally, and socially valuable.

But the ability to engage with and create porn as an anti-capitalist strategy is not an option for everybody, and it also reflects the race, class, and gender privilege of some producers. As Mireille Miller-Young (2014) writes, Black women use alternative economies such as sex work to access upward social mobility in a broader context of feminized poverty: "Commodifying one's own sexuality is part of the strategic and tactical labor black women use in advanced capitalist economies" (182). Similarly, Sophie Pezzutto notes that trans women often choose mainstream work because indie productions do not pay enough to cover their bills. Even industry fame does not necessarily result in material benefits. As Casey Kisses remarks to Sophie, "We are always in mansions, yes, but do any of those mansions belong to me? No" (Pezzutto 2023, 32). Still, producers with low budgets can find nonmonetary ways of exchanging something meaningful and useful to performers. Jiz Lee (2016) argues that content trades can provide long-term income through ongoing royalties, support new producers who do not have start-up capital, and offer "the potential for a more level playing field" (66). In her essay "Queer Porn as Postcapitalist Virus," micha cárdenas suggests that worker-owned cooperatives have the potential to distribute profits more equally among communities. cárdenas (2014) writes, "If queer porn producers and performers want to move the genre forward as a postcapitalist possibility, then queer porn sites should be structured around collective ownership, decision-making and capital distribution" (114).

In addition to worker cooperatives, some pornographic projects act as fundraisers for community projects. From San Francisco, Jiz Lee's Karma Pervs raised funds for human rights, health, community projects relating to reproductive and sexual health, LGBTIQ needs, and sex worker rights. In the United Kingdom, Blake and Nimue Allen's 2015 caning fundraiser raised money for Backlash, an anti-censorship organization advocating for freedom of expression. In Australia, Gala Vanting donated her work to Holly Zwalf's 2015 performance *Engorged: Fucking (with) the Maternal*, which features a series of artists and parents documenting their journeys in queering parenthood with profits being donated to Grandmothers against Removals, a protest against the ongoing removal of Aboriginal children from their families (Sperring and Stardust 2019).

Professional Sexperts

Interventions of indie producers transcend the screen. The producers I spoke to were actively engaged in cultural discussions about sexual health, communication, and consent. While a number of authors have expressed concern about porn's prescriptive effect in supplying audiences with a narrow repertoire of sexual scripts, performers and producers I interviewed were passionate about pornography's potential to educate viewers about body diversity, pleasure, and safer sex. Porn projects were being pitched as educative projects, porn stars were leading in community health promotion campaigns, and performers were holding sex education workshops. Performers were using their scenes to document negotiations of safer sex, the definition of which continues to change with new technologies and treatments, such as pre-exposure prophylaxis (PrEP) and antiretroviral therapies (ART) that now result in undetectable viral load. In Anna Brownfield's 2016 film *The Bedroom*, she features "sex through the ages," with all six sex scenes set in one bedroom from the 1960s through the 1990s, tracing the emergence of the contraceptive pill, the HIV epidemic, the boom in vibrators, and the emergence of online sexual encounters.

In Australia, this trend represents an extension of a long history of community engagement and peer education as part of our response to HIV throughout the 1980s. Australia's unique partnership approach to HIV was led by sex workers, trans folk, gay men, and people who use drugs, and it resulted in federal and state health departments funding local community organizations to engage in health promotion and outreach (Midwinter-Pitt 2007). Sexually explicit material was used in the early nineties by the Victorian AIDS Council (VAC; now Thorne Harbour Health) and the AIDS Council of NSW (now ACON) in health promotion targeting gay men, and the eroticization of safer sex became a hallmark of gay men's HIV prevention (Leonard and Mitchell 2000). VAC issued postcards depicting gay pornography where readers could scratch off a "censored" notice to find health promotion messaging. In 2014 *Dirty Queer* magazine partnered with *Dude Magazine* and the Peer Advocacy Network for the Sexual Health of Trans Masculinities (PASH.tm) to bring out US trans porn star Buck Angel for a series of screenings and workshops that took a pleasure-positive approach to community-led health promotion.

Funding for sexually explicit material targeting women did not occur until more recently, but when it did, porn performers were featured in health promotion material that combined art, health, sex, and community. I spoke to ACON's then community engagement coordinator Viv McGregor about their unique sexual health project for lesbian, bisexual, and queer women, which ran from 2012 to 2018, using photography, video works, profiles, and interviews with porn performers for health promotion. The project sought to meet the needs of what bisexual, bi-curious women, and women who have sex with women who are presumed heterosexual. It targeted women engaged in group sex, blood sports, water sports, and sexual practices that pose an increased risk of sexually transmitted infections or blood-borne viruses by mailing information on safer sex, play piercing, and blood packs; running skill-sharing workshops; hosting film screenings; and encouraging sexual health testing (Constable and May 2012; Albury 2015). In our interview, Viv described the erotic art and interview material as "the honey to bring people in, to provide this sort of sex-positive space to explore sexuality which then includes sexual health."

Porn performers are active in adult sex education, holding instructional workshops in adult stores and kink spaces. They also support educational programs and media literacy among young people by deconstructing and analyzing porn. In the absence of comprehensive sex and relationship education, being competent in mediated sexuality has been identified by Australian researchers as a crucial part of healthy sexual development (McKee et al. 2010). In 2015 Helen Corday worked alongside Fitzroy High School in hosting five community forums, including "Pornography and Teenagers: Developing Porn Literacy" (run twice due to high demand), where porn performers spoke alongside sexologists, family planning professionals, and psychologists. Helen told me afterward about her positive feedback from other health professionals on the panel: "The presence of a porn performer . . . removed the skepticism the

FIGURE 1.6. Film still of *Yes, We Fuck!*, directed by Raúl de la Morena and Antonio Centeno, which traces the lives of six people discussing sexuality, disability, connection, attraction, and politics. The film won Best Documentary at the Berlin Porn Film Festival in 2015.

teenagers had toward community concern and lent credibility to the sexual health nurses in the eye of the teens." That same year, Clare Watson's sold-out theater piece *Gonzo* brought together four teenage boys in conversation with Helen and Gala Vanting. Instead of representing young boys as blank slates on which media is projected, *Gonzo*, based on peer-led focus groups among teenage boys aged twelve to eighteen in Melbourne, depicts teens as conscious and critical consumers. In a conversational, improvised scene with Gala and Helen, the teens asked questions about the labor conditions, whether they were having a good time, and how they maintain romantic relationships. They wanted to know if the activities were consensual and paid attention to whether the performers were using lubricant. The play explores the role of pornography as part of healthy sexual development where it is de-coded, not prescriptive, and where young people have the conceptual tools to navigate it.

The investment of porn performers and producers in health promotion does not suggest that pornography should be a substitute for comprehensive population-level sex education. As Nic Holas said to me: "To say that pornography doesn't have a role in sex education is being a bit willfully ignorant, but I also believe that it shouldn't take the place of coherent sex education and holistic sex education from . . . when we are charged with that responsibility as a way of disciplining us, that's problematic . . . [pornography] shouldn't be the primary text."

To minimize the risk that their work would become prescriptive, some performers are taking steps to increase transparency. The practice of documenting the explicit negotiation of consent has become a common practice in indie porn. Porn performers in my study described actively role modeling consensual negotiation in their behind-the-scenes footage. Sensate Films practiced content forecasting, letting viewers know in advance whether the performers in a scene were an off-screen couple, particularly experienced, fluid bonded, or had negotiated certain activities in advance. Mistress Tokyo, an experienced dominatrix, said

> I tell people when I negotiate with them before the scene starts in my professional sessions what my requirements are, as a person who can't know everything that the person is feeling. I can't speak for them, so I think that showing pre-scene negotiation and post-scene aftercare is a great thing. I think that mid-scene negotiation is really great as well. I think that for some people that will ruin the fantasy and you won't have those people buying your stuff. But I think that's a risk you have got to take.

Such moments of requesting permission for physical contact "are at the core of queer pornography" according to Grace Sharkey (2018, 141). She identified key objects that reoccur within queer porn texts, including "the gloved hand," "the bottle of lube," and the Hitachi magic wand (139), which not only reference safer sex but also speak to "understood narratives about queer intimacy in which bodies may require subtle roadmaps" (142). These initiatives are part of a broader movement in which porn stars have created public resources on sex and consent, opening up important conversations about safe words, withdrawing consent, pressure, coercion, and nonconsensual sex.

Post-pornographies

Indie porn may well be the business model of global tech companies who outsource production and control the major distribution infrastructure. Not all indie producers are trying to revolutionize the system—some are just trying to survive it or gamify it. But a diverse influx of new creators are not simply accepting "business as usual." Indie producers are engaged in world-making practices, making interventions into the processes of porn production, representation, and distribution. Many are issuing fundamental challenges to the ways porn is produced, valued, and categorized. Although these interventions are influenced by the economic, legal, and tech cultures in which they emerge, producers I interviewed are invested in changing the sexual scripts in public and private spheres; in affirming the diverse bodies of their audiences; intervening in conversations about sexual health and consent; and in archiving community subcultures and histories that might otherwise go unrecorded. They aspire to value time, intimacy, and experiences rather than specific sexual activities; they decenter explicit sex as the core of eroticism and queer the cis-normative taxonomy of sex that locates erogenous zones only in the genitals; and they are demanding that performers are valued in material ways that reflect their contributions. These approaches are confounding for regulators because they defy existing categories of classification. They contest the dominant circuits of porn distribution, cultivating their own economies, audiences, and networks. These findings demonstrate that pornographies are far more than, as suggested by regulators in chapter 3, "dirt for dirt's sake." They illustrate that indie pornographies matter, and their considerable contributions ought to be taken seriously.

Getting Our Hands Wet

I am lying on one end of a massage table, naked from the waist down. My head is nestled on the shoulder of Wendy Delorme, a French porn artist and star of Émilie Jouvet's *Much More Pussy: Feminist Sluts and the Queer X Show*. We are in a light-filled dance studio in Neukölln, Berlin, surrounded by thirty people in a circle. This sold-out workshop is part of the annual Berlin Porn Film Festival. We have limited audience numbers to maintain some sense of intimacy over the next four hours while we engage in live fisting and squirting demonstrations.

Our workshop collaborators are BDSM practitioner Gala Vanting and performance artist Sadie Lune. Gala and Sadie are known as "pleasure activists," for their interdisciplinary blending of sex work, art, education, and activism. We are four queer femme porn performers hailing from Australia, France, Germany, and the United States. Sadie—who is known for stage performances in which she invites audience members to view her cervix through a speculum— facilitates the audience, finding yoga mats for people to sit on, fielding questions, and introducing the workshop with a group breathing exercise. It's the third of three interactive, experiential, live sex education workshops I've facilitated, and it is pitched to "those with cunts and people who fuck them."

Gala has prepared a montage of squirting videos and sourced anatomical drawings that illustrate how G-spot ejaculation works. The most useful diagrams don't come from medical textbooks, but from resources produced by women pornographers, sexologists, and sex educators, such as Deborah Sundahl, Tristan Taormino, and Cyndi Darnell, who released an instructional video series titled *The Atlas of Erotic Anatomy and Arousal*. Gala's curation of porn highlights includes Christian Slaughter's *Biodildo*, in which Jiz Lee begins squirting as KAy Garnellen punches their vulva, and Heartless Productions' *Qustom Queer Qommandos*, in which Parker Reed squirts all over his custom pink guitar.

I'm hydrated to maximize the quantity I can squirt. I take probiotics to minimize the chance of thrush and abstain from sex for a brief period to ensure I'm not swollen or sensitive. I have been practicing at home with an EPI-NO—a silicone pelvic floor trainer used to prepare the perineum for stretching to minimize the risk of vaginal tears. The device was a gift from my stripper friend Cherry Pop after she used it to prepare for the birth of her baby. We talk about preparation: placing cotton wool under long fingernails inside a glove to avoid abrasions; removing nail polish to reduce the risk of bacterial vaginosis; finding hypoallergenic lube for sensitive skin, and glycerin-free lube to reduce the risk of thrush. I have had recurrent urinary tract infections since I was a child, so right before the demo I make a deliberate point of excusing myself to duck into the toilet and empty my bladder.

Like all sexual encounters, we never know what our bodies will be up for on the day. We explain to participants that our vaginal elasticity, lubrication, and capacity are affected by hormones, scar tissue, childbirth, menopause, medication, and trauma and that our relationships to them shift throughout our lifetime. We decide to present this lack of certainty not as a limitation, but rather as an opportunity to discuss why we deliberately avoid goal orientation. We decide to meet our cunts where they are at and expect no more from them than they are willing to provide in the moment.

In the end, our performance anxiety is short-lived. The four of us are seasoned show ponies—we take pleasure in the wonder of our bodies, and I am comfortable enough with a fist inside me to take questions about warm-up, crowning, and technique. During the demonstration, I take pride in standing up, rotating, and even walking backward on all fours, dragging my fister behind me as a means of demonstrating the strength of vaginal muscles and suction.

People circle the table along different vantage points. One of the participants is nursing her newborn baby. "How does that feel for you?" "How do you know when to enter?" "Can you actually feel the cervix with your knuckles?" "Can everyone squirt?" This interactivity is one of the most dynamic and compelling parts of the workshop. As we are lit under fluorescent lights and in close proximity, participants can hear our breath, watch us check in, shift positions, and ask us questions. This skill set of body awareness and frank communication is one we have each learned from sex work.

Wendy Delorme and Zahra Stardust in a live fisting demonstration at the Berlin Porn Film Festival 2015, also featuring Sara Svärtan Persson (*left*), Gala Vanting (*middle*), and Marije Janssen (*right*).

Films and diagrams aside, the ritualistic aspect is what feels most unique to live demonstration. Later, Gala describes the event as "one of the most moving and reverent atmospheres I have witnessed." Marije Janssen, one participant who runs porn film festivals in the Netherlands, told us afterward: "So many people think of fisting as something aggressive, something the receiver almost has to endure, in a way. But to really see, right in front of you, the care, intensity, and intimacy is a huge eye-opener." Meanwhile, another participant, Sara Svärtan Persson, described the atmosphere as "welcoming and open. It felt safe, as well as intimate."

As porn stars, representations of our sexual selves are widely accessible, and our lives are often treated as a kind of public utility. Because of this widespread cultural entitlement to our bodies, carving out space for intimacy, even within this modestly sized workshop, feels like a crucial act of self-care. As Gala lies down for the squirting section, I stand at the top of the massage table and put my hands on her chest. From here, I can touch her hair, hold her hand, or just be close. We have spoken in advance about the importance for Gala of having her whore family around her in a protective bubble when she performs in a public space. For a moment, the audience is quiet, and Sadie is at work. We hear Gala's breath and, in time, the sound of her ejaculate falling on the sheet. The participants are peering in for a better view. "I invite you to come and sniff my squirt," Gala said, smiling, at the end of the workshop. As Wendy and I begin to pack up our materials, a queue of participants forms, leaning in to sniff Gala's wet patch.

2

Imagining Alternatives

Production Values and Ethics

"It's about the process, not just the product" may be the catchcry of the feminist porn movement. At a time when intimacy coordinators are increasingly hired (and, post-#MeToo, sometimes legally required) on film sets in order to ensure the safety and well-being of actors, porn performers—who have long been practicing intimacy facilitation—are developing innovative visions and processes for best practice ethics on intimate sets. In the absence of formal codified workplace health and safety (WHS) standards or industrial protections, indie pornographers are creating their own blueprints, pioneering and role modeling ethical processes from recruitment through to production, marketing, and distribution. The ethics described by my participants goes far beyond the WHS concerns of regulators.

Below I outline how the ethical interventions of indie porn producers constitute a "radical rethinking of what occupational health policy is imagined to do" (Berg 2021, 180). The ethics my participants describe build from key bodies of knowledge, including sex worker rights, HIV activism, feminist care ethics, disability justice, anarchism, and anti-capitalism. These wisdoms influence their approaches to rights, performer experience, labor organizing, collective decision-making, accountability, consent culture, and sexual health. I suggest that these interventions resemble a "prefigurative politics" (Daring et al. 2012, 255) whereby social movement actors are making new worlds by taking active steps to create and live them. These movements think beyond the law to *prefigure* alternatives to the existing system. While indie pornography movements are deconstructive—offering critiques of current systems of regulation—they are also *generative*: imagining, articulating, and building new ways of doing and relating.

Precarious Protections

When Helen Corday discovered that the former Australian porn website Abby Winters ("happy, healthy and natural girls getting naked") was selling her scenes to third parties, she was concerned. Having expected that her material would be available only on one website, behind a paywall, she was not adequately informed that the scenes could subsequently be sold and used in unanticipated contexts. Helen did not feel equipped to report this to the regulatory body Fair Work Australia because the content was being produced in Melbourne, where production of so-called objectionable content was criminalized. Instead, when private negotiations with the company G Media failed, Helen went online: She wrote a personal blog piece about their unethical practices. It was then that Helen was approached by the *Herald Sun*, a tabloid newspaper that, instead of reporting on the industrial issues at stake, used her blog as part of a series of sensationalist articles campaigning against pornography. These articles eventually led to the prosecution of Abby Winters and their subsequent relocation to Amsterdam.

When I spoke to Helen she told me she felt that the combination of tabloid media and porn stigma meant that her original concerns about onselling content to third parties and transparency in performer contracts were totally eclipsed. She surmised, "We can't have public conversations about industry standards" because when internal discussions go public, media itself plays a punitive role and performer grievances are used as ammunition to justify increased law enforcement instead of improving worker rights: "That whole episode is an indication of the problem of criminalization and stigma in the media around these issues, that any real discussion about ethical standards was just lost."

When I spoke to Robbie Swan, one of the cofounders of Eros Association, he recalled that the articles were pitched in such a way that they demanded police attention.

> That case was brought to trial essentially by a crime writer for the *Herald Sun*, Keith Moore. . . . I'm not sure about what his personal agenda was with that, but he got a bee in his bonnet, you would have to say, and he wrote stories claiming that young women obviously above age but between eighteen and twenty-three, twenty-five, were making films of themselves, and they were selling them online to G Media. Now, the story he wrote in the *Herald Sun* was very provocative and basically accused the police of not doing anything about it. He wrote a second follow-up story as well. The police really couldn't ignore it.

The precarious legal position of pornography in many countries poses barriers to the open and transparent development of labor standards for porn workers. Even where production is legal, appropriate WHS standards and/or industrial rights are lacking. Criminalization of production and laws that prohibit association make it difficult for performers to collectively and openly organize, unionize, or mobilize for fear of identification, discrimination, and arrest. Speaking out about poor experiences on set is risky for performers, as it plays into regulator fantasies of risk and danger while rarely leading to positive outcomes. Even in countries where the production of pornography is legal, such as the United States, regulation is disproportionately focused on preventing STIs and HIV transmission, such as proposing mandatory condom use.

And yet, in my interviews, performer iterations of WHS extended far beyond sexual health into the provision of adequate food and water, the choice of scene partners, adequate air-conditioning, pastoral care, and cultural safety. In our interviews, performers shared salient concerns about industrial rights issues: the content of their contracts, privacy of their information, and processes for dispute resolution. Some were concerned about what Luna Trash referred to as "creepers," "predators," and the "dodgy guy with a camera" taking advantage of models and believed that decriminalization would provide greater transparency for performers to share safety information. The kinds of ethical concerns described by participants extend beyond the fantasies of WHS projected by governments.

Performers indicated little faith in government to develop appropriate standards for the industry. Angela White, who had worked in Los Angeles at

FIGURE 2.1. Sex School Berlin is an explicit sex education platform founded by An-narella Martinez-Madrid. The sex worker– and sex educator–led site presents "how-to" content on topics such as consent, communication, sexual health, and identity. It features (*from left*) Bishop Black, Parker Marx, Sadie Lune, and Lina Bembe. Image by Natália Zajačiková.

the time regulators proposed mandatory condom use, reflected: "I wouldn't want anything to be overregulated where it became impossible to actually produce, which is what they're kind of proposing with Measure B in the States, where people would essentially have to wear hazmat suits to perform."

In our interview, porn scholar Alan McKee cautioned against having undue faith in "the hands of politicians," given government's track record and its lack of insight about the industry, asking, "How much would you trust the government to decide what is desirable practice in sex work?" Suggesting that regulators may use a rhetoric of protection in order to justify further criminalization, he added, "People aren't treating you well enough; therefore we're going to make it illegal to do what you're doing." Performers expressed concern about what McKee (2016) has described as "the exceptionalist approach to pornography." In creating onerous requirements that do not exist in other industries, governments are "setting up an impossible standard" that would not be feasible to comply with. Noncompliance, then, is used to provide justification for abolition of the industry. It is for these reasons that indie porn producers are creating their own informal standards of production.

Rights, Care, and Ethics

The focus on ethics in production has been precipitated in part by the international sex worker rights movement, with greater numbers of sex workers moving behind the camera and performers speaking out about their on-set experiences. Over the past four decades, sex workers have framed many of their claims using a language of constitutional protection and human rights. Gail Pheterson's anthology *A Vindication of the Rights of Whores* and the World Charter for Prostitutes' Rights adopted at the first World Whores Congress in Amsterdam in 1985 paved the way for sex worker movements to advocate for decriminalization, WHS standards, and industrial rights protections (Chateauvert 2014). More recently, the mobilization of a rights discourse for porn performers is particularly stark in the United States, where the Adult Performer Advocacy Committee, a California body made up of porn performers, provides its Performer Bill of Rights (Adult Performer Advocacy Committee, n.d.b). Porn performers have also contributed to the Free Speech Coalition's INSPIRE program (Industry Newcomer Support Program) heralded by performer outreach advocate Lotus Lain, which informs, shares resources, and provides awareness and guidance for new or prospective performers. In Australia, Eros Association developed its Adult Media Production Standards in 2018, outlining the basic rights of performers on a porn set, including expectations, amenities, and payment.

In addition to the frameworks of rights, the ethical processes of porn production described by my participants resemble a feminist ethic of care. A field of normative ethics that concerns how we ought to act, feminist ethics of care developed in the late seventies and early eighties in response to the misogyny evident in traditional moral philosophy. Feminists critiqued the centering of culturally such masculine traits as autonomy, hierarchy, and fairness, which situated "human beings as free, equal, independent and mutually disinterested, a conception claimed by some to be contrary to the experience of most women" (Jaggar 1991, 81), and instead focused on the value of such culturally feminine traits as interdependence, community, connection, sharing, absence of hierarchy, and process (Jaggar 2013). The focus on performer experiences and alertness to their emotional health and well-being closely resembles care ethics categories of attentiveness, responsibility, competence, and responsiveness (Tronto 1993). Performer concerns with accountability, feedback processes, transparency, and dispute resolution reflect the turn toward justice in more contemporary feminist ethics (Held 2018).

For example, Angela White described how producers should consider "anything from what makes [performers] feel comfortable in terms of air-conditioning, whether they're hot or cold, whether they're hungry, making sure they've had enough to eat or drink, making sure that they feel up to the scene on the day." Being attentive like this requires a devotion to learning what the other person might need without projecting one's own needs. In her advice to potential porn producers, Michelle Flynn blogs that they should do some self-reflection on their experience and familiarity with the industry before deciding to produce so that they don't put "people's safety in jeopardy." She recommends that potential producers "earn your stripes and know what your role is before you place yourself at the helm." Her approach values the labor of performers rather than expecting them to be a free pool to tap into: "It's so important to be sensitive to the needs and concerns of people working in a sexual and potentially vulnerable space, and those who have been in that space themselves are especially well equipped to empathize. Put yourself in the performers' shoes as best you can; don't ask them to do anything you wouldn't do yourself."

Black feminist care ethics teach us that care must extend beyond the self, beyond individual luxury, and beyond capitalist logics and instead constitute a form of political activism, connection, and resistance to an anti-Black and capitalist world (hooks 2001; Piepzna-Samarasinha 2018). Sex worker ethics are informed by an intimate knowledge of sexuality and labor. Sex worker activism is "inextricably related to struggles for the recognition of women's work, for basic human rights and for decent working conditions" (Kempadoo and Doezema 1998) as well as situated in a history of antiwork and anti-capitalist politics (Mac and Smith 2018; Hester and Stardust 2019). Sex worker activism also developed against the backdrop of the gay and lesbian liberation movements of the 1960s, the sex wars between second-wave feminists and s/m lesbians in the 1970s, and the HIV epidemic of the 1980s. In my interviews, performer-producers described an ethics that valued insider knowledge and lived experience. Gala, for example, believed that her experience as a performer informed her ethics as a producer: It "helps a lot in developing your code of ethics: understanding what it means for you to distribute your work wherever and however you do." Angela White described the value of being a *current* rather than a *former* performer because it meant she was still in tune with and had an "insight into performer needs." Performers brought a heightened sense of the stakes of offering up something intimate and valuable to a politicized public. There was an *affinity* here between performers—a level of empathy, investment, and accountability that came with shared experiences or collective stakes.

Consent Cultures

While some anti-pornography feminists have argued that women cannot consent to participate in pornography at all, feminist porn producers have made efforts to make the casting process as transparent as possible in an effort to support informed decision-making. Performers I spoke to were concerned with full and frank disclosure about on-set expectations and contractual obligations. Michelle Flynn referred to this practice of "full disclosure," meaning that performers are provided with transparent details about the scene in advance of the shoot, including information on how long they will be required to perform, whom they will be performing with, what acts they will be expected to perform, what they will be paid, whether there will be behind-the-scenes interviews, and how many people will be present. The BIPOC Adult Industry Collective are demanding also that performers be told the title of the film in advance so that they do not agree to contribute to a film only to find out later that it employs racist marketing terminology. Daisy Ducati, for example, recalled participating in an interracial shoot and then two weeks later seeing the DVD titled "Black Wives Matter" (McGowan 2020).

Performers I interviewed raised additional aspects that were relevant to them, including clarity about what happens to the footage following the shoot, how the footage would be edited and distributed, and whether the scene could be sold in full (rather than just licensed) to a third party. This could include honest information about where the content could potentially end up, including the real risk of porn piracy, and whether the producer has a policy to address content theft. This information was relevant to performers' decisions about what their labor power was worth to the producer. If the scene was for worldwide distribution or open access on tube sites rather than for festival use only, this may impact a performer's decision about their payrates. Having this information well in advance of the shoot would mean that performers would have time to review their contract, raise any issues, and negotiate terms and conditions before filming begins instead of producers "upselling" (asking the performer to do more explicit acts) on set while the camera is rolling.

To some extent, this shift represents a response to stereotypes of the casting couch, a genre of pornography in which the power difference between performer and director is eroticized and performers may be pressured into impromptu sexual acts as part of the casting process. In order to avoid situations of duress or exploitation, it was important to some interviewees that they not actively recruit for their projects but, rather, let people come to them on their own initiative. As Domino from *Slit* magazine said, "We only want content from people who want to share it." Sensate Films told me, "We work with people who have self-nominated. So they don't come to us from an agency or anything. They find out about what we do and they come to us." This strategy aims to draw people to their project through word of mouth as a "vouching" system for reputation. It also means that performers find their way via community, scene-connectedness, and sexual networks. For example, Cat O'Nine Tails started her website Shot with Desire by shooting content of her friends in the punk and queer scenes. Potential performers came to Nic Holas through his work in porn, sex parties, or his Scruff profile. For producers who did not necessarily share the same sexual networks, a more formal recruitment process was necessary. Larger businesses I spoke to did advertise but often had a built-in cooling-off period prior to shooting.

Producers described feeling a responsibility toward new performers and allocated additional time to discuss the implications on their lives, including the potential impact of stigma on employment, family life, child custody and relationships, and any legal risks. Producers described going beyond their formal obligations to provide a legal duty of care. There was an awareness that the stigma attached to pornography warranted additional care. When shooting her feature film *The Band*, Anna Brownfield described how one woman changed her mind two days before shooting was set to begin. Anna's response was "My attitude is the more information, the better. . . . I'd rather people be there because they actually want to be there." This ethic prioritizes the well-being of performers, however inconvenient businesswise. Theme Fatale Lucie Bee felt the onus was on the producer to provide up-front information, precisely because once the material is in the public domain, it becomes difficult for anyone to control: "We need to be having those conversations with people because I think some people waltz into porn thinking 'I'm going to make a bit of cash' and then it's going to disappear on the internet and no one will see it. That's not what happens. . . . Once this is on the internet, it's on the internet, and we could take it down tomorrow, but someone's probably illegally downloaded it a bunch of times and it's not going to go away. There'll be screen shots; there'll be everything."

Clarification of the minimum requirements that need to be performed in order to be paid also was seen as part of responsible practice. Madison Missina felt the need for transparency around what constituted "completion" of a scene prior to shooting, particularly in relation to orgasm: Would she be paid if she didn't orgasm? In some cases, she felt that producers' expectations, informed by gendered conventions, were just assumed rather than explicitly negotiated. Transparency in advance gives performers opportunity to negotiate terms and engage in collective bargaining.

FIGURE 2.2. Shine Louise Houston (*left*), founding producer and director of Pink and White Productions, CrashPadSeries.com, and PinkLabel.tv, behind the scenes of filming *The Crash Pad* with Goddess Ixchel and Ray. In Shine's view, "There is power in creating images, and for a woman of color and a queer to take that power . . . I don't find it exploitative; I think it's necessary." Image by CrashPadSeries.com.

Risk, Safety, and Sexual Health

Performers' discussions of sexual health are also informed by an ethic of care centering on performer choice between a range of risk-reduction strategies. New technologies in STI/HIV treatments and prevention have changed definitions of safer sex, meaning there are now multiple means of reducing the risk of transmission, from the use of prophylactics, such as condoms, gloves, and dams, to serosorting (sorting sexual partners per HIV status), the use of PrEP to prevent HIV transmission, and the use of the treatment as prevention (TASP) technique whereby a person living with HIV can maintain an undetectable viral load. My interviewees were concerned with having opportunities to negotiate strategies that suit them and being provided with free personal protective equipment rather than the imposition of one safer sex method.

These approaches are quite different from regulatory models in other jurisdictions, such as in Los Angeles, where performers are required to undergo STI/HIV tests every fourteen days and have a negative result before being eligible to shoot. The current Performer Availability Screening Service (PASS) system run by the Free Speech Coalition provides a testing protocol and centralized database for checking clearance to work. While this system is reasonably effective (there has not been a case of on-set transmission of HIV since 2004), requirements for performers to be HIV negative assumes that people living with HIV cannot have safe, ethical, responsible, or pleasurable sex. Testing has been criticized as a sole prevention tool because window periods mean that recent infections will not be detected. Testing can incur a cost to the performer and also relies on trust in one's co-performers being safe off set following their latest test. While regulatory measures have sought to mandate one type of safer sex method (for example, condom use), these attempts fall behind the latest scientific developments in risk-reduction tools.

While these rigid models are particular to the LA mainstream porn industry, indie creators in the United States often work outside the commercial talent pool, using fluid-bonded lovers with their own safer sex agreements or providing performers with a range of resources to choose from rather than dictating what safer sex looks like. Australian performers similarly are concerned with having genuine choice over their safer sex practices. It is further of concern that STI/HIV prevention methods remain voluntary and confidential. Nic Holas, an HIV activist, spoke to the threat of forced medication and removal of a worker's right to choose their own risk reduction strategy. Angela White raised the concern that producers might offer a choice but then stop hiring people who choose to use condoms, dams, or gloves. Performers also were suspicious of an overinvestment in biomedical solutions to HIV: "We can't just default to a pharmaceutical solution when what we have is an ethical problem," Nic Holas told me. "I don't know that paperwork is the smartest way for us to protect ourselves."

Some producers provided free safer sex barriers with nonallergenic, latex-free and paraben-free options. Sensate Films supported the decision-making of performers. As Gala described,

> So what we have at Sensate is a form in which the performers involved in a scene agree to various options in regards to sexual health and protection. So, if they are fluid-bonded already and they don't wish to make use of safer sex supplies, they are able to elect that. If they want to do mutual testing, they decide that amongst themselves and we witness the test. And then we also make whatever supplies they might need available to them free of cost. So that kind of encapsulates my attitude towards that, which is basically that the worker chose their own conditions and the workplace supports this, and proactively finds information they might

need to make those decisions and provide the equipment necessary to carry out whatever choice they've made.

In conversations with my interviewees, they made it clear that it was important for producers to allocate sufficient time and space for performers to negotiate their scenes and to protect the confidentiality of their health status. Dick Savvy described having "a pretty intense discussion about the scene" at least two or three days beforehand around negotiating safer sex: "There's no way in hell that I want to put someone at risk." Nic Holas discussed the ethical considerations of serodiscordant sex:

> If I was shooting a scene in which I had two people of different statuses—I knew, for example, that I had a pos guy and a neg guy performing together, that for me is a big ethical conversation that needs to involve those two performers. That's really where it begins and ends. It's what those two performers are comfortable with and comfortable with doing. . . . I have a bigger responsibility than just HIV and just sexual health, but also to mental health and safety and personal safety for both of those two performers. . . . If fear of contracting HIV or the risk of contracting HIV is one of those things that affects that end game, then the shoot needs to be postponed or altered.

Part of supporting a performer's own decision-making was also protecting the confidentiality of their health status, particularly in light of reports of hook-up apps selling data on the HIV status of their users (Christian 2018). In 2011 the legal names of fifteen thousand porn performers were leaked from the Adult Industry Medical Healthcare Foundation (AIM) database by a disgruntled ex-performer/director; some had their addresses, the names of family members, and the details of their STI/HIV status published online on Porn Wikileaks. AIM was sued for patient privacy violations and went out of business. In our conversation, Nic Holas believed that respect for the privacy of performers "is a piece of the puzzle that's been missing from a lot of discourse around risk and sexual safety."

Privacy for Exhibitionists

My interviews indicate that performer control over their own images is an essential part of ethical production. When porn performer Mia Khalifa launched a petition in 2019 for her videos to be scrubbed from Pornhub and Bang Bros, her campaign spoke to multiple legal and ethical issues facing online sex workers: unfair contractual terms, inadequate privacy protections, and a lack of avenues to address piracy and nonconsensual intimate imagery. Since a Motherboard investigation exposed the scraping and distributing of a large volume of sex workers' OnlyFans content in 2020, this conversation has reignited. Performers I spoke to were concerned about their content being screenshotted, capped (recorded), or reposted elsewhere as well as the risks of doxing, trolling, stalking, harassment, malicious flagging, scraping, and data mining. Risks of production are heightened with the broader increase in digital surveillance: Geolocation devices on smartphones mean that posting on social media could notify authorities and bring risk of raids; mandatory data-retention laws requiring ISPs to keep records of phone calls and emails risk providing government with potentially incriminating details; the use of facial recognition technology to verify performers connects their performer and legal identities. As Alexander Monea (2022) writes, "escaping the scope of digital surveillance is near impossible" (1).

In our interview, former Scarlet Alliance CEO Janelle Fawkes recalled a number of cases where sex worker IDs were used by former business owners to blackmail them. The legal and immigration statuses of porn performers can make them vulnerable: Madison Missina described an experience in which a producer she had worked with contacted the US Department of Homeland Security about her sex work when she was there on holiday and reported being deported with a ten-year ban. These experiences are consistent with recent research. Vaughn Hamilton, Hanna Barakat, and Elissa M. Redmiles (2022) examined the impact on sex workers across seven countries who had moved from in-person to online-only work during the COVID-19 pandemic and found that, while there were benefits to online work, the public visibility also introduced new risks: "greater digital exposure, burnout, and loss of control" (21).

The risks for performers are salient with archival projects to digitize queer and feminist pornography archives. While many queer, feminist, and independent porn projects have been intended as subcultural community materials, sold in hard copy at discreet local venues, recent digitization projects may raise privacy risks for performers. Controversy has emerged about the ethics of digitization of *On Our Backs*, a lesbian sex print magazine, surrounding the benefits of making this iconic publication digitally accessible while being mindful of whether performers have given consent for their image to be used in new contexts and new media (Groeneveld 2018). Xavier Marz, who works in a straight job outside his queer community work, described being hyper aware of the vulnerability given the political environment: "I think when you're queer and you're out there and you're sex positive and you're appearing in things, those things last forever, especially with the internet. Shit is so Google-able." Giving performers control over their image involves a tacit recognition that their labor elicits personal risks.

An ethics of care, affinity, and accountability extends to post-production, including into the conscious use and marketing of the product. Some produc-ers gave performers the opportunity to review and approve content after it had been edited. Luna Trash, for example, had a policy of deleting all con-tent that was not approved by the performer: "Nothing will be printed unless they completely are totally happy . . . even if you end up with one photo left from the whole shoot." Gala described how she had selected, "down to the shot," the footage she appears in for Sensate Films "completely on my own terms." This emphasis on self-determination and self-representation is driven by performer-producers who have a lived experience of the repercussions of losing control over one's image online. Luna recalls, "I've had really negative experiences with men's magazines and I'm not doing them ever again for that reason. . . . They just send off the images, and you look and you're like, 'Why would you pick that photo?'" In magazines such as *Picture, People,* and *Pent-house,* models might not see their images until they buy a copy from a retailer. Building in processes for performers to approve their images (or at least input into the decision-making) recognizes that detached business practices can have real-world impacts on the emotional health of performers.

Given the risks of piracy and discrimination, some producers I spoke to gave performers the option of deciding their level of exposure in advertising, in-creasing performer control over where their images could be sold or shared. For example, Howard's model release sought permission to use the material for broad-based marketing: "We don't onsell without the permission of the contributor . . . we don't just commodify that image and spread it all around the internet at our whim like a lot of producers do." Sensate Films went fur-ther, giving performers choice from a range of options for marketing, includ-ing "whether you need your face to be out of promotional things." These prac-tices were a practical recognition of the realities of porn stigma. Standard model releases afford producers rights to exploit the image and its likeness in perpetuity. In Madison Missina's experience within mainstream porn, model releases have been standard "company gets everything," allowing producers to use the footage for maximum profit and visibility. In contrast, given the op-tion, performers might ask that their image be used only in hard copy but not online, only within its original context, not as part of advertising material, or for only their body shots to be made public while their faces remain behind a paywall.

Limits on future use of the material were more common in smaller sized projects where the scale facilitated more frequent communication and closer working relationships. Xavier Marz described how at *Dirty Queer* magazine "we've had people go in and say, 'I want to cross that bit out.' We're like, 'Sure, absolutely.'" Smaller operations offered a level of personal and community responsibility that may be more time-consuming within a commercial context. For example, *Slit* noted that "in most formal, or in bigger productions, there's a much more formalized approach to getting release forms and consent for the reproduction of images. And in *Slit* we mostly relied on the fact that we had personal relationships and developed personal relationships with each of the contributors." People knew each other through "six degrees of separation," which allowed for contact and discussion: "It enabled a kind of informality that is perhaps not as possible when we're talking about bigger arrangements."

Attention to privacy also means putting in place systems that reduce the risk that a performer's identity documents can be misused. Although there are no formal legal standards in Australia outlining what information and identification producers need to collect, Australian producers often borrow from the United States. The 2257 Form (a model release form), originally enacted and struck down following the Meese Commission on pornography in 1986 and then reintroduced in 1990 as part of child protection legislation, seeks to prevent child sexual abuse material by requiring producers to keep detailed records. The 2257 requires producers to collect two sets of photo identification, performer aliases, addresses, signatures, and Social Security numbers and to publish the date and location of shoot, the name of the custodian of records, and the location in which this paperwork is held, which cannot be a post office box and must be a residential or business address. US producers themselves have criticized this system as placing solo and home-based producers at risk of stalking and harassment (see Taormino 2006), and the Free Speech Coalition has challenged it in court as being unconstitutional.

Sex workers themselves are sharing strategies to protect their privacy. Gala Vanting had partnered with sex worker technologists Assembly Four to produce a digital security resource for sex workers. Janelle Fawkes suggested alternative methods of verifying identification to reduce misuse of information or harassment. Instead of storing ID, she suggested an analog process whereby an ID was sighted by a number of witnesses who signed to verify the person's date of birth. Gamer geek Lucie Bee suggested there should be stipulations about how long a producer could hold your ID, for what purposes, where they would store it, and who could access it. Legally, a 2257 Form can be securely discarded after seven years; however, fear of fines and of prison sentences for failing to have paperwork can act as a barrier to producers ever destroying

FIGURE 2.3. Jet Setting Jasmine and King Noire, who operate the award-winning website Royal Fetish XXX, offer practical advice on kink, communication, race, gender, relationships, parenting, and polyamory in their "Porn and Politics" column in *HoneySuckle* magazine. A licensed psychotherapist, mental health educator, and intimacy coordinator, Jasmine supports porn performers navigating intimacy, trauma, and cultural identity. Image by *HoneySuckle* magazine and Royal Fetish XXX.

them. Others suggested confidentiality agreements to ensure that producers do not disclose sensitive information learned during the shoot, such as a person's serostatus. Pink and White Productions has partnered with Takedown Piracy to offer digital fingerprinting (enabling a video to be uniquely identified) so that producers can more easily identify copyright breach and issue takedown requests. As more platforms move toward digital verification, privacy risks are one of the key workplace issues facing performers. In 2023 the European Sex Workers Rights Alliance published the report "Toward Safer Intimate Futures," in which they described the level of risk management sex workers are required to do as "victim blaming enacted by technological design" (Qin et al. 2023, 14).

Responsible Consumption

Ethics in production also extends to how scenes are marketed to consumers. The producers I spoke to were eager to present performers as multifaceted human beings. As Michelle Flynn remarked, "These are performers; they're not commodities. You know, they're people." Luna insisted that the women in *Trash Dolls* "were performers, artists, creative individuals." Although the inclination to sell performers' tastes and preferences is explored more critically in chapter 5, an ethics of care extended to *humanizing* performers. Luna tried to pick creative questions in her interviews that would elucidate the performers' status as multidimensional beings rather than focusing only on their genitals: "We wanted to show that these are smart, intelligent girls." Similarly, Cat O'Nine Tails focused on performers' "unique beauty and individuality." She said, "I'm never going to write 'Look at this slut that's really down with it, and she only opens her mouth for cock, the stupid bitch' or some crap like that. I never ever write anything disrespectful about the people that have posed for me." Producers aimed to show respect for the performer as an individual, paying attention to how each wanted to be portrayed.

Producers then employed various mechanisms that gave cues to consumers about how to read and interpret their texts, from marketing materials to the monitoring of forums. Consumers were invited to engage according to the values of the site and encouraged to make positive and generous comments about the performers. Howard reported that his sites were designed in a way that encouraged this: "We don't ever trivialize their contributions, and we want the customers to understand that." When I spoke with Garion Hall, founder of Abby Winters, he believed this could in part be achieved by the presentation and layout of his site, which he said "tends to attract people who share our values and certainly are less likely to say dickhead things on a public forum anyway." Helen Corday believed there was also a role for "educating the consumer to be respectful." On some sites, performers wrote their own artist bios and chose the information they wanted to share, which meant their representations were not mediated by the producer. For example, *Slit* "favored an approach which was a record of conversation rather than a lot of editorial." This focus was on giving performers a platform to speak for themselves instead of a producer projecting their own fantasies.

Of course, this was not a foolproof method. As Nic Holas reminded me, "We are not in control of the way that the material we make is interpreted" or "what the viewer projects onto that pornography." The possibility always remains of "misogynist or homophobic or empty queer filters being applied on top of that otherwise beautiful, honest work." These steps nevertheless remained structural safeguards to protect performers. Producers had different ways in which they moderated forums, from approving comments before they went live to deleting comments they thought were nasty or demeaning. For example, Howard practiced retro moderating on his large site, which meant that "everything gets published before we get the chance to moderate it." He described times when staff would write to members "and explain to them why it's not an appropriate thing to say about this person who's just put themselves naked out on the internet for the world to see." Garion Hall couldn't recall ever removing a comment from a customer but noted a time when a member had commented on a model's weight, and the model had responded with "a big fuck you." In this case these men relied on the labor of customers and other models joining the discussion to effectively school the member. Leaving models to defend themselves and retroactively removing comments was a strategy utilized by these large companies, which hosted a significant amount of content. It relied on producers identifying what is hurtful and standing up for their models. However, smaller projects could take a different approach. Helen Corday, a former model for alternative Australian erotica sites, was more proactive when she started her solo site: "I didn't put a comment [function] on the videos because it was more important to me that there never be a moment where a performer might be insulted." This issue of moderation on digital platforms and its challenges about who bears responsibility for managing risk is not isolated to porn websites. However, for producers, encouraging responsible consumption was a core aspect of their approach to ethical production.

Conflicts in Compliance

Industry conversations about what constitutes ethical production practices reveal a number of tensions: between the interests of workers versus producers; between accountability to performers versus governments; about who needs protection and from what; and about the status of porn as work. While performer-producers described a community-based, worker-led ethics of care, based on a politics of affinity and a framework of accountability, nonperformer producers described a duty and responsibility to protect performers via compliance with legal obligations. Producers had to protect themselves from liability and many saw paperwork as an effective way of demonstrating their ethical processes.

For example, Michelle Flynn saw the collection of identification and records as a critical step in ethical production as well as having standardized processes and checklists for accountability. Having previously worked for Abby Winters before she went independent, Michelle said that recordkeeping was "drilled into me for the last nine years." When we spoke about whether there was a tension in recordkeeping in a criminal environment because it posed risks of incrimination, she replied, "Yeah. But I would rather be incriminated for shooting someone consensually that is over eighteen than potentially being incriminated for shooting someone under eighteen. But that's the trade-off, right?" This concern is illustrative of the political climate in which pornography is being produced—fear of producing pornography featuring minors was ever-present, given the need to protect children and young people, its heavy criminal consequences, and the repeated media portrayal of pornographers as exploitative, irresponsible, and predatory.

Similarly, the discreet processes of recruitment (as one producer described them, "clandestine") occurred largely in response to the criminalization of production, serving to avoid legal consequences for advertising. But recruitment also included a gatekeeping function in determining who was eligible to participate, which Howard described in our interview as "responsible recruitment." Howard spoke about meeting legal requirements to ensure all performers were adult, but he also went further, using an intuitive judgment about potential participants to "assess them for suitability." Howard, who was not a performer himself, described his process as follows:

> If there's anything obvious that comes up then the interviewer is trained to discourage them, or to turn them away, or put mechanisms in place to prevent them getting involved, and those might be people that present as being desperate for money, and usually they're identified because they'll say that—their attitude will be, "Look I just urgently need some money; what do I have to do to get it?" Or if they're under the influence of drugs or alcohol then we sort of usher them out the door without asking for any commitment to participate, and usually they don't come back. So there are signs that we look for, people for whom this is not a good idea. The other one is their career choice. If they tell us that they're training to be a teacher, for example, we'll advise them that it's probably not a good idea to get involved, or if they ever want to run for public office, same thing really.

These considerations recognize the risks of stigma on the lives of sex workers, ensuring that consent is informed (and sober) with opportunities to consider its future impact. However, such deliberation processes also raise questions about decision-making and agency. Sex workers have criticized producers' reluctance to hire people who are only "there for the money" and their expectations that workers are there for anything other than the money. Sex workers who live in chronic pain and who manage their pain with drugs— pharmaceutical or otherwise—can still be capable decision-makers. People who use drugs have also spoken out against paternalistic judgments about how they spend their money: Elena Jeffreys (2007) notes that people working in other professions, such as lawyers, are not accused of being forced to work in the legal profession to support their drug use. The protectionism of producers goes further than legally required. Rather than taking a harm-reduction or health-promotion approach, in their paternalistic distancing from sex workers and people who use (illicit) drugs, they gatekeep who can make the decision to use their body for work and potentially increase their stigmatization.

Similar tensions were evident in cases where performers wanted their footage removed from a website. Performers expressed interest in establishing a clear process for taking down content should they change their mind. However, some large companies had a policy that they would only remove content if it had been live for a certain period (for example, ninety days) so that the company could earn exposure and income from its release. Performers reported that other companies required them to pay back the money they earned during the shoot. These conversations in part were about the status of pornography—questioning whether it should be treated like other forms of media production with enforceable contracts, where an artist would have difficulty recalling their work after signing a release and receiving consideration, unless there were specific remedies written into the contract. Performers suggested that the stigmatized status of pornography called for a more nuanced approach to consent, and some saw this behavior as image-based abuse. They positioned their consent as dynamic, something that could be withdrawn at any stage. They were invested in producers having clear, up-front policies in place about what steps (if any) were available to them, and at what stages of publishing and distribution they could elect to recall their image.

Discussions around the appropriate process for protecting sexual health also demonstrate disjuncture between an ethics of care and producers' legal obligations, which could sometimes be in conflict. Producers were concerned about their duty of care to prevent STI/HIV transmission on set and a desire to send a message that, as one producer put it, "We care about performers; we care about modeling safe sex." When that burden on an employer is set in legislation (for example, in some states employers are required to demonstrate that they have taken reasonable steps to minimize the risk of STI/HIV transmission), the risk then becomes that producers may start collecting (and storing) copies of test results or even requesting on-site testing. The need for producers to prove that they have taken all necessary steps to ensure safety could have unintended consequences for performers and has the potential to undermine public health objectives.

Questions of ethics and compliance raise questions of accountability. Although producers felt a sense of legal responsibility and professional duty, they

FIGURE 2.4. Porn academic and femme gimp Loree Erickson pictured in the poster for her film *Want*. Loree, a pioneer of queercrip porn, is building intimate bonds within her care collectives and among her scene partners and fellow activists. Image courtesy of Loree Erickson.

expressed a willingness to be answerable to performers and a readiness to account for their decisions. This sense of accountability was especially visible among producer-performers, who straddled the multifaceted role of recruiting, producing, screening, and living within sex worker communities. Helen Corday reflected, "I feel like I answer to my community, and I'm open to it. I answer to sex workers primarily." Many producers invited performers to provide feedback following the shoot about their experiences with a view toward adapting their production practices accordingly. In their accounts of what constituted ethical production, performer-producers were less concerned with what governments identified as their legal responsibilities and more concerned about being adaptive to changing community values.

Doing It Ourselves

Current regulatory models that see pornography only as something to restrict access to are inadequate in addressing the needs and protections espoused by porn performers. In the context of this lack, producers turn to other jurisdictions for guidance and paperwork on how to safeguard their businesses.

Meanwhile, performers and producers are participating in a dynamic process of developing ethical approaches to content production and distribution, sharing practices and strategies across continents. Their approaches are works in progress that adapt and respond to changing social norms and critical conversations. What constitutes ethical porn is neither static nor uncontested. Dialogues about ethical porn production borrow from other social movements and philosophies as well as look both locally and internationally. In doing this, producers and performers are engaged in a process of creating new blueprints and prefiguring alternatives.

The intimate, experiential knowledges that performers hold shape their ethics in relation to health, work, privacy, care, and justice and call for rethinking current approaches to regulation. Regulators and policymakers could learn a great deal from listening to the nuances of these ethics and by being guided by the initiatives of these stakeholders. Indeed, it is the responsibility of regulators to do so. But in the spirit of DIY culture, porn communities are not waiting for regulators to catch up or to protect them; they are taking it into their own hands, building their own processes, and doing it themselves. As I have shown in this chapter, performers are leading the way for us to think about ethics in a way that could benefit workers' movements in other industries.

Part II

regulatory fantasies

What Happened to Our Squirt?

I am lying on a sofa in a custom pink latex cincher. Madison Missina hovers above me in a polka dot–trimmed two-piece. We are on the set of the 3D production *Blonde*, a collaboration between Madison and Pop Porn 3D as part of her #safesexissexy campaign. We are dressed in latex for the occasion to promote the use of condoms and dental dams on film. We ask the cameraman to take close-ups as I drizzle saliva and lubricant across the translucent dam and Madison uses her mouth to slide a condom over my glass strap-on cock.

Madison and I have something in common: We are both squirters. We move through the scene in anticipation of how we can incorporate an extravaganza of double gushing into the shot. It's in-your-face visibility to the max, and the coordination and orchestration of it delight us. I feel her gloved fingers inside me and the texture of her thigh-high PVC boots beside me as my climax builds. My heart rate quickens; I brace myself and squeeze—and squirt directly at the cameraman. Wow, I think, I can't wait to see what this looks like in 3D!

Not long afterward I receive a copy of the DVD. Excited to see our scene, I watch it at home and wait for the finale. It doesn't come. In fact, neither of our ejaculations nor the two clitoral orgasms we had afterward were included in the final cut. We certainly enjoyed ourselves, but where is the visual evidence of our orgasmic pleasure? Classification is the answer. The editors had preemptively cut the squirting in fear of it being "refused classification" (in other words, censored) by the Australian Classification Board on the basis that it was either urination (a prohibited fetish) or merely "revolting or abhorrent phenomena." The clitoral orgasms appeared to be collateral damage, cut in the desire to keep one long sequence instead of editing the climaxes back in after cutting the squirting. The producers' concerns were not unfounded. In 2010 Australian Customs refused the import of films featuring G-spot ejaculation.

Pop Porn 3D would have had to pay the classification fees twice if it had to re-edit, so in this case they chose the safe and preventative path: self-censorship.

It wasn't the first time my body had been edited to conform to classification standards. In various issues of *People* and *Picture* magazines between 2010 and 2013, I opened copies at my local newsagent to find my labia minora digitally removed. To meet classification requirements that prohibit "indiscreet genital detail" in unrestricted magazines, editors had developed routine airbrushing practices for "indiscreet" vulvas (those with long inner labia) in which they were, in industry terms, "healed to a single crease" (Barnett 2010). The Classification Board also reportedly suggested that small breast size could imply that models were "underdeveloped" and therefore underage and might then lead to publications and films being refused classification on that basis.

How does one arrive in a context in which our bodies and bodily functions are prohibited from view? In 2014 I traveled to the Eros Foundation archives at Flinders University Library to find out. The restricted collection is a goldmine of correspondence, submissions, posters, newspaper articles, DVDs, VCRs, and cassette tapes dating back to the 1980s. During that decade, Christian Democrat Rev. Fred Nile had launched a campaign to ban all X18+ content nationwide. A staunchly conservative politician, Nile later made headlines when he ordered his staff to watch adult videos on parliamentary computers in the name of "research." The national adult business association, Eros, had engaged in innovative political lobbying strategies to prevent the ban, including bringing porn stars to Parliament House and sending pornographic videos directly to members of Parliament (the films were even tailored to their portfolios—*Liquid Assets* to the treasurer, *Love Letters* to the minister for post and telecommunications).

At the time, porn producers could technically use government funding to produce films. Under the Austrade Export Market Development Grant, the government paid 70 cents of every dollar over ten thousand dollars spent on promoting Australian-made films to export markets. However, when one producer, John Lark, applied for funding to subsidize his porn series *Down Under*, Catholic senator Brian Harradine (1989), concerned that the material "promotes sexually promiscuous AIDS high risk behaviour" and that "Australia's international image is at stake," successfully convinced the government to exclude businesses marketing X18+ films.

Throughout the nineties, Eros changed tactics and campaigned to introduce a new federal classification category, "Non Violent Erotica" (NVE), through a private members bill. NVE was essentially a compromise that would permit state governments to prohibit X18+ but still allow Eros members to legally sell some narrow forms of explicit content. NVE did not represent a political vision for an ideal regulatory framework; its most contentious clause was the prohibition of fetishes. As it later appeared in the guidelines (Australian Government 2005, X18+):

> No depiction of violence, sexual violence, sexualised violence or coercion is allowed in the category. It does not allow sexually assaultive language. Nor does it allow fetishes or depiction which purposefully demean anyone involved in that activity for the enjoyment of viewers. Some consensual practices, however, are not allowed in this category. These include consensual depictions of fetishistic behaviours such as body piercing, applications of substances such as candle wax, golden showers, bondage, spanking or fisting.

Backlash to the policy came from BDSM and kink communities who believed they had been sold out as part of a political compromise. Porn scholar Kath Albury gave evidence that NVE would "pave the way for government sanctioned discrimination against sexual minorities who are not breaking any laws" (Senate Legal and Constitutional Legislation Committee 2000, 15). But despite community discontent, the bill received multipartisan support and passed through the House of Representatives in 2000.

Then something unusual happened. On the eve of the Senate vote, Harradine held a parliamentary screening of his private collection of sex films, which included Buck Angel's *Transsexual Adventures* and Max Hardcore's *Going South* and *Black She-Men*. No one questioned how an anti-abortion, anti–stem cell-research, anti–marriage equality politician came to possess such a collection of titles. But the screening served its purpose—Prime Minister John Howard reported being disgusted by the content, and as a result, the sale of X18+ content remained illegal in the states, and the federal X18+ category was amended to exclude fetish.

Eros complained that politicians themselves were breaking the law by screening potentially refused-classification (RC) pornography in Parliament House. The attorney general was asked on notice whether members of Parliament were exempt from having custody of prohibited, unclassified, or RC materials. There were scandalous news articles—the *Canberra Times* headlined one article "Police Inquiry into MP's Porn Show" (Lawson 2000)—but no politicians were charged. Parliamentary officials insisted the screening was covered by parliamentary privilege. Two decades later, Eros are still lobbying to remove the prohibition on fetish from the X18+ category. And Madison and my squirt never appeared in 3D.

3

Criminal Intimacies

Regulatory Trends and Transgressions

Porn performers around the world continue to draw attention to ill-conceived approaches to government regulation of pornography. In 2016 performers in Los Angeles protested Proposition 60 being considered in the California Senate, which sought to make condoms mandatory in all pornographic scenes. Performers marched down Sunset Boulevard chanting "our bodies, our choice," pointing out that the bill would allow private citizens and consumers to sue producers (including sole-trading performers) when condoms were not visible, regardless of actual STI risk or transmission, meaning that their legal names and home addresses could be made public, increasing risk of stalking and harassment (Calvert 2017). Two years earlier, hundreds attended an infamous face sit-in outside the Palace of Westminster in London, holding signs like "Squirt doesn't hurt!," "Shame on you, we come too!," "Urine for a shock if you expect us to stop!," and "I reserve my right to the English vice!" as part of a mass demonstration against the Audiovisual Media Services Regulations 2014 that the protesters considered "sexist" (Press Association

FIGURE 3.1. Protesters lead a face sit-in outside the Palace of Westminster in London advocating against the Audiovisual Media Services Regulations 2014, which prohibited such acts as facesitting, caning, water sports, and G-spot ejaculation in video-on-demand pornography. Image by Rex.

2014). The protest followed changes to the law on video-on-demand content in the United Kingdom, which prohibited the depiction of female ejaculation, watersports, spanking, facesitting, and fisting (Petley 2014). Performers continue to critique these top-down regulatory approaches, which are characterized by their being out-of-touch with the ways that people actually have sex, their misdiagnoses of the problems, and their inability to actually improve the situation for performers.

A closer look at the trends, patterns, and regulatory attitudes toward pornography allows us to situate such government approaches within a distinct lineage—one with an obsession with body fluids, a phobia of fetish, antiquated understandings of safer sex, and desperate attempts to maintain the place of sex within heteronormative, able-bodied, cis-centric configurations of intimacy. All the while, such approaches involve confiscating and destroying precious pornographic artifacts and preventing the production of content that could actually disrupt normative sexual scripts. At the same time, the regulatory framework promotes disrespect for the law and provokes pleasures in criminal intimacies. Regulators' futile attempts to maintain a socio-sexual order coexist alongside their inability to control proliferating sexual content. In my interviews, porn producers were vocal and exuberant in their critiques of the law, referring to it as out-of-touch. The law was, at times, irrelevant to producers; at others, an unreasonable rule that invited disobedience. These findings speak to the law's productive power, eliciting the generation of alternative ethics and standards. Producers found gratification in their contempt for unjust laws, their transgression of discriminatory prohibitions, and their status as sexual outlaws.

Containing the Threat of Democratization

Current attempts to regulate pornography form part of a long-standing attempt to contain a perceived threat of democratization. Modern pornography is a relatively recent invention, coinciding with the invention of the printing press, which brought the possibility of sexual, irreverent, or iconoclastic materials enjoying mass distribution and wide circulation (Hunt 1993, 9–10). Although depictions of sexual and erotic practices can be traced back to ancient civilizations, such as the sexually explicit frescoes of ancient Greece and Rome, they did not attract the same categorization as pornography does now. The sequestering of pornography from other forms of art, literature, and daily artifacts, its labeling with the Greek etymology *porni* (prostitute) and *graphein* (to write), and its designation to a separate archive began with the archaeological excavation of Pompeii in the eighteenth century. Sexually explicit images and objects were considered both "too valuable to be destroyed . . . too provocative to be displayed" (Dean, Ruszczycky, and Squires 2014, 2), and the term *pornography* was revived to justify these objects' distinction from everyday culture. We can understand this moment as the origins of our current X18+ category.

Pornography—in this new iteration—also emerged as part of what philosopher Michel Foucault (1998) called a "steady proliferation of discourses concerned with sex" in the nineteenth century (18). The taxonomies of sexual perversion that developed during this time through disciplines of psychiatry and sexology remain replicated in current classification categories. While cultures of Rome, China, Japan, India, and the Arab-Muslim world have explored sex through an *ars erotica* (erotic art), Western societies approached pornography through *scientia sexualis*, a scientific approach concerned with "eliciting the confession of the scientific truths of sex" (Williams [1989] 1999, 3; Kurylo 2017)—one which was exemplified by the focus on "maximum visibility" (or, the money shot) in commercial pornography.

What constitutes pornography—whether it be images, film, art, or advertising—has long been contested. Current debates around whether key texts or images do indeed constitute pornography persist precisely because *pornography* functions as a broad *rhetorical tool* that can be employed to serve various political purposes. Historian Walter Kendrick (1996) consistently places quotation marks around the term *pornography* in order to remind readers that "what is being talked about is not a thing but a concept" (xiii), a regulatory category created, invented, and determined by law and policymakers who have the power to classify what kind of knowledge and material is considered obscene, offensive, dangerous, or harmful. Despite the ambiguity of the category itself, regulators approach pornography as something that is contagious and corruptive.

Debates today about differentiating between pornography and art are the legacy of crises over new technology. The category of pornography has come to exist in reference and opposition to art, pornography functioning as a pejorative term serving to preserve and maintain the status of art. Art historian Kelly Dennis (2009) describes how, during the nineteenth century, photography was posing a challenge to art; nude paintings were seen as "leaving room for the imagination," while photography—and, by extension, pornography— was seen as "too real," "too close," and its "immediate materiality and mass availability" threatened to corrupt the masses (2). We see the same conceptual distinctions still being debated in the twenty-first century: Microblogging site Tumblr's 2018 ban on "adult content" prohibited photos, videos, or GIFS of real-life genitals but permitted "artistic nudity," such as illustrations and sculptures. Now, with the emergence of generative art apps, such as DALL-E, that automatically generate avatars and images, the line between art and porn is just as blurry. Although some companies have been quick to claim that sex-related words cannot be processed, image generators such as PornPen have emerged to make increasingly realistic explicit art.

This concern with realism and explicitness (and its purported potential for corrupting women and children) has persisted into the twenty-first century with the development of digital technologies, with various practices employed to diminish their effects (such as pixilation), and with software employed to detect and restrict access to explicit content (for example, the tool introduced by Instagram in 2017 to automatically blur "sensitive content"). With moving pictures, video cassette recorders, digital cameras, webcams, live streaming, and now virtual reality pornography, regulators continue to fear the capacity of technology to bring subjects closer to graphic reality. This is especially the case now that viewers have become users, interacting with content creators

FIGURE 3.2. Japanese sculptor and manga artist ろくでなし子 or 碌でなし子 Rokudenashiko ("good-for-nothing girl") was prosecuted for obscenity in 2014 after emailing data that could be used to make 3D prints of her vulva.

and coproducing content. As Dennis (2009) describes, digital technologies on portable devices "continue to invite touch" through practices of scrolling, selecting, and keying (2). The ability of viewers to *interact* with media has been a key differentiating factor in the classification of computer games as compared with films: In Australia, R18+ computer games were not available until 2013.

Regulators have been concerned less with the content of pornography itself and more with its potential availability. In Japan, when artist Rokudenashiko (Megumi Igarashi) was found guilty on obscenity charges for sharing the data from a 3D scan of her *manko* in 2016, it was not her art objects that were deemed obscene. She had been using silicone molds to produce dioramas and an entire kayak in the shape of her vulva, which she paddled along the Tokyo River. Rokudenashiko was prosecuted for the *online availability of her digital data*—the 3D scan of her vulva. The primary concern of the obscenity charges was with the restriction of publication, dissemination, and circulation of this data and its capacity for influence. Ironically, Mark McLelland (2018) points out, the only people who downloaded and reproduced the data at the time were the police.

Regulatory Trends

Over the past two centuries, various kinds of moral panic have been mobilized in regulatory approaches to pornography. Regulatory framing has shifted from narratives of obscenity and indecency (characterized by high-profile trials in England and the United States that sought to remove sexually explicit materials from circulation) to discourses of harm and injury (including the anti-pornography ordinance proposed by Catharine MacKinnon and Andrea Dworkin in Indianapolis that would enable women harmed by pornography to sue for damages in civil court). Subsequently, regulators began to assess sexually explicit material on the basis of offensiveness and community standards (which have positioned procreative, vanilla, able-bodied, and heteronormative intimacies as benchmarks). Even the European Union Parliament proposed a resolution to ban all forms of pornography in the media (Committee on Women's Rights and Gender Equality 2012).

As porn performers have become more vocal about their experiences on set, anti-pornography advocates have turned their attention to what they perceive as the deleterious effects on consumers, constructing a moral panic of porn addiction that they claim threatens heterosexual society, relationships, and coupledom: Between 2016 and 2019, sixteen US states passed resolutions declaring pornography a public health crisis (Webber and Sullivan 2018). Some states have begun positioning pornography as a form of sex trafficking, and in 2020 California bill AB 2389 sought to license, fingerprint, and background-check porn performers. (As first proposed, the licenses would only be available to people over twenty-one and would require performers to undertake special training every two years on human trafficking, safety, and workplace rights.)

Others have developed a preoccupation with so-called extreme pornography, such as the UK ban on acts that are likely to result in serious injury to a person's anus, breasts, or genitals. Concerned with young people's exposure to pornography, numerous western democracies are now trialing or implementing age verification systems to restrict access, including through facial recognition, behavioral profiling, and identity matching. At the same time, in some jurisdictions, young people engaged in sexting may be liable for producing and disseminating child abuse material of themselves. Although the language and the framing shifts—from obscenity to protection to health—the regulatory desire to control the production, sale, and consumption of pornography continues. The narrative of children's exposure remains a popular "rhetorical trope [that] is leveraged" (Monea 2022, 9). However, despite fifty years of academic research into the effects of pornography on consumers, there is not a lot of reliable data about whether porn consumption leads to greater pleasure or sexual literacy because studies have conflated kink with violence, confused correlation with cause, and focused on the relationship satisfaction of monogamous couples rather than on pleasure (McKee et al. 2022).

Attempts to regulate pornography have often resulted in poor outcomes for both porn performers and consumers. The attempt to criminalize so-called extreme pornography in the United Kingdom, for example, has captured consensual BDSM activities in its definitions of extremity (Petley 2009; Attwood and Smith 2010; Antoniou and Akrivos 2017). The California bill discussed above initially proposed that performers undergo background checks (listing the past three years of their criminal history), be fingerprinted, and obtain licenses with their legal names and addresses on the public record (Kingkade 2020), which the Adult Performers Actors Guild claimed would criminalize workers and pose serious privacy risks. Databases of porn consumer profiles are susceptible to being leaked, hacked, sold, tracked, and misused (Blake 2019), and many of the proposed age estimation techniques elicit serious privacy and feasibility issues, as well as significant racial and gender bias in biometric approaches. Some clinical psychologists and scientists have critiqued the invention of *sex addiction* and *porn addiction* as having no scientific basis. Instead, they note that the most common factor in reports of porn addiction is religiosity and argue that individuals reporting addictive use could be better conceptualized by considering internal and external conflicts and desire discrepancy (Ley, Prause, and Finn 2014). They have also made a suspicious note of the large, lucrative treatment industry that has conveniently boomed along with this new addiction.

Pornography laws have further been used as part of racial oppression and colonization. In Australia, pornography was prohibited in certain Aboriginal communities following the Northern Territory Emergency Response (NTER) in 2007. Under the guise of addressing child abuse, the Australian government sent the military into remote Aboriginal communities and initiated the quarantining of welfare benefits, compulsory government acquisition of land, removal of customary law, and increased police presence as well as suspending the commonwealth's Racial Discrimination Act 1975. As part of the intervention, the possession, control, or supply of X18+ materials became a federal offense punishable with fines of up to AUD$11,000 and two years in prison. The NTER was described as a "war" on Indigenous people, a "form of racialized combat" that used biopolitical population management to sustain colonial sovereignty (Tedmanson and Wadiwel 2010, 7). The ongoing criminalization of possessing pornography among Aboriginal communities in the Northern Territory illustrates how racialized and paternalistic ideas inform which communities are seen as responsible enough to self-govern and how porn regulation is deployed as part of a settler colonial project. In *Black Witness*, Darumbal and South Sea Islander journalist Amy McGuire calls the "unabashedly racist" policy "the most extreme example of media-driven policymaking in recent history" (2024, 46).

Dirt for Dirt's Sake

Early case law on obscenity (under which pornography offenses were regularly brought) positioned pornography as at once dangerous (with the potential to deprave, influence, and corrupt) and at the same time empty and valueless (prurient, irredeemable, deficient). The common law offense of obscenity can be traced back in England to the Obscene Publications Act 1857, which provided for the seizure of obscene and pornographic materials. In the case of *R. v. Hicklin* (1868), the Court of the Queen's Bench found that a publication may be obscene if it had the "tendency . . . to deprave and corrupt those whose minds are open to such immoral influences, and into whose hands a publication of this sort may fall." Obscenity law was adopted in the United States with the enactment of the Comstock Act of 1873, which banned information about family planning, abortion, venereal disease, and contraception. After adopting the Hicklin test, the US Supreme Court later redefined obscenity in *Miller v. California* (413 U.S. 15 [1973]), with reference to whether a text "appeals to the prurient interest," is "patently offensive," and "lacks serious literary, artistic, political, or scientific value." Although pornography has been distinguished from obscenity, the two are regularly conflated. Regardless of its ability to elicit physical responses from its viewers—its "carnal resonance," as Susanna Paasonen (2011) has called it, to *move* people, to laughter, to sadness, to arousal—pornography continues to be situated in the public imaginary as lacking social importance or merit. Despite its capacity to *touch* its viewers emotionally, pornography continues to be positioned as base and unworthy, as requiring external value to redeem its status into something socially meaningful.

As courts across Western democracies looked to international jurisprudence, definitions of obscenity traveled and adapted and began making reference to "dirt." Australia adopted the Hicklin test, and in the 1948 case of *R. v. Close* ([1948] VLR 445), the High Court held that although the standard may vary from time to time, there does exist "a general instinctive sense of what is decent and what is indecent, of what is clean and what is dirty" (465). This reference to "dirt" was adopted by the Canadian Supreme Court in *R. v. Brodie* ([1962] S.C.R. 681), where Judge Judson described obscenity as "dirt for dirt's sake, the leer of the sensualist, depravity in the mind of an author with an obsession for dirt, pornography, an appeal to a prurient interest" (704). Brenda Cossman argues that this language of "dirt" in obscenity law sees "a clear distinction made between good and bad sex—a binary opposition between clean and dirty, decent and indecent. Bad sex is dirty sex" (Cossman et al. 1997, 109). Although the Canadian Supreme Court moved away from dirt and toward a test of harm in the decision of *R. v. Butler* ([1992] 1 S.C.R. 452), the spectacle of dirt continues to inform obscenity and now classification law in Australia.

In her book *Purity and Danger* (1966), anthropologist Mary Douglas develops a theory on "dirt" which argues that it is a conceptual category that operates to organize and maintain order. Rather than relating to disease or cleanliness, dirt, writes Douglas, is "essentially disorder . . . matter out of place" (2). Although the regulation of pornography has moved away from obscenity offenses to classifying content, with the relevant test becoming one of community standards, classification still reflects similar themes of dirt and disorder, and still treats sex as matter out of place. Subsequent to *Close*, the Australian High Court in *Crowe v. Graham* ([1968] 121 CLR 375) moved to assess whether material is obscene in relation to community standards as well as the manner and extent to which it "transgress[es] the generally accepted bounds of decency" (395). In this case, Judge Windeyer distinguished between people working in pornography and ordinary, decent-minded people, placing people who sell sexual materials as outside the community. He described community standards as "those which ordinarily decent-minded people accept. They are not what those who peddle obscenities and indecencies urge should be accepted" (399).

In this iteration, porn consumers and producers are positioned as *outside* rather than part of communities—they are matter out of place. If a language of dirt is used to maintain an order in which (public) sex is not a part, this order is also upheld by references to decency and modesty. In the Australian case *Pell v. National Gallery of Victoria* ([1998] 2 VR 391) regarding Andres Serrano's artwork *Piss Christ*, which featured a photograph of a plastic crucifix submerged in the artist's urine, Judge Harper referred to "obscene" as something "unduly emphasizing matters of sex, crimes of violence, gross cruelty, or horror, so as to offend against the common sense of decency" and "indecent" as something "right-minded persons would consider to be contrary to community standards of decency" or "an affront to sexual modesty" (392, 394). These references to modesty, decency, and right-minded people are largely a test of middle-class manners. They uphold an order that positions sex (and body fluids) as belonging in private rather than public space.

This history exposes how the moral sensibilities of regulators often clash with the community standards of porn performers, producers, and consumers. Despite being persistently situated as outlaws, sex workers have interrogated the idea that they exist *outside* of and *separate* from the community. While porn "peddlers" continue to be cast as a threat to the community, population surveys suggest that looking at pornographic material appears to be reasonably common. The Second Australian Study of Health and Relationships interviewed 9,963 men and 10,131 women aged 16 to 69 nationwide and found that 84 percent of men and 54 percent of women had looked at pornographic material in their lifetimes, and few respondents reported being addicted to pornography or having experienced bad effects from viewing it (Rissel et al. 2017). As regulators grapple with classifying online content, no longer can they think of community standards in terms of geography: Instead, they must consider virtual community standards across borders (McKee, McNair, and Watson 2014). Rationales for criminalizing production make far less sense when people are producing and selling images of themselves.

Is the Reasonable Person Kinky?

At various points throughout the twentieth century, many countries made an official move away from censorship regimes to classification frameworks, renaming their regulators and claiming not to prohibit content but simply to assess it. In Australia, for example, the advent of national classification legislation in 1995 was supposed to signal a shift away from morality-based obscenity and indecency laws toward community standards. However, classification laws inherited the language of obscenity and indecency case law, describing "revolting or abhorrent phenomena" that are "gratuitous," will "demean," or are "offensive" to the standards of "morality, decency and propriety." Rather than disappearing, offenses for publicly selling, distributing, and exhibiting obscene, offensive, or indecent material are still found in state summary offenses acts and criminal codes.

In my interviews, producers believed that classification laws did not reflect current community standards. One producer who focused on depicting women's pleasure remarked, "I don't think anything that I shoot is objectionable or offensive." Feminist porn producer Anna Brownfield said that even for people who appeared sexually conservative, "once you have a little scratch under the surface you discover they're actually quite sexually open in terms of what they think is acceptable to see." Howard, who ran three subscription websites, made a similar assessment, "I would estimate that probably half of Australians are having sex that we could not legally film and publish in Australia." Their responses echo the concerns of many feminist legal scholars who have long critiqued the figure of the white, cisgender, heterosexual, able-bodied man as the benchmark of reasonableness, neutrality, and objectivity in assessing what is offensive, degrading, or abhorrent.

My interviewees were blunt in their reactions to the regulatory framework. Many were professional sexperts with an everyday working knowledge of bodies, sexuality, and politics. Many were performers; two were sex therapists and another two held gender studies degrees. Brownfield referred to classification law as outdated. Another producer commented, "I think they are operating in a world that maybe existed forty years ago" and thought that customs officers interpreting G-spot ejaculation as urination showed "a blindness or a willingness to misunderstand." Similarly, Aeryn Walker said, "People clearly don't understand what's going on in reality, or possibly basic science" and that customs officers were out of touch with women's anatomy. Xavier Marz from *Dirty Queer* magazine said, "I just imagine those censorship boards being like a series of white bread sandwiches . . . just cookie cutter suburban."

Seasoned professionals with lived experience in BDSM, sex work, and queer politics, many producers were skeptical of laws that pathologized deviance or perversion. As sex worker activist Gala Vanting put it, "This is deeply archaic shit." When we discussed criminal penalties for publishing indecent material, Sindy Skin laughed at the ambiguity of the term: "What's 'indecent'? For the recorder: I'm rolling my eyes ridiculously." There was a sense that the experiences of policymakers were wildly divorced from sexual cultures. In Cat O'Nine Tails's words, "What a bunch of backwards old men really. . . . Like seriously, have you ever made love to a woman? Do you actually know how her body works? Come on."

Behind this exasperation is concern among feminist and queer producers for culturally relevant community standards. Cat, a qualified sex therapist, was concerned that Australia was behind international standards since even the American Psychiatric Association's *Diagnostic and Statistical Manual of Mental Disorders* has now accepted that fetishes do not necessarily constitute mental illness. Gala Vanting said that the lack of comprehensive sex education in Australian public schools meant "I don't actually trust these people to tell the difference between [ejaculation] and urination." A director of one queer porn film festival believed that the prohibitions on fisting and golden showers were

FIGURE 3.3. Chelsea Poe in *Fucking against Fascism* (Trouble Films), profits from which were donated to Trans Lifeline and Black Lives Matter. Image by Courtney Trouble.

inherently queerphobic. Fetish practices have long been documented among gay men, lesbians, queers, and sex workers (Rubin [1991] 2011, 232; Crozier 2012). "I feel like it's sort of blatantly queerphobic, homophobic, pervert-phobic, everything. Golden showers, for instance, I mean, are a really common practice, I mean definitely amongst gay men. . . . I mean I think anyone who knows anything about gay culture, gay subcultures, knows about that . . . and of course fisting is a really common practice amongst gay men and queer women as well, but because it's not, you know, procreative sex, it's also [seen as] this really threatening practice."

For Gala, depicting BDSM practices, fisting, or G-spot ejaculation was important because "these are in my community. That's what happens. And that's how you fuck. Or it's one of a million ways in which you fuck." She believed it was important "to have those opportunities to see those things represented, to understand how they work, to feel in any way that they are normal." Xavier Marz from *Dirty Queer* magazine believed that the situation reflected the hypocrisy whereby men believed they could best represent women's interests. "Look at our fucking minister for women!" he exclaimed, referencing former prime minister Tony Abbott, who stated publicly that women were physiologically unsuited for leadership and appointed himself as minister for women. In this context, producers have little faith in elected representatives or their appointees to read the temperature of contemporary community standards.

Public Sex and Porn Film Festivals

While porn film festivals abound in Europe and parts of North America, the screening of sexually explicit films in public is largely prohibited in Australia. Although some exemptions exist for cultural, documentary, and community films, sexually explicit films are not eligible. (Despite this, there have been a handful of inconsistent classification decisions whereby films with sexually explicit material have been granted waivers or classified as R18+ instead of X18+. Films such as *Irreversible, Anatomie de L'Enfer, Romance,* and *Shortbus* have been classified R18+ by the classification review board despite containing explicit sexual activity.) One might envisage that, given their emphasis on documenting subcultures and educating audiences, many DIY porn films could be considered documentary or cultural and be integrated into public film festivals. Indeed, the value of sex in public is encapsulated by the founder of the Berlin Porn Film Festival, Jürgen Brüning, who describes the festival name as a deliberate decision "to place pornography into bright daylight" (Meier 2015, 291). But instead, by sequestering sexual media into a separate category that is to be consumed in private, pornography itself is positioned as being outside culture, as something that does not belong.

In 2013 Travis Matthew's film *I Want Your Love* (which featured explicit homosexual sex) was refused classification to screen at the Melbourne Queer Film Festival (MQFF), the largest and oldest queer film festival in Australia. It formed part of a long historical clash between queer cinema and the legal concept of "the reasonable person" (Huntley 1995; Kincaid 1998). In my interview with Stuart Richards, author of *The Queer Film Festival: Popcorn and Politics* (2016), he recalled how the film had screened at queer film festivals around the world before being refused: "The feedback for *I Want Your Love* was that there wasn't enough narrative substance to require the explicit sexual scenes, which I think is very subjective. But I honestly don't think there was much difference between *I Want Your Love* and *Sexing the Transman.*"

This need for sexual media to contain narrative substance is a legacy of obscenity legislation that requires prurient material to be redeemed by literary or other merit. Writing on classification decisions in relation to trans and gender-diverse films, Accadia Ford (2016) notes that *Sexing the Transman,* a documentary film directed by Buck Angel exploring the sexuality of trans men, received an exemption presumably because of its documentary features. When we discussed the exemption refusal for *I Want Your Love,* Richards emphasized its implications for the filmmakers, festival organizers, and communities. Due to the limited budget, minimal staff members, and volunteer base of the nonprofit MQFF, appealing the decision would have been beyond their labor capacity. But further, it foreclosed avenues for communities to financially support local queer filmmakers. As Richards describes it, festival censorship created the conditions and incentives for film piracy, with the result that the film became available via less ethical distribution methods: "I think it was also disappointing because that film was still accessible within Australia. It got all this free publicity. But that film was on a lot of free-to-access VOD sites—Pornhub, X videos; that film was still floating around—so a lot of people were still watching this film, but it was through an alternative distribution method where the filmmaker didn't get any money."

This process of quarantining sex from visible spaces has been documented in both physical and virtual geographies as a zoning practice, often with a "devastating" impact on sexual subcultures (Berlant and Warner 1998, 551). During our interview, Viv McGregor, who coordinated the lesbian and same-sex attracted women's health project at ACON, noted the importance of visual representations of sexuality in building community and finding belonging. She argued that queer film festivals were particularly important given the closing down of physical spaces—bars, clubs, warehouses—that have historically been sanctuaries for lesbian, queer, and bisexual women due to gentrification, the economic climate, and women having less disposable income. In the view of my interviewees, film festivals were spaces that fostered community building, critical conversations, and collective identity. Richards explained:

> I think the queer film festival does two things. One is they provide exhibition of films that otherwise wouldn't be able to be screened . . . a lot of the queer films on Netflix for instance—they're very much standard dramas or standard comedies, mostly gay or lesbian characters—mostly gay—and a lot of the more alternate film forms and other identities in the queer community don't get that distribution outside the queer film festival.
>
> And on top of that is having that shared identity. And that's something that a lot of the promotions, director's statements, and mission statements are all about, promoting that community space, where it's not just about the film you're watching—it's also about being in that space, the queue lining up, the festival bar, the MQFF does speed dating, and then panels, parties, and all these other events around the actual screening. So that is the primary purpose of the QFF—it's a community atmosphere.

A director I interviewed from one queer porn film festival stated that festivals were also important in capacity development and encouraging emerging, amateur, and community filmmakers "to plant a seed for people actually producing their own work locally." Other interviewees described the value of watching intimate material together in producing desire and communication. Jack Sargeant, a film scholar who had curated counterculture, cult, and underground cult cinema, described how sexually explicit material could be integrated with other subcultural content in programming: "In my experience in the underground film world going to film festivals there'll be everything from music documentaries to student films to films about sex to stoner comedies, horror films—there's no set genre."

Sexually explicit material is situated as *outside* all other film content, as something so distinct from general filmic representation and so separate from everyday culture as to not only warrant its own category but also attract a raft of special restrictions and penalties around its screening. The positioning of public sex as what Mary Douglas would call "matter out of place" acts to reinforce an existing cis-heteronormative order. While queer intimacies are screened out of public view, heterosexual intimacies that are "less commonly recognized as part of sexual culture," such as "carrying wallet photos, buying economy size," are normalized (Berlant and Warner 1998, 555). Intimacy becomes linked to coupledom, sexuality is confined to the bedroom, and queer forms of sexual sociality are penalized.

Fears of Fetish

The amount of time, energy, and voyeuristic attention that lawmakers spend obsessing over sexual fetishes in order to prohibit people from enjoying them is a paradoxical phenomenon. First, it is symptomatic of what Ummni Kahn (2014) calls a "vicarious kink": The constant focus on taboo sexuality and sadomasochism in the socio-legal imaginary is perverse in itself. Second, it is representative of Linda Williams's (2004a) concept "on/scenity," whereby representations of sex that were once obscene (off the public scene) become on-scene when politicians themselves become the "unwitting pornographer, pandering the very material [they] would censor" (3). Third, it positions fetish as abject in order to preserve a sociosexual order that is "articulated by *negation*" (Kristeva 1982, 6). While pornography is frequently accused of being homogeneous and plastic, the regulatory framework itself restricts the kinds of practices that tangibly illustrate that the performers are human—that they bleed, ejaculate, and urinate—and produces orgasm-centric, cis-heteronormative, and ableist models of sexual connectedness. The same is true of the online environment. As Alex Monea (2022) writes,

"The porn industry's deepest darkest secret isn't that porn is exploitative, socially corrosive, or a catalyst for misogynistic violence—though these can all be true. It's that porn is *boring*. . . . Porn is boring because it's caught in a heteronormative filter bubble" (8).

The prohibitions on depicting fetish content in the United Kingdom and Australia have significant potential impacts for performers, consumers, and the public. For example, in Australia, the X18+ category prohibits the depiction of both violence (broadly interpreted to capture BDSM content, rough sex, and dirty talk) and fetishes (via a detailed list of prohibited activities, including fisting, golden showers, piercing, bondage, and candle waxing). The irony is that violence is permitted in all other classification categories (including the G category, which is available to minors). Violence is prohibited even where it bears no relation to the sexual activity or appears unrealistic: One of the world's highest grossing porn films, *Pirates*, was originally refused classification because it involved a scene with two skeletons fighting. The prohibition on fists (and presumably stumps) makes obvious that the regulations are not only heteronormative, but ableist (Thorneycroft 2020), as the guidelines forbid the use of "a non-sexual part of the body that gives sexual gratification," which reduces sexuality to the genitals and ignores the creative and innovative ways in which people with disabilities find pleasure.

In addition, X18+ films cannot include anyone who "appears to be" under age eighteen (regardless of whether they actually are under eighteen), which has led to the prohibition of slash fiction, hentai, and literotica depicting consenting adults (see McLelland and Yoo 2007). In 2013 Victorian police charged queer artist Paul Yore with child pornography, excising seven images from his *Everything Is Fucked* installation with a knife. Yore's work, a commentary on capitalism, sexuality, and culture, involved psychedelic tapestry, collage, and kitsch objects, including unicorns, phalluses, rainbows, children's faces, fountains, dildos, and an image of teen pop star Justin Bieber's face. Yore was later acquitted, and police were ordered to pay his legal costs.

Why are fetish practices so threatening to regulators? In her theory on abjection, French Bulgarian philosopher Julia Kristeva (1982) describes the abject as something that sits between life and death, a thing that gives rise to horror, disgust, fear, and revulsion. She argues that these visceral reactions are responses to a threatened breakdown in meaning caused by the loss of distinction between the self and Other. Giving examples of rotten food, corpses, sewerage, and open wounds, she describes such states as existing on the border between life and death (2). These liminal, transitory spaces evoke concern because their ordinary context is disrupted, and they do not respect borders

FIGURE 3.4. Queer artist Paul Yore outside the exhibition *It's All Wrong, but It's Alright* (2019), a mixed-media installation comprising found objects and reclaimed materials. Dark Mofo festival, Black Temple Gallery, Hobart, Tasmania. Image by Chris Crerar.

or rules (4). The abject, then, threatens regulators' understandings of a cis, hetero reality and prompts them to distance themselves from kink to stabilize their own worldview.

Perhaps the real offense of BDSM, then, is that it reminds regulators of the corporeality and fleshy possibilities of their own bodies, a mortality they are not ready to face. Body piercing literally opens the flesh, allowing for the letting of blood; golden showers open the bladder to let the inside out; fisting involves reaching deep into the body, knuckling up against internal organs. This is not to say that these practices are dangerous. Rather, they remind the viewer of the materiality of the body: Fisting is reminiscent of birth, and yet the fist can also be reminiscent of violence; blood is a life force, yet its existence outside the body can also signal injury; defecating is necessary for health and is also waste exiting the body. Kink practices are somatic; they test the thresholds of one's body. Candle wax is capable of burning the skin; spanking can cause capillaries to burst and leave bruises or welts; bondage practices like asphyxiation remind us of our own vitality: that breath is life.

Sexual practices that legislation treats as degrading or violent may have an entirely different significance for those involved. As Michael Warner (2000) writes, "Queer culture has long cultivated an alternative ethical culture that is almost never recognized by mainstream moralists as anything of the kind" (viii). While some anti-pornography advocates have associated kink with degradation, shame, and humiliation, for many in kink communities, BDSM and fetish practices represent relationships of trust, with a strong emphasis placed on boundaries, consent, and communication. A number of texts discuss protocols of initiation, negotiation, consent, skills, and safety in BDSM cultures (such as Langdridge and Barker 2013). Many of these practices may be about sensation play, higher states of being, catharsis, healing trauma, leaning into subspace, or testing emotional and physical thresholds. Margot Weiss (2011) describes the feeling resulting from flogging as being "like the relaxation of a deep tissue massage, the high of eating spicy food, or the cognitive release of meditation" (x). Fisting, for example, potentially challenges heterosexism as a practice that is not phallocentric. It provides anal/vaginal/throat eroticism with "intensity and duration of feeling, not climax" (Halperin 1995, 101). As Dinesh Wadiwel (2009) eloquently writes, "The practice is by nature gentle and . . . requires care and skill on the part of its practitioners . . . an elaborate web of communication strategies" (495–96).

Despite these embodied understandings, body fluids are selectively understood by regulators as waste, contaminants, and pollutants rather than as evidence of life, hydration, or pleasure. They are read according to misogynist and homophobic double standards: Semen is generally considered acceptable (even where it is spilled rather than procreative), while G-spot ejaculation and menstrual fluids are largely prohibited. In her research on period porn, Laura Helen Marks (2013) suggests that "perhaps menstrual blood is too abject, too connotative of violence, of death, while semen connotes life, creation, and reassures the self." However, not all semen is seen to connote life. Even where gay sperm has life-affirming qualities, including the ability to literally "Fuck the Dead Back to Life," as advertised on posters for Bruce La Bruce's *LA Zombie* (McGlotten 2014; McGlotten and Vangundy 2013), gay sperm can be seen as representative of death. After *LA Zombie*, in which a gay zombie is able to resurrect the dead by having sex with their wounds, was refused classification for the Melbourne International Film Festival in 2010, the director of the Melbourne Underground Film Festival advertised that they would screen the film instead. His house was raided by police (Sparrow 2012, 86). The media outcry and cultural backlash against barebacking or "raw sex" in response to the Treasure Island Media films *Viral Loads* and *Teenage Truvada Whore*, which depict sexual cultures among serodiscordant gay men (as Nic Holas described it in our interview, "HIV meets youth. Scandal"), illustrate that HIV stigma (and homophobic discourses of infection and contagion) are still alive in porn regulation (Dean 2009 and 2015; Scott 2015).

Laws that conflate kink with violence seriously limit opportunities for health promotion in film. The inclusion of instructional, educative interviews or on-screen negotiations can actively model ways to navigate mutual pleasure and safer techniques. And yet prohibitions can create inconsistencies between what is lawful in practice and unlawful on-screen. As Sindy Skin said to me in disbelief: "I think that what blows me away is that as a dominatrix I have people coming to me and asking for this service, and it's between two consenting adults. It's safe, sane, consensual as we like to say in BDSM. Yet does this mean if I was to film the session and then give it to the guy, does that mean that I've done something illegal?"

While kink communities have since moved toward the term *risk-aware consensual kink* (rather than relying on "sanity"), Sindy's point about the law's inconsistency is important. Sole emphasis on representation, regardless of whether negotiation and consent are evident in the scene itself, effectively removes all consideration about performer experience, and it removes the ability of performers to give consent that is specific and dynamic. As Brenda Cossman and colleagues (1997) write, "Repressing the representation does nothing to address the underlying material conditions under which these representations may have been produced" (44).

"We're Going to Destroy the Whole Thing"

What then happens to pornography that is removed from public circulation? A recurring theme in my interviews was producers' sense of loss when their valuable content was confiscated or destroyed by law enforcement. I spoke with Amy Middleton from *Archer* magazine, a "journal of sexual diversity" and print publication about sexuality, gender, and identity established in 2013. *Archer's* second issue, which featured a cover image of two boys, one of whom was topless, was deemed as inappropriate for sale and removed from newsagent shelves. Although the image was not sexualized, it was removed after some retailers believed it should be wrapped in plastic. Technically, opaque wrapping is only required for publications that are not suitable for public display, but this response employed stereotypes about homosexuality as contagious or predatory. In returning the issue, retailers tore off the front cover, effectively destroying the magazine, which Amy described as a "brutal" and "heartbreaking" practice (Middleton 2014). In our interview, she described how this had led the magazine to narrow its distribution pathways: "It was like this really

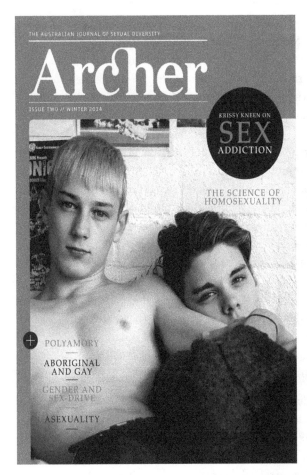

THE AUSTRALIAN JOURNAL OF SEXUAL DIVERSITY

Archer

ISSUE TWO // WINTER 2014

KRISSY KNEEN ON
SEX
ADDICTION

THE SCIENCE OF
HOMOSEXUALITY

+ POLYAMORY

ABORIGINAL
AND GAY

GENDER AND
SEX-DRIVE

ASEXUALITY

FIGURE 3.5. The
second issue of *Archer*
magazine, the Austra-
lian journal of sexual
diversity, was removed
from newsagent
shelves with the front
cover torn off for being
deemed inappropri-
ate for sale. Image by
Charlie Brophy.

barbaric process, and probably publishers like Fairfax don't really notice that
cost, but for us it's just not sustainable. So now we do very targeted distribution. We only sell a couple here and there for where we think they're going to
sell, rather than risking them and the artworks."

The selective enforcement of pornography laws and the large gray area of
interpretation leave producers in a state of uncertainty and anxiety. In Australia
there remain heavy penalties for producing, selling, exhibiting, advertising, importing, or exporting unclassified X18+ or refused classification (RC) material.
Police right of entry and search and seizure powers are incredibly broad, and
in some cases, courts may order the destruction or forfeiture of films and publications. For example, in Victoria making objectionable films for gain brings a
penalty of up to two years' imprisonment while possessing commercial quantities

of RC films (which may feature consensual sex involving fetish) results in a ten-year penalty. When G Media was prosecuted in 2009 for producing content in Melbourne, the Eros Association noted that, as part of the investigation, police visited young adult performers at home, threatening to charge them.

In my interview with Robbie Swan from Eros, he reported that raids, arrests, and fines for adult retailers overwhelmingly coincided with politicians' electoral campaigns and regularly followed tabloid press articles about cracking down on pornography. Such raids can bring enormous financial costs for retailers, sometimes sending them into bankruptcy or causing them to lose their homes. In 2010, when adult retailer Darryl Cohen was imprisoned for three months for selling unclassified and RC films in a retail outlet on Oxford Street in Sydney's gay district, police confiscated four thousand DVDs. Of these, only thirty-eight films were subsequently rated X18+ and five were deemed as RC simply because of homosexual BDSM material (Barnett 2010).

Customs restrictions that prohibit importing and exporting objectionable material also make it difficult for producers to sell, share, and network internationally. In our interview, porn producer Howard described how both his personal and professional material was confiscated by the Australian Customs and Border Protection Service despite being lawful content:

So I had been in Europe making content, on holidays, but also making content for our websites, and I backed all of my footage up and posted a hard drive home as a backup, and it didn't arrive back home, and I thought that it was lost in the mail. Months later I got a letter from customs saying that they've seized this hard drive and that they believe that it contains material which they believe is child exploitation material. . . .

So I rang them up and said well, "What's this about?" The only thing I could think of was that I had filmed a girl in the UK masturbating in a bed which was an antique cot. She'd made a bed out of an antique cot, and she was quite small in stature, and I thought perhaps that they'd perceived that we were trying to depict that she was a child or something. But that wasn't it at all. What they'd picked up was a series of photos of an American girl, and she'd actually emailed them to me for publication on one of our sites, and it was just a series of photos of her naked, and they weren't explicit. And they appear to have picked up on the shape of her breasts, shape of her nipples particularly.

So once they described the pictures to me I said, "Yes, I know who that is." I said. "Well I have her ID on file; she's 23 years old, so can I just send you the ID and will you send back the hard drive?" And they said, "No, it doesn't work that way." And this is just a customs officer so they're not trained, or they would have some minimum training in how they police this. And of course, they're always going to err completely conservatively. So in their view if anything even could remotely fall under the classification of depicting a person that could be under eighteen then they will just black ban it. And that's what they've done here; they've just looked at this girl and said, "Oh, look, she's obviously over eighteen, but with those breasts, perhaps, you know, she could be construed as being young."

So they said, "Look, the only thing you can do is take us to court, but we warn you, it will be a huge media event." And I said, "Well, on that drive are all my holiday photos. You know, most of what's on that drive's not even porn. Can I have a copy of that?" And the answer was "No, we're going to destroy the whole thing."

The confusion among customs officials (not to mention residents or international visitors) about what constitutes illegal pornography (whose breasts and what fluids meet the threshold) means that the material identified and captured is broad in scope. Howard felt confident that a court would have decided differently but was deterred by the expense and publicity of a court process. Criminalization poses further barriers to producers utilizing justice avenues. In some cases, police have not taken their claims seriously. When producer Anna Brownfield sought to make a police report about an individual who was stalking, harassing, and making death threats against her, police said to her, "Well, what do you expect in your industry?"

Costs of Compliance

As I demonstrated in chapter 1, many indie producers aim to create material that is diverse, inclusive, and accessible. Yet working within the legal framework involves self-censorship (omitting sexual practices and compromising political visions), personal expense (traveling to different jurisdictions), not being able to recruit or advertise locally, and working in isolation with limited opportunities for collaboration. Without a supportive legal structure performers have less choice and autonomy in the kinds of work they do. Compliance can also involve significant financial expense. In the past, producers and retailers have faced exorbitant licensing fees for selling sexual content that were completely disproportionate to the actual administrative costs and effectively acted as a punitive tax to discourage the industry while raising revenue (see Sparrow 2012, 62). Making porn legally requires class privilege, access to capital, and/or residency in urban centers, which contributes to a pornographic landscape that is predominantly white (Gregory 2017). The entry cost can deter independent operators, discouraging diversity and favoring big production companies with discriminatory hiring policies. The legal framework thereby creates a class of criminalized people who cannot afford to comply and are vulnerable to police harassment and arrest.

Angela White reported that because producers need to look elsewhere for location and talent, Australian pornography then ends up lacking cultural distinctiveness:

> For the most part I can't use Australian talent unless they're overseas. It makes it very difficult to work with other Australian performers, and there is something unique about Australia and Australian people. There's no denying that. So you do miss out on what kinds of things those performers bring to the table that maybe a US performer wouldn't. There's also the fact that I can't showcase beautiful Australian landscape. I can't give jobs to Australian people as a small company. I have to take my money elsewhere, so in terms of the economy I'm, you know, I'm putting my money overseas.

The prohibitive legal framework contributes to the dominance of US porn and the importing of a US brand of indie pornographies rather than developing localized iterations. Anna Brownfield lamented the lack of opportunity to screen her films for local audiences: "In terms of sale, it means that my product goes overseas and it doesn't really get seen here at all by Australian audiences, except through various distribution channels online. So it limits my ability to reach my homegrown market, which is a little bit sad."

As a result, some producers I spoke to had or were considering relocating offshore. Howard reflected: "We're considering going overseas to produce as well because there are places where we could happily produce things like BDSM, golden showers, power play, that sort of thing. But financially it's a huge burden."

The legal framework also limits producers' capacity to produce hard copy, tangible content in a variety of visual mediums. For Gala Vanting of Sensate Films, this was a significant loss: "Our desire really is to explore intimacy in all formats . . . we really enjoy making things that you can hold in your hand; we love the texture of those things and think that those elements are part of the erotic experience of consuming porn and erotic art."

Meaningless Consultation

Where porn performers and producers have tried to engage with law reform, they often cite inadequate consultation, polarized public debate, and political compromise. Public consultation and law reform processes in representative democracies work to maintain a social order that prevents marginalized communities from direct participation and representation in decisions affecting their lives. When I asked porn producers about their experiences engaging with law reform, none had been invited for consultation, though some had proactively sought out opportunities to write letters to politicians expressing their concerns. In addition to the emotional labor of educating civil servants and politicians, consultation brings risks of self-incrimination for producers. As one feminist producer said, "It would be really nice to be able to be more open and politically active, but there is that ongoing fear of prosecution that gets in the way." As a result, many of the intricate discussions about the personal effects of regulation happen within industry: "The only times that I have conversations like this are with peers," Gala Vanting told me. Performer-producers felt a sense of injustice about governments not making sufficient effort to ask or invite them to have a say. As performer-producer Kim Cums said sarcastically, "Nobody ever consults anyone that's actually involved in any aspect of it. Thanks politicians; it's just our lives and livelihoods, but you don't have to ask us any questions at all." Because producers feel disenfranchised from and disillusioned with the law-making process, the valuable insights accrued through their work often remain within the industry rather than being used to inform policy.

Because of the lack of meaningful consultation with porn performers, political debates about pornography largely center on polarized arguments: socially conservative positions that emphasize the harm of pornography and purport to protect women and children by preventing their exposure to or participation in pornography, and liberal positions that advocate for an unfettered right to freedom of speech that adults should be able to see, read, and hear what they wish. When I spoke to Kim Heitman from the digital rights organization Electronic Frontiers Australia, he observed that the debate has been "distorted" and "hijacked by the middleman": "The debate has been entirely between the people who don't want pornography being sold and the people who make cash from selling the pornography created by other people . . . so we get the situation where the children aren't being protected; it's the people who allege they speak for the children whose views are heard. It's not the sex performers and the sex workers who are heard; it's the people who sell their product."

The polarized framing of discussions of pornography (harm versus freedom of expression) by two opposed lobby groups illustrates how a multifaceted issue can become watered down. The voices of performers, producers, and consumers are often muted or silenced during debates on pornography law reform. Issues repeatedly raised by my interviewees about selective policing, the misuse of their personal data, lack of privacy protections, piracy of their content, domination by tube monopolies, the need for workplace health and safety standards, barriers to accessing industrial rights, and the prohibitions on kink content are all eclipsed. By positioning pornography in such narrow adversarial terms, particularly using rights-based approaches centered on speech and harm, legislators defer responsibility for structural issues that shape power in the media landscape.

Approaching pornography law reform through the lens of speech has serious limits. For example, in 2018 a private member's bill (the Freedom of Speech Legislation Amendment [Censorship] Bill) promised reforms that the adult industry had long been campaigning for: It proposed to remove the prohibition on fetishes, permit advertisements that deal with sex, remove restrictions on online X18+ content, and remove prohibitions on the possession, control, and supply of pornography in the Northern Territory. While these would have been welcome and long-overdue changes, they were part of a suite of bills that attempted to lower the threshold for racially vilifying speech. The bills proposed to remove restrictions on speech that offends, insults, humiliates, or intimidates a person or group of people because of their race, color, or national or ethnic origin. The bills did not address the ongoing Northern Territory intervention (its welfare quarantining, acquisition of land, and targeted policing leading to disproportionate incarceration) that Aboriginal communities continue to resist. They did not address such issues as work health and safety standards for performers, antidiscrimination protections, avenues for justice, industrial rights, decriminalization, or destigmatization. Instead, by framing the problems of pornography regulation as only having to do with free speech and censorship, law reform efforts completely missed the core issues in need of attention.

The likelihood of meaningful reform is further stifled by politicians' concerns about retaining their electoral seats—decriminalizing production and sale is unlikely to be a popular party platform at election time. In my interview with Terry Flew, who acted as chair of the Australian Law Reform Commission's National Classification Scheme Review, he reflected on the potential for porn law reform: "So often I think change in this area happens to some degree by subterfuge and by the application of other laws. For instance, if you wanted to convince a conservative government to liberalize laws in this area, you'd point to reducing red tape and government spending and getting the classification board to focus more on matters of larger community concern. That would be the sort of pitch that you'd make."

Flew noted the difficulties of bringing bipartisan change with such a regular turnover of state politicians, in a context in which ministers would "start turning their head down and looking at their notes and avoiding any sort of eye contact." In his experience working on classification law reform, he reported that "several attorney generals were completely surprised as to what the actual laws were [that] they had responsibility for." His view was that reform was most likely to be "relatively piecemeal and ad hoc" and come via framing decriminalization in terms of a reduction in red tape or redressing the misalignment of federal classification and state criminal laws. However, the risk is that in appealing to economic benefits for legislators and pitching solutions that are expedient and safe for them, the reform process becomes about what is convenient for politicians rather than beneficial for the stakeholders, and the political asks become dangerously diluted.

Disrespect for the Law

Because content may be produced, uploaded, sold, and viewed across multiple countries, it presents jurisdictional challenges. As one feminist producer asked, "Why should I follow Australian classification rules when the vast majority of my audience is actually American?" Alan McKee, Brian McNair, and Anne Watson (2014) have asked, "Whose community standards, and which communities should prevail in policy-making around the regulation of the Internet[?]" (164). While the internet is generally governed according to geographical location, these authors demand regulators pay attention to virtual "suburbs" whose membership is determined on shared values. My interviewees spoke of standards in their various (kinky, sex worker, sex-positive, queer, porn) communities. "There's a queer ethics I think," said Xavier. "In general, the queer community is a lot more open to things that are potentially considered extreme by the mainstream because the kind of sex we have is so demonized anyway." Gala Vanting believed her communities had some shared political values: "They are interested in the rights of adults to make their own decisions, to choose what they're exposed to, to process that information and that imagery with their own lens (rather than someone else's lens bending it). Other things that I think are valued are freedom of expression, democratization of things like desirability and production (of anything, whether that's art or media), and anti-oppression."

Some participants espoused a libertarian approach, emphasizing the autonomy of the individual to follow their own interests unless they were infringing upon the rights of others, naming age and consent as the relevant factors. As Mistress Tokyo put it: "If you're offended by it, don't watch it. You know, if you don't want to see someone fisted, pierced, pissed on, then don't watch it. It's really bloody obvious to me." Others emphasized the more normative aspects of queer and feminist community standards in depicting safer sex, making consent visible, and offering content warnings. Domino spoke about certain practices being celebrated in queer communities given their history of criminalization and stigma: "In producing *Slit* we just couldn't understand why having images involving penetration were controversial, or images involving oral sex, or piercing, or BDSM, and there were some images with bruises and whips and needles. And so, I guess that's reflective of how we understood, at the time of producing *Slit*, the queer community standard is open to diverse sexual practices. From our own experience of involvement in the queer community and sex-positive community it's like, public sex is acceptable, and in fact it's great, you know?"

This celebration of nonnormative intimacies did not come without a sense of responsibility. Producers often signposted their material to provide users with advance information about the nature of content. Gala Vanting recalled, "We've explained that the people in this film are established partners or are fluid-bound or have done this before. Sometimes we say explicitly that the scene has been negotiated in advance, and the film depicts these kind of acts, so that a person that [may be] potentially triggered by that or is concerned about consent in BDSM has that information before they see the film."

In our interview, Terry Flew commented that these discussions were productive because they illustrate the value of co-regulatory projects and because, on their own, states are ineffective in understanding the nuance of community standards: "I think the ethical porn movement, that's a really important thing . . . like all things online, the capacity for community self-governance is important. And recognizing the internet emerged largely outside of state jurisdictions, the state is always going to be a somewhat blunt instrument through which to develop standards."

I asked my interviewees about the possibility of developing industry standards on pornography production and sale. One producer felt that, because regulators are so divorced from the material realities of production, standards should be developed by people within the industry: "It definitely shouldn't be done by people that don't know anything about pornography or the industry, absolutely not, because I feel like that's probably currently what's happened and that's the problem." Others didn't trust government to be involved at all, given their track record: "The practicality of that makes me nervous—who would fund it, what interests would be reflected, what level of community consultation would actually take place?" Others noted the tension between what producers might advocate for versus what performers might advocate for and voiced concern that it could be too driven by business. One interviewee was equally dubious about the prospect of codifying queer community standards, primarily because queer is an anti-identity category that is relational. Domino reflected that "community doesn't necessarily mean progressive— and nor does lack of regulation."

We ought not take for granted the current regulatory approach as if it is the only possibility. Cindy Gallop (2013), who runs the website Make Love Not Porn, argues that instead of blocking porn, governments should support and actively fund porn entrepreneurs who want to disrupt dominant representations of sex. They could do this, she suggests, by ensuring that banking institutions and hosting services stop discriminating against adult businesses and by providing financial subsidies to independent producers. In Sweden, Mia Engberg received approximately eighty thousand dollars from the Swedish Film Institute for her *Dirty Diaries* series in which she invited artists and filmmakers to make their own feminist porn using mobile phone cameras (Sabo 2012, 182–83). It is not unimaginable that other governments could fund the production of sexually explicit films through arts initiatives and grants—but in the meantime, producers are not waiting for government funding or endorsement.

Pleasure in Transgression

Porn producers' distrust of the law and their attempts to circumvent it should be understood as speaking to the poor design of the regulation and as a call for its reassessment rather than being read as an impetus for stronger enforcement. Classification, customs, and criminal laws play a central role in the *construction* of normative sexuality. Classification law actively engineers specific types of bodies that can be viewed—bodies with large breasts and neat labia, bodies that do not participate in kink or fetish, able bodies that experience pleasure through set erogenous zones, and bodies that do not bleed or leak or squirt. Restrictions on the production, sale, distribution, screening, possession, and consumption of pornography reinforce public sex as matter out of place, while heteronormative manifestations of intimacy permeate public life. Indie porn can therefore be seen to function as a queer world-making practice in the face of criminalization and pathologization.

Pornography laws misread and misunderstand the social, political, and cultural meanings afforded to sexually explicit films and the kinds of political projects I detailed in chapter 1. While the law retains a progressive narrative of reflecting community standards as they evolve, its conservativism and rigidity are out of step with contemporary attitudes toward sexual practices and the globalized nature of porn production and distribution. The law is not apolitical: Pornography and the law have a history and genealogy that inform one another, and its categories reflect political compromise. Porn regulation operates as a form of messaging that is often initiated at specific moments driven by media or electoral politics.

The heavy-handedness of the law is illustrative not of its effective regulatory grip, but instead of its *lack* of control over its subjects, who see the law as unjust and, in many cases, irrelevant. The current framework is so contested that it risks producing high levels of noncompliance, exemplified by the deliberate organizing of resistance screenings of pornographic films and the development of community processes of signposting and self-governance. However, the law, via the threat of both custodial penalties and fines as well as selective policing, administrative decision-making, facilitation of malicious complaints, confiscation of hard drives, deletion of content, and destruction of artwork, still has real constitutive effects on how porn producers and performers operate.

Meanwhile, the regulatory framework has produced new investments in criminal intimacies. Prohibitions, as Tim Dean (2011) reflects, "may be regarded as soliciting their own transgression rather than simply forbidding it" (71). Defiant portrayals of such prohibited activities as fisting and squirting are examples of what Kristeva (1982) describes as the "erotization of abjection" (55), and they reflect our sexual pleasures in being outlaws. In its failure, the law invites transgression and generates conditions that are ripe for resistance.

Diversity Washing

In March 2016, to coincide with International Women's Day, tube site Pornhub launched a female director series, asking female directors to share their work—for no remuneration but for mass exposure. Pornhub pitched its offer as an altruistic measure to promote "women-friendly porn" and showcase how the industry had evolved. Female directors were invited to become a Pornhub "content partner," creating individual profiles and providing free content in return for public promotion. Pornhub planned to promote the series in anticipation that the traffic would translate to earnings for female directors by directing viewers to their individual sites.

Indie producers across Australia, the United States, Europe, and the United Kingdom mobilized—initiating contact with one another in a scoping exercise with a view to making a collective decision about how best to respond. Most producers approached this offer with suspicion. Given that small producers were being asked to provide free content that would generate advertising revenue for a billion-dollar company, Pornhub's venture seemed more like a capitalistic endeavor than an altruistic contribution to International Women's Day.

These producers were wary of Pornhub's business practices. At the time, it was owned by Canadian company MindGeek, which owned eight of the top ten tube sites and was defending a piracy lawsuit for allegedly charging for access to pirated videos on Pornhub Premium. MindGeek had deliberately devalued companies through piracy and then bought up large production companies. French journalist Ovidie's 2017 documentary *Pornocracy: The New Sex Multinationals* exposed MindGeek's anticompetitive business practices and their business strategies to avoid copyright and taxation laws in order to monopolize the market.

Feminist producers in this group were dubious about being used as part of a respectability campaign for a company whose CEO had recently been arrested pending ongoing investigations. Producers were skeptical about becoming embroiled in an attempt to clean up Pornhub's image and how that would impact a movement advocating for ethical practices of production and distribution. The promise of potential traffic did not create much incentive: Those who participated in the trial partnership found that it resulted in increased traffic but few sales. One producer described it as a mere "carrot on a stick." Some were not convinced that Pornhub wouldn't sell their scenes as premium content under their new business model. But the core issue at stake was something else: the corporate co-optation of feminist pornographies.

"Aren't they just looking out for their own best interest?" asked one producer. "Aren't they exploiting a niche market in 'ethical' content?" asked another. "Isn't this creepy?" "Isn't it greenwashing?" "Isn't it pinkwashing?" Feminist pornographies were not simply a formula to "add women and stir"; they were not solely concerned with increasing the number of women as directors and consumers. Around the world one fundamental tenet was being iterated: Feminist pornographies are about the process, not just the product. While feminist producers were often guided by the comfort level of performers in deciding whether their images would remain behind a paywall or be used in marketing, contracting with tube sites risked losing control of the product. Under this model, feminist content could be featured next to misogynist, racist, or transphobic taglines. There was no guarantee that the content would be removed on request. Entering into a content partnership with Pornhub would effectively endorse the company's practices, perhaps offering them the most valuable gift of all: a sign of approval. As one producer warned, "The best way to stop a subversive movement is to buy it. The best way to kill feminist porn is to swallow it."

On the other hand, independent producers were struggling financially due to legal and administrative barriers to selling content online. The market monopoly enjoyed by tube sites made them hard to avoid for producers wanting their content to be seen outside their immediate circles and by a broader audience—Pornhub at the time boasted up to sixteen million active users per day (by 2019 it was twenty-two million). Was it worth "sleeping with the enemy" if it meant exposure of the work? Or, alternately, was there a way to leverage this offer and subvert it? We were all working—to some degree—within a capitalist framework anyway. Ideas emerged to minimize the damage: Perhaps it wouldn't cost us if we provided trailers or safe-for-work videos that are already free online. What if we uploaded videos discussing the importance of paying for porn as a primary indicator of ethical consumption? Attuned to the varied financial positions of producers across the globe and the need to hustle to meet their bills, there was a general sense among indie producers that any response should speak to the larger political and economic framework in which this initiative is pitched rather than single out producers who chose to be involved out of economic necessity. For some, engaging with Pornhub was unavoidable. It is a conglomerate, after all. The danger of Pornhub's offer was to pitch us against one another; the challenge of the movement was to maintain a united front.

The political moment also presented producers with an opportunity. International Women's Day provided a chance to speak out against the impact of tube sites on independent production, about the effect of piracy on individual performers, about the culture of entitlement among audiences for free content, and about the nuances of ethical content that are glossed over in media. We could take a stand as a collective, with strength in numbers: an open letter? Discussions about finding trustworthy journalists were tempered by the commercial risks of speaking out. In an industry already steeped in stigma, and in which media reporting is notoriously polarized, trust in media was low.

The moment illuminated the need for alternative distribution platforms and channels to share feminist content; counter channels where feminist pornographies would not be swallowed up and consumed by the offer of a campaign, where producers could retain control over the context and integrity of their content, and where profits could be distributed back to independent producers and their performers. A tempting response here, as one producer proposed, was to build our own version of the same thing: "Where are the feminist tube sites?" they asked. The prospect of a consolidated platform was appealing but not that simple.

Although a tube site featuring feminist content would no doubt be appealing to consumers (a number of us had been approached by entrepreneurs seeking to establish something similar), to mirror the model of existing tube sites would still be merely playing their game, on their terms. Some producers were concerned that having any investment in mass appeal and mainstream publicity would only dilute our integrity as independent directors. If we are so eager for exposure and profit, surely this is going to taint our decision-making and ability to scrutinize and critique industry practices. It was time to step outside the frameworks offered by big business and redefine our own terms of reference. One producer exclaimed emphatically, "We are not just niche content; we are meant to be a political movement!"

Pornhub's offer was not the first or the last time feminist producers were faced with an opportunity for political compromise. Eighteen months later, a women-run company called Bellesa came under attack from performers and feminist producers for pirating films for their free porn site pitched as "Porn for Women." Bellesa's founder boasted that she had "found a way to bring women porn they'll actually enjoy without draining their bank accounts." Porn performers started to file complaints under the US Digital Millennium Copyright Act asking to take down content. Australian porn performer Kim Cums tweeted, "It's not free content. It's stolen content. You are no better than PornHub, Imgur, or Reddit." San Francisco–based performer Jiz Lee tweeted, "Stealing porn empowers no one. And to pirate specifically from female producers in the branding of 'porn for women.' . . . Shame on @BellesaCo."

Pornhub has not avoided criticism in the following years. Although Ethical Capital Partners has recently been engaging porn scholars to consult with performers about their needs and experiences, Pornhub's belated policy changes—including the step to verify content creators—have historically been prompted by financial and reputational incentives. In 2020 Pornhub implemented a verification process within seventy-two hours of Visa and Mastercard threatening to withdraw payment services from the site, following accusations that it was hosting nonconsensual content and child abuse material. Pornhub has engaged in visible corporate social responsibility campaigns, including making donations to social justice organizations and public statements in support of #BlackLivesMatter. However, the site maintains a racialized tagging system that treats whiteness as the normative benchmark and requires performers of color to use racist tags like "ebony" and "interracial" in order to remain visible and earn income. Between 2022 and 2024, based on the Pornhub Tracking Exposed study of its personalization algorithm, Pornhub has faced legal actions in Italy and Cyprus for its alleged breach of the EU's General Data Protection Regulation (article 9) on the basis that it was nonconsensually collecting and processing users' personal information, including users' sexual preferences, browsing practices, and viewing histories.

4

#NSFW

Online Privatization, Sanitization, and Gentrification

Many independent producers originally moved to online distribution precisely to avoid the misogynist, ableist, racist, cis-centric, and heteronormative classification systems they were faced with. They began hosting sites internationally and marketing to consumers abroad through member-based websites, video-on-demand, and direct-to-user sites. Motivated by economic opportunity, legal necessity, and the hope of avoiding ethical compromise, some producers espoused the techno-utopian aspirations of Web 2.0 and the affordances of convergent media. However, they soon found that platforms were not necessarily less regulated or more permissive than national classification schemes. Rather, the standards for sexual content on privatized platforms were just as onerous, unjustified, and potentially even more out of touch, with less transparency in decision-making and fewer avenues for recourse. While user-generated content may have diversified pornography, it resulted in the centralization rather than the redistribution of infrastructure, power, and wealth.

Shifts from national classification of broadcast media (a one-to-many model of mass communication via the silos of radio or television) to platform mediation of convergent media (in which new technologies have enabled more devices, platforms, and networks through which to distribute content) created new challenges. With community standards being determined by corporate entities rather than government agencies, the threshold test for content moved from *obscenity and offensiveness* to *profitability and reputational risk*. This shift is of concern because of its underlying foundations in homonormativity, ableism, and racial capitalism—it marginalizes bodies and sexualities where they are deemed to be unprofitable, unproductive, or high risk. This matters because private platforms operate as gatekeepers of public space with the power to control what we see and share yet without the transparency and accountability required of government or media.

Further, in navigating online space, performers and producers are incentivized to self-censor, to present a white, slim, hetero, binary, able-bodied version of their gender and sexuality that is compatible with the market-driven architecture of privatized platforms, resulting in narrow articulations of gender, race, bodies, and desires. This has produced the paradoxical situation in which sex industry businesses, despite having historically facilitated the commercial growth of online platforms, are facing widespread erasure and thereby enabling free tube sites to dominate the market and place individuals at risk of economic precarity. The proliferation of tube sites and targeted advertising brings new political challenges for indie porn producers in how to remain both visible and viable.

Fantasies of Democratization

The transition away from static websites to the second generation of the World Wide Web brought technologies for user-generated content, participatory cultures, collaborative modification, and social networking sites. The abundance, affordability, and intuitiveness of such new communication technologies as camera equipment, computers, and webcams blurred the distinctions between performers, producers, distributors, and consumers. Pornography has historically been a "major promotor of new communication technologies," with porn producers being early buyers and users who accelerated the distribution of VCR and CD-ROM (Coopersmith 1998, 95). Sex workers were early pioneers who designed, coded, built, and used websites and cryptocurrencies to advertise and transact in a context where print advertising was criminalized (Barrett-Ibarria 2018). Sex industry businesses helped online platforms flourish by populating them with content, increasing their size and commercial viability. Sexual communities were actively building virtual subcultural spaces and peer-to-peer networks, using self-representations as means of identity-formation and connection (Jacobs 2007). Some believed that the proliferation of alternative, independent, amateur, and user-generated content on the web promised to democratize pornography (McNair 2013).

However, online space was never the free domain espoused by some early internet pioneers. A swathe of books now demonstrate how human prejudices have consistently been programmed into datasets, coders, and algorithms. Safiya Umoja Noble's *Algorithms of Oppression: How Search Engines Reinforce Racism* (2018) documented systemic racial bias in Google's search engine. In *The Digital Closet: How the Internet Became Straight* (2022), Alexander Monea describes how a thirty-year "war on porn" has suppressed LGBTQ+ content and embedded heteronormative bias. As privatized platforms take on the role of content regulation, distribution has become largely regulated by intermediaries: payment processors, hosting services, and streaming platforms. To obtain broadest reach, remain visible, and earn money, content needs to attract likes, clicks, rankings, and traffic, and producers have to strategically shape their scenes into material that can be safely sold in an attention economy.

Rather than being a techno-utopian space, new communication technologies merely represent a fantasy of democracy. Astra Taylor (2014) argues that the "new order" resembles not a revolution, but a *rearrangement* of power whereby giant tech companies have replaced media moguls as gatekeepers and advertising revenue techniques have simply adapted. Companies such as Google, Amazon, Apple, and Microsoft (who earn more than the entire gross domestic product of some countries) have transformed themselves into businesses that provide essential online infrastructure—both hardware and software—that others rely on. Capitalism, writes Nick Srnicek (2017), tends to restructure itself through new markets, technologies, forms of exploitation, and means of accruing capital. These companies are transforming the global economy through what he describes as "platform capitalism" (22). The deliberations of feminist producers described in the "Diversity Washing" vignette illustrate the dilemmas for alternative producers in intervening in a system without being swallowed up.

Discourses of participation, visibility, and democratization in relation to sexual identities therefore need to be approached with caution. As Rosemary Hennessy (2000) writes, they "need to be considered critically in relation to capital's insidious and relentless expansion" (112), which can simply co-opt and subsume social movements. Alternative pornographies can become part of this machinery and should be read, argues Katrien Jacobs (2004), "in light of capitalism's tendency to control ownership, control 'edgy' content" (79).

The digital divide between users is not necessarily reduced, but rather exacerbated with new communication technologies: While increased access to digital equipment promised more diverse content, the distribution methods were geared toward generating private wealth for corporations (Marwick 2007). The centralization of data and content under big tech has since prompted a democratic turn toward Web 3.0, an internet iteration renowned for blockchain technologies, horizontality, and decentralization, though this result is not without its own environmental and other problems.

Discrimination in Payment Processing

Denial of financial infrastructure is a regulatory technique used to deter the production and sale of pornography online. Refusals of service, disproportionate fees, and administrative blocks to setting up bank accounts, establishing payment processors, and withdrawing funds create disincentives to independent porn production and pave the way to monopolization by porn tube sites, those that can afford to give away free content and are able to monetize theirs through advertising. Independent producers who run their own websites, where they would ordinarily be reaping more of the profits, report obstacles to actually selling their content.

In our interviews, producers reported institutional discrimination from Australian banks that refused to process transactions for porn websites. As Howard told me, "They just won't touch it." Sindy Skin, who hoped to start a platform for Australian producers to host their material collaboratively, was refused by St. George, ANZ, and Commonwealth banks. Kim Cums, who ran her own subscription site, reported that her bank wouldn't deal with digital content at all and that she had problems getting paid out by crowdfunding platform PiggyBankGirls. Luna Trash reported that working with cash as a stripper meant "I haven't been able to get any loans" for her alt-porn *Trash Vixens* endeavor. Cat O'Nine Tails felt that banks have unrealistic requirements for credit card processing for small businesses, impairing their ability to get small products off the ground: "They wanted huge up-front fees and a business plan, and they expected a massive turnover—and when you're starting out that's never going to happen." Such refusal of service was not limited to Australia. After relocating to Amsterdam, G Media, owned by Abby Winters, had their Dutch bank account abruptly canceled—after five years—because, they were told, their company "no longer fits within [our bank]'s client profiles." Another producer reported being subjected to special conditions and requirements that other customers were not: "We had an account closed recently because we were unable in a particular time frame to convince the billing company that the money that was coming from our website was not being used to fund terrorism."

Without national banks processing payments for porn, producers turn to international billing companies that specialize in processing adult content. However, the two main companies my interviewees used, CC Bill (in the United States) and Verotel (in Europe), require proof of an address either in the United States or Europe, thus causing Australian producers to have to set up legal entities overseas in order to access payment processing. The expense and networks necessary to complete this process, from setup costs to relocating to obtaining a business address, can become obstacles for individuals without up-front capital. While smaller billing companies, such as Zombaio, have catered to Australians in the past, their user support was often unavailable, and in 2015 they changed owners and failed to pay out funds to account holders. At the time we spoke, two interviewees reported still being owed money from Zombaio. Some porn sites have since turned to cryptocurrencies to avoid financial discrimination, as generally their fees are lower and there is less risk of being deplatformed. However, cryptocurrencies still bring privacy risks for sex workers, as they document legal names and transactions, and require significant digital literacy to use.

If a producer is successful in securing payment processing, they are often charged higher fees because billing and credit card companies deem adult sites as being at high risk of charge-backs and fraud. For example, at the time of my interviews, Verotel charged €500 per annum and CC Bill charged US$1,000 per annum just to operate the site, on top of the average 12–16 percent cut they took from all sales, plus the international transaction fees a producer has to pay to receive payment. Sindy Skin calculated that to sustain an account with Verotel and cover her costs, "I would need to make [AU]$3,000 to break even before making any profit, and that's every year to cover the costs and everything, and that's not even including my time of coding." Higher fees apply regardless of whether the sites actually have higher rates of charge-backs: One feminist porn producer who had been running sites since the early 2000s told me, "It doesn't matter that I've been running my business for this long and I've actually got less charge-backs than car rentals." Lux Alptraum (2014) suggests that this alleged risk may not be about the account holders themselves, but rather that banks decide providing services to porn producers puts *them* at risk of losing their conservative clients.

As my colleagues and I argue elsewhere, this is an issue of discrimination by design, stemming from classist, racist, transphobic, and whorephobic laws and policies. The wars on trafficking and terror, in addition to the criminal-ization of sex work and restrictive migration policies, have resulted in oner-ous obligations on banks to prevent money laundering and human trafficking through consumer surveillance. These wars have produced the conditions for both police and financial institutions to work in tandem to restrict financial services to sex workers. In their attempts to algorithmically identify instances of sexual servitude, illegal activity, and trafficking (politicized concepts with contested definitions and racialized histories in preventing Asian migration and miscegenation), they have relied on broad proxies (from cash withdrawals to online payments) that pick up a range of actors (from sex workers to adult businesses and activists organizing mutual aid fundraisers) (Stardust et al. 2023). Instead of addressing any of the root factors around labor exploitation, the privatization of financial infrastructure and the rise of intermediary power have instead accelerated historically discriminatory practices of assessing risk and creditworthiness: gatekeeping wealth rather than distributing it.

Some scholars have found evidence of shifts in the economic structure of pornography in transparent fee structures offered by streaming sites. In his re-search on "Porn 2.0" about amateurs uploading their content to XTube, Sharif Mowlabocus (2010) notes that performers are paid monthly a standardized 50 percent of net profits "irrespective of content, body type or sexual prefer-ence, [or] prices" (78). However, Australian performers/producers described significant hurdles in receiving payouts from international companies. Cat O'Nine Tails described her billing experience as "a four-year nightmare," with "convoluted" processes for payouts involving "always about three middlemen." Sindy Skin, who used the amateur and fetish porn website Clips4Sale, said, "You have to have a minimum of $150 of credit in your account before you can even withdraw from Clips4Sale, and then it costs you about $50 each time." Kim complained that "there's always some sort of road block or loophole that you have to jump through." To be paid sometimes required a physical US address, as some sites would only pay via US check, "or you can only get like a prepaid card, which then has a two dollar transaction fee every single time that you use it, and by the time that you have paid all of your fees to all of the people that are all paying high-risk adult fees to MasterCard, Visa, you've like lost 90 percent of your profits, in which case it's like, 'Why am I producing any-way?' Because I'm making like a dollar off a $10 video."

Many online payment processors refuse adult content altogether, their terms of use sparking debates about who can make money online. Overnight changes in policy or targeted crackdowns on users mean that performers and producers have had their accounts suspended and their funds forfeited, sometimes up to thousands of dollars. For two decades, sex workers have spoken out in online media, with headlines such as "How the Financial Sector Is Making Life Miserable for Sex Workers" (Horn 2014) and "How PayPal and WePay Discriminate against the Adult Industry" (Stryker 2018). In 2021 social media sites AVNStars and GayVN both announced they were ceasing payments to sex workers due to banking discrimination. To a large extent this is also determined by the credit card companies themselves. American Express refuses porn transactions completely (*Economist* 2015), and Visa has previously implemented a $750 annual fee for adult businesses (Lubove 2003). In 2015 MasterCard announced it was implementing a worldwide ban on customers placing adult advertisements on Backpage.com, and in 2021 both Visa and MasterCard withdrew their services from Pornhub. MasterCard placed further restrictions on adult content, preventing anonymous content and requiring documented age and identity verification for all people depicted.

In 2022 porn researcher Val Webber found that 90 percent of surveyed sex workers experienced detrimental effects to their livelihood as a result of MasterCard's restrictive policy. This "entrenched pattern of systemic discrimination" continues to operate, says sex tech author Violet Blue (2015), despite being found to violate constitutional rights in the United States, and does so in a way that "disproportionately denies financial opportunities for women." According to Blue, "For nearly a decade, PayPal, JPMorgan Chase, Visa/MasterCard, and now Square, have systematically denied or closed accounts of small businesses, artists and independent contractors whose business happens to be about sex. These payment processing authorities have also coerced websites to cease featuring sexual content under threat of service withdrawal, all while blaming ambiguous rules or pressure from one another."

In response to such policies, performers and producers find new forms of digital payment via wish lists and gift cards as well as through offline sales: *Slit* magazine reported being "pushed off PayPal," meaning they had to "resort to much more informal means" of offline distribution. The barriers impact financial viability for independent and small producers and create disincentives to making porn altogether. Combined with criminal laws prohibiting sale, production, and advertising in most states of Australia, it is increasingly difficult and expensive for individuals to directly *sell* pornography on their own sites (and, importantly, their *own terms*). The denial of financial services to independent producers then creates opportunities for tube sites to monopolize the market by streaming free (sometimes pirated) content and for platforms to take advantage of performers by taking predatory commissions. As I explored in "Diversity Washing," producers then face a dilemma of whether to give their content to these companies, accept their nonnegotiable terms of use, and relinquish control of their product, all in return for traffic.

Flagging, Screening, and Detection

Social media platforms are largely governed by their terms of use, which bind users to operate within agreed conditions. Social media platforms have received criticism from users about their poor privacy policies, the unilateral amendment of terms and conditions, and their imposed definitions of community standards. Terms of use are not necessarily reflective of legal standards or technical requirements, in part because sites operate with an international user base. Instead, the policies reflect, as Yoel Roth (2015) argues, "normative judgments about proper self-presentation and community formation" (414). These standards are not politically neutral (Jillian York calls them "silicon values," as they reflect the tech bro culture of Silicon Valley); nor are they collectively determined or debated with participation from the user base. Rather, they are imposed from above and exported across the globe.

They are also unevenly enforced—Meta employs an XCheck content review system that whitelists celebrity and popular accounts and exempts them from many of its rules (Díaz and Hecht-Felella 2021). This double standard in enforcement means that sex workers, strippers, and pole dancers are disproportionately affected while celebrities continue to flourish (see Are and Paasonen 2021). Further, Meta has coded the hypersexualization of plus-size Black women into their algorithms, creating a racial and size hierarchy determining which bodies are flagged. In 2020 model Curvy Nayome launched a petition to stop Instagram from censoring fat Black women, noting that *Playboy*'s images of slim white women remained up. The campaign prompted Instagram to review its nudity policy in relation to plus-sized bodies.

The terms of use of billing companies, platform providers, and hosting services draw upon legal distinctions between unlawful/lawful activities but also at times widely depart from them in prohibiting activities that are legal to perform, on or off camera. Although pornography laws differ per jurisdiction, corporations tend to take the most restrictive legal frameworks as their baseline. In a political climate in which sex itself is risky business, representing scandal and inviting complaint, companies do not want to be seen to be endorsing commercial or nonnormative sexual practices. Their requirements are not necessarily based on law, but rather on *reputational risk*—the potential of bad publicity, a tarnished reputation, or public outcry that would reduce the market value of the company or prompt the loss of their investors. The problem of corporate governance is that, as Terry Flew (2015) writes, it is "overlaid with that of how to grow the user base of commercial sites, build brand identity, and increase revenues and shareholder value, while recognising tensions that exist between user niches and the much-vaunted mass audience" (15–16). In decision-making about content, corporations, driven by commercial motives, appeal to conservative values because they don't want to isolate their advertisers or jeopardize their revenue stream.

An interesting example can be found in Verotel's ban on blood in video content. Verotel's prohibition may be intended to avoid depictions of sexual violence, but it also prevents the portrayal of menstrual porn. Failure to secure credit card billing because of such policies has led to the closure of sites like BloodieTrixie.com and Furry Girl's EroticRed.com, which portrayed people having sex or enjoying their bodies while menstruating (Marks 2013, 2). This example demonstrates how online corporate "policing of content goes far beyond what is legally required" (Crawford and Gillespie 2016, 412). While it may be necessary to preclude nonconsensual sex or sexual violence, having sex when menstruating is certainly not illegal, and in Australia depicting it isn't either. In her book *Periods in Pop Culture* (2012), Lauren Rosewarne differentiates between menstrual porn made for men, which fetishizes menstrual sex, and menstrual porn made for women, which focuses on real blood and challenges dominant representations of menstruation (123, 139). Filipina-American May Ling Su's website OnMyPeriod.com promotes healthy menstrual practices, sharing ancient folklore and moon blood rituals and herbal and nutritional support. In our interviews, Helen Corday said she believed that depicting menstruation as desirable in pornography was politically important: "I just think it's aesthetically beautiful and sexually arousing, and I think that's an important thing for women; lots of women are disgusted by themselves, and my love of it is something I really wanted to share . . . because lots of people are in a lot of pain and shame around menstruation that's really unnecessary."

Prohibitions on certain body fluids are also evident in the terms and conditions for some webcam sites, and where they draw the line is particularly interesting. One study of BongaCams, LiveJasmin, and Chaturbate illustrates that the sites reject the idea that they facilitate sexual expression or even work (Stegeman 2021)—they are consistent in the delusion that they do not participate in sexual economies. The rules for webcam performers on MyFreeCams include a list of activities that are "forbidden" on camera as a "zero-tolerance violation." These include a range of body fluids (breastfeeding, lactation, urination, menstrual bleeding, enema play, vomiting) as well as activities (penetration of the vagina or anus with items "not meant for sexual simulation"—an unclear term itself). These activities are listed alongside unlawful and non-consensual activities, such as rape, bestiality, incest, involvement with minors, and impaired consent, without differentiation and as if they are analogous (MyFreeCams Wiki). While these appear to be arbitrary distinctions, like the classification laws I discussed in chapter 3, they are consistent in their attempt to maintain the symbolic integrity of the cisgender, heteronormative body. Where bodies act in ways that destabilize cis-normative heterosexuality (and where they find pleasures in the fluids, orifices, and functions outside this model), they are designated as abject and pathological, conflated with violence and removed from view. Performer Sophie Ladder has embarked on the painstaking process of compiling a detailed spreadsheet of adult site restrictions, reviewing such sites as XHamster, CamSoda, ManyVids, and Fansly, listing which words and content are forbidden from clip sites, live stream sites, fan sites, tube sites, sexting services, and social media (Ladder 2022).

To enforce their terms of use, platforms utilize a mix of reporting tools, user controls, and algorithms to flag and detect prohibited content. Verotel and CC Bill run monthly screening compliance software to pick up keywords. Users have complained about the limitations of automated systems for determining acceptable content and their potential to capture unintended material in the process. Aeryn Walker, a cosplay enthusiast, had a scene flagged wherein she was a vampire using fake blood because the site prohibited the use of blood, regardless of whether it was realistic. Angela White spoke of the blanket bans on words like *force* (which meant she could not depict forced orgasms, a distinct pornographic genre) and *drinking* ("I can't say I was drinking a glass of water . . . I can't drink someone's squirt or ejaculate"). Angela believed these blanket rules, regardless of context, "make legitimate conversations impossible" and that important dialogue about sexuality is made invisible and becomes unspeakable.

One feminist producer, Ms Naughty, has publicly discussed how she was asked to remove blog content because it discussed a celebrity (Oprah Winfrey talking about porn), and it was against her biller's terms of use to discuss celebrities on an adult site. When PinkLabel.tv posted about altsHIFT's film *Love Your Cunt* (a celebration of genital diversity) on Twitter (now "X"), their post was removed and the account temporarily suspended for "hateful conduct," prompting a discussion about acceptable language: "Does 'cunt' break the rules?'" (Clark-Florey 2019). In 2022 the Oversight Board overturned Meta's decision to remove two Instagram posts for allegedly violating Instagram's "sexual solicitation" and "nudity" policies. Fundraising for top surgery, the posts

FIGURE 4.1. PinkLabel.tv's post promoting altsHIFT's film *Love Your Cunt* (starring Kali Sudhra and Ivy de Luna) was temporarily removed from Twitter in 2019 for violating the rules against "hateful conduct" with its phrase "Your cunt isn't on trial; your cunt is the fucking judge!" Image by AltsHIFT Films, courtesy of PinkLabel.tv.

featured two trans and nonbinary people who were bare chested with their nipples covered. These cases do not represent random mistakes or enforcement errors, but rather exemplify a far more systemic and predictable pattern.

Aside from the obvious impacts on people's access to gender-affirming health care, media, and conversations, these policies result in the loss of a dynamic cultural archive and the sanitization of online space. In 2018 micro-blogging site Tumblr, a haven for fan fiction writers, independent sex workers, and kinksters, announced it would no longer host adult photos, videos, or GIFS with "real-life human genitals or female-presenting nipples" or any content depicting sex acts. Tumblr's definition of what constitutes permissible adult content (illustrative but not "real" nudity) preserves a class-based and fallacious distinction between art and pornography. They only permit "exposed female-presenting nipples in connection with breastfeeding, birth or after birth moments" and in "health-related situations, such as post-mastectomy or gender confirmation surgery." Aside from the paradoxical task of ascertaining which nipples appear to be "female-presenting" (a fraught exercise lacking any utility), these policies restrict representations of women's bodies to their reproductive functions, repeat the tired framing of women's bodies through medical lenses, and equate nudity with sexuality.

The fruitless task of designing an algorithm that attempts to identify whose nipples are "female" is inevitably going to fail simply because not all nipples are gendered and not all nipples are gendered in a way that is coherent to the cis-normative configurations of machine learning classifiers. The absurdity of this cisgendered fixation is best exemplified by Courtney Demone's social media campaign #DoIHaveBoobsNow?, which follows her journey on hormone therapy, testing out at what point her breast tissue would become detectable as "female" and warranting of censorship.

Decision-Making and Content Removal

While the nebulous term *pornography* has, in the past, been applied to a range of analog products (from advertisements to clothing to music videos), it is now applied liberally to various kinds of digital networked intimacies. It extends not only to sexual content but also to anything peripheral to it, from emojis in online chats to external links on user profiles. For example, as part of enforcing their prohibition on "sexual solicitation," in 2019 Meta (then Facebook) began removing chats featuring eggplant and peach emojis when used in certain configurations alongside sexual conversations. In 2022 Linktree closed accounts of users overnight if they included URLs of not-safe-for-work (NSFW) websites. In addition to detecting keywords, platforms also use sentiment analysis tools that attempt to analyze tone, intent, and emotion behind text as part of content moderation systems. However, these tools often fail to understand subcultural nuances in language and dialect. For example, researchers examined a sentiment analysis technology called Perspective only to find that tweets by drag queens on Twitter rated higher for "toxic speech" than tweets by white nationalists (Oliva, Antonialli, and Gomes 2021). This is not to say those tweets were more toxic, but that the software confused what the authors describe as "mock impoliteness" (a strategy LGBTQ people use to cope with hostility) as inherently toxic language. This tool does the same with sex worker rights terminology—when I typed "whore power" (a common sex worker rights phrase) into Perspective API, it came back with a 72.53 percent likelihood of being toxic. This programming does not ensure healthy dialogue, as it promises, because these predictions are often used with little oversight to flag and remove sex workers' content, including where words like *whore* have been reclaimed. It certainly does not eradicate the whorephobia that underlies many platform community standards. This is a common problem with such a black-and-white approach to content moderation: User surveys on social media takedowns indicate that trans people frequently have content removed that discusses transphobia, and Black users frequently have content removed relating to racial justice (Haimson et al. 2021).

The lack of transparency in arbitrating community standards is no more apparent than when the decisions of platforms are challenged by users. My interviewees were concerned that their livelihood could be undermined by a single complaint, however unwarranted, without justification. Howard remarked, "You only need a very small number of people to complain, and they have the power to control what a large number of people can do, or see, or talk about." One notorious Instagram user, known as Omid, has been on a series of campaigns to report porn performers' Instagram accounts and have them deleted despite not showing any nudity or sex (Fabbri 2019). As a result, producers have erred on the side of caution in what they share, in both online and offline contexts. Speaking about their approach to curating *Dirty Queer* magazine, Xavier recalled, "I've had some heated discussions about really wanting to include an image and specifically not including that image because it just had the potential—because I feel like all it would take is one complaint from one person."

Sometimes terms of use are deliberately broad to provide discretion for the corporation in permitting or removing content without explanation. In an illustrative example, Ms Naughty had all of her promotional videos removed from Vimeo in 2013. She wrote asking them to define what constituted sexually explicit content so that she could edit her work to meet their terms. She asked:

> If you can see genitals, is it explicit? If you can see nipples, is it explicit? Only female nipples or male nipples too? If the subject deals with sex and if the actors are nude and simulating sex, is that explicit or porn? How do you know the difference between simulated and real sex if you can't see genitals? If it *looks* artistic, does that make a difference? If the images exist purely to arouse, is that porn? Even if there's no nudity in those images? What if someone gets aroused at, say, images of feet?

The questions are pertinent. In 2016 Erika Lust's film *Do You Find My Feet Suckable?* was removed from YouTube despite containing no nudity or sexually explicit material—only foot sucking. In their response to Ms Naughty, Vimeo did not elaborate on any criteria or definitions of explicitness in their decision-making and made it clear that, as a private company, they have no obligation to host anything that doesn't "interest" them (Ms Naughty 2013). "As I mentioned, we review each video on a case-by-case basis and therefore there is no exclusive definition that we use to determine whether or not a video violates our Community Guidelines. Our moderation team has agreed that the removed

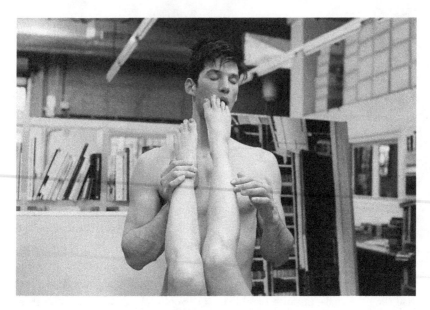

FIGURE 4.2. *Do You Find My Feet Suckable?*, an XConfessions film by Erika Lust, was removed from YouTube in 2016. Image by Rocío Saucedo.

videos did indeed violate our Community Guidelines, and we are not interested in hosting them on Vimeo."

Unlike the classification board or the courts, whose decisions can be reviewed, who are accountable to the public, and who are generally expected to follow precedent and publish reasons for their decisions, private regulation provides little transparency in decision-making. Vimeo's definition is so vague as to be reminiscent of US Supreme Court Justice Potter Stewart's famous quote in *Jacobellis v. Ohio* (378 U.S. 184, 197 [1964]) that he could not define pornography, but "I know it when I see it." The arbitrariness of their decision is highlighted by the fact that, in 2015, music artist Peaches released her video clip *Rub* on Vimeo, which includes nudity, sex, and an orgy with some of San Francisco's best-known queer porn stars. This clip remains online and has been marked by Vimeo as "mature," which suggests differential treatment depending on whether the person uploading is viewed as an artist or a pornographer regardless of the content of their work. This reinforces the status of pornography as, in Kelly Dennis's (2009) words, a "moral and aesthetic regulatory concept" that is conceptually distinguished from art or culture (6).

In the refusal of Vimeo to provide reasons or criteria for their decision-making, we can see what Kate Crawford and Tarleton Gillespie (2016) refer to as a "monarchic structure" of governance in which "a plea can be made, but the decision to remove or suspend is solely up to the platform" (422). While Ms Naughty could engage in limited discussion with Vimeo to provide an explanation or seek clarification—she even wanted to edit her content to meet their standards—she cannot negotiate her terms of use. Vimeo is not obliged to provide justification, and evidence of the issue is effectively removed from public debate. Crawford and Gillespie argue that flagging mechanisms, where they leave no room for "users to qualitatively describe the reasons behind the flag" (422), obscure public debates about what constitutes offensive content and leave no room to articulate concern or air disagreements that are actually "vital public negotiations" (413).

Instead, they ask whether the action of flagging and decision-making should become more public or even open to debate. They reference Wikipedia discussion pages on which the content is openly debated and "backstage discussions" are visible over time (421–22). In this model, which they describe as "antagonistic pluralism," the public can access a "history of debates about a particular video, image, or post," providing a space for "objections and counterobjections," and it would "recognize that social media sites are not only about individual content consumption, but also intensely relational, social spaces where debates over content and propriety play a role in shaping the norms of a site" (422–23). In this model, important discussions over community standards can be played out (and recorded) in the public sphere. This would be a useful move, given that international governing bodies are becoming increasingly concerned about automated content moderation. In 2021 the UN special rapporteur Irene Kahn published a note on freedom of opinion and expression that specifically recognized that "the policies of digital platforms also seek to censor women's sexual expression, including prohibiting nudity and 'adult content.' Because automated content moderation is unable to identify nuance, content can be wrongly removed or blocked" (26).

Historically, classification boards have focused on very specific issues (sex, violence, nudity, drug use) as the basis for restricting access to content. But what if classification and content moderation standards stopped seeing sex, nudity, or drug use as harmful and instead issued warnings for phenomena like sexism, racism, or ableism, which are undoubtedly triggering, alienating, and harmful? What if platforms and film boards notified users that content featured themes of colonialism, white fragility, toxic masculinity, the war on drugs, or the prison industrial complex to recognize the devastating reach of these structural harms? Indeed, there is a new push to "classify consent" in film and television. Citing scenes from such television series as *Bridgerton* and

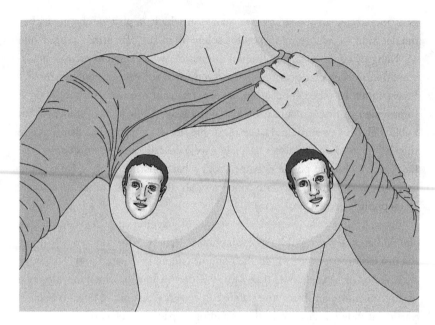

FIGURE 4.3. Sex worker artist Exotic Cancer critiques Meta's nudity and sexual solicitation policies using CEO Mark Zuckerberg's face to censor "female nipples." Image by Exotic Cancer.

such films as *The Devil Wears Prada*, the nonprofit organization Consent Labs argues for scenes depicting nonconsensual acts to no longer be trivialized as comedy or romance and instead to be accurately labeled as featuring nonconsent. There would, of course, still be practical issues in identifying such content at scale as well as the risk of critical, subversive, or parody content (or nonverbal consent) being flagged erroneously by algorithms. But it speaks volumes about the values of platforms where they flag sex but not sexism.

Preemptive Editing and Compatible Bodies

Corporate regulation at the point of entry to the market affects what people create at the level of production. Restrictive terms of use, screening software, and hidden decision-making have a chilling effect, discouraging people from expressing particular representations. Producers already edit their content to meet classification requirements—Angela White described how her labia were "healed to a single crease" in Australia, photoshopped with pubic hair in Germany, and pixelated in Japan to meet classification requirements in each country. Michelle Flynn cut her footage into soft and explicit edits to meet TV broadcasting requirements, including editing out erect penises. Gala Vanting identified a gap between what she would like to make and what's possible to show and navigated this through a mix of self-censorship and overseas distribution. The risks of content removal and the time-consuming labor of having to reedit footage mean that producers cut and slice their raw material into palatable products. It is the sanitized versions of the work that get the exposure. The full scene, if it contains particular body fluids or sexual practices, can rarely be screened, sold, or hosted, and those bodies and sexualities potentially become invisible.

In addition, performers themselves can refrain from certain activities because there is nowhere to screen or sell the footage. Individual sex workers, queers, women, and kinksters, become self-disciplining subjects *responsible* for gatekeeping and policing their pleasures to be marketable, safe, and low-risk. The individual can take on the corporate values of these companies at the level of the body. Over time these "business as usual" editing practices risk becoming normalized. This cultural engineering affects the social and political landscape too: It affects who is seen as desirable and can foreclose sexual possibilities. The kind of pornography that is then produced may not be safe for work (depending on your vocation), but it is *safe for the market.*

This matters significantly because depictions of queer sexualities and women's body fluids become relegated to small, underground, subcultural (and criminalized) spaces. They are then visible only among select audiences or through word of mouth. If we think back to the aspirations of queer and feminist porn, to *intervene* in the categorization and valuation of certain bodies, these goals are thwarted by the segregation of adult content as distinct from other art, media, and cultural spaces. In addition, it deters participation from particular communities in public online spaces. In their study on queer women's experiences using Tinder, Instagram, and Vine, Stefanie Duguay, Jean Burgess, and Nicolas Suzor (2018) found that the "patchwork platform governance" of these sites "significantly limited queer women's ability to participate and be visible on these platforms, as they often self-censored to avoid harassment, reduced the scope of their activities, or left the platform altogether" (237). The result is an erasure of sexual minorities from public space as cultures that do not belong.

As platform users struggle for online visibility, they can boost their status by presenting as palatable versions of themselves. Alice Marwick (2013) argues that the architecture of social media incentivizes personas that are "highly edited, controlled, and monitored, conforming to commercial ideals that dictate 'safe-for-work' presentation" (5). In her ethnography on webcam girls,

Terri Senft (2008) similarly found that workers must use "self-presentation as a brand in an attention economy" and market themselves as microcelebrities in order to "prop up" capital (25–26). This is particularly the case for porn sites that rely on consumer voting practices for performers to be paid, where performers engage in free labor in the hope of earning an income. Luna Trash stated that when she and Dolly started Trash Vixens, they were upset by the system used on SuicideGirls; you could upload a photo set to the site but get paid only if consumers voted you as the "set of the day."

> Before the voting system they used to get girls of all shapes and sizes in . . . eventually it was just the skinniest prettiest girls. They weren't getting any of the plus-size girls in anymore because they'd get voted down. Yeah, so that whole diversity [thing] ended up being lost a bit because of the voting system . . . and then it's sort of giving the power to the consumers, which they love because then they get their say and they get that power from it. Then that takes the power away from the contributors, I think.

Even if such sites may have a diverse pool of contributors, the systems and techniques for sorting content privilege a particular type of body. In her research on Reddit Gonewild, where users upload naked pictures of themselves, Emily van der Nagel (2013, 1) examined the systems of user rankings, voting, point scoring, and algorithms to determine which content was placed most prominently at the top of the site.

> Although hundreds of photographs of naked bodies are submitted to reddit gonewild each day, only a few appear on its "front page." Which of the photos feature depends on not only who posts photographs and who votes on them, but also on technological codes (reddit's algorithms, interfaces, and user accounts) and cultural codes (guidelines, social norms, and "karma" points) that operate alongside these actions. When technological and cultural codes are taken together, they reveal an amateur pornography site that appears open and inclusive, but is instead closed to all but the few who fit the amateur pornography ideal: young, white, slender and female.

Angela Jones has found similar results in her work on camming. In an article titled "For Black Models, Scroll Down" (2015), she describes how camming sites are structured by classism and racism, finding that "whiteness increases erotic capital" (795), with Black models receiving a higher camscore (a measurement of monetary success) when they adopted a white feminine

FIGURE 4.4. The Algorithmic Justice League's "AI versus Drag" workshops encourage users to contest the binary gender of facial recognition algorithms, confusing them through the use of experimental drag makeup. Image by the Algorithmic Justice League.

aesthetic. Then, because the site creates a status hierarchy, ranking performers according to their earnings, those with lower camscores faced decreased visibility and therefore decreased earnings. Jones points out that "many of the highest-grossing models on this website (all white), may not realize that their position at the top of the page is buttressed by the black women at the bottom of the page" (794–95). In these ways, the very function of these interfaces relies upon the racialized labor and economic subjugation of women of color.

In another example, a study of user-generated amateur videos on YouPorn found that rather than facilitate more diverse representations of gender and sexuality, the amateur content adhered to a masculine, heteronormative porn script. The marketing of the films as real life worked to reify and naturalize "a politically conservative gender ideology" (Van Doorn 2010, 411). Even if we all had the means to participate, the kinds of bodies visible are those that are popular, trending, and algorithmically amplified.

On top of manifesting a corporate ethic and presenting oneself in a way that is likely to generate clicks, visibility, and income, Mark Coté and Jennifer Pybus (2007) argue that users of social media "must become compatible with the needs of contemporary capitalist reproduction" (99). In his work on XTube, Mowlabocus (2010) notes that XTube "offers advice on being an efficient labourer" to amateur porn performers, suggesting that new users post content as often as possible in order to boost their visibility and increase their sales (83). Online pornographic subjects, then, must be *coherent* and *productive* to the system of racial capitalism. If one's body or sexuality is unprofitable, inefficient, or risky, one cannot enter the marketplace and faces barriers to participation. In our interview, film studies scholar Jack Sargeant remarked, "It's really sad and frustrating, but I think [corporations] are only censoring until they see they can make money; then they won't."

Purging Sex Industry Businesses

The threat of removal is constant and pervasive for sex workers. In 2021, after having relied on sexual content for its rapid growth for five years, OnlyFans announced it was banning "sexually explicit" content from its platforms. Although it backtracked and suspended the policy within days, the announcement highlighted how vulnerable sexual content creators were to the whim of company decisions. One of the most significant catalysts for recent crackdowns on online sexual expression has been the passage in April 2018 of the Stop Enabling Sex Traffickers Act (SESTA)/Allow States and Victims to Fight Online Sex Trafficking Act (FOSTA) (HR 1865), which amended the Communications Decency Act of 1934. Codified as Chapter 5 of Title 47 of the US Code, this act previously included an immunity clause (Section 230) specifying that "no provider or user of an interactive computer service shall be treated as the publisher or speaker of any information provided by another information content provider" ((c)(1)). Section 230 was considered to be one of the foundations that allowed for growth of the internet, freedom of speech, digital commerce, and user-generated content. It also previously protected administrators of digital platforms from being held liable if user-generated content violated US laws.

Since passage of SESTA/FOSTA, however, Section 230 cannot be used as an immunity defense if the published content breaches US sex work or sex trafficking laws. These two amendments create a mechanism for civil action to be undertaken against a site by or on behalf of those who were advertised. Further, a new section makes it an offense to own, manage, or operate an "interactive computer service" (or conspire or attempt to own, manage, or operate an interactive computer service—which can include ISPs, hosts, and content developers) "with the intent to promote or facilitate the prostitution of another" (HR 1865, sec. 3(a)). These changes effectively make it unlawful for an owner, manager, or operator of a website to knowingly allow sex workers to advertise, or even to allow platforms to be used for sex workers to share information. They have also had a transnational effect on porn performers and producers around the globe who use US-owned digital platforms, regardless of whether or not they reside in the United States.

Now with a legal incentive, platforms have preemptively begun changing their terms of use and removing adult content in anticipation of legal action. Survivors against SESTA documented the following in 2018: Craigslist had preemptively removed its classified personals section; Reddit had closed down subreddits, such as /escorts and /sugardaddy; Google Drive had begun deleting explicit content and locking out users; Google Play had updated its policy to ban explicit content, including "promotional images of sex toys"; EventBrite had changed its terms of service to exclude events that constitute or promote "explicit sexual activity or pornography"; Microsoft's terms of service (relevant for Skype, Xbox, and Office) had been updated to say that "inappropriate content," such as nudity, may result in suspensions or bans; Facebook had released a new policy prohibiting sexual services, including "escort services, prostitution, filmed sexual encounters, sexualized massage," and other acts, such as "paid domination service"; and a number of escorting sites had closed down entirely. As Kendra Albert (2022) of the Harvard Cyberlaw Clinic points out, technically, this kind of content should not be captured by FOSTA at all; rather, case law to date suggests that FOSTA is concerned with direct advertising and the arrangement of in-person sex work.

Even before FOSTA, refusing service to adult performers and businesses was discrimination that passed as acceptable. Former Apple CEO Steve Jobs publicly stated, "We do believe we have a moral responsibility to keep porn off the iPhone" (Cossman 2013, 63). In 2015 Google announced it would ban explicit material from its blogging service (though this was later retracted) (Curtis 2015). Amazon removed porn stars' wish lists without warning, resulting in porn performers losing their account balances (Dickson 2014). Crowdfunding sites such as Kickstarter and GoFundMe prohibited adult content. Sex was seen as a risk to business: one homeowner complained that gay porn stars had used her Airbnb home as a film set, worried that it "could damage her house's image as a rental property" (Howell 2016). A porn performer's crowdfunding for a medical campaign was removed even though it was unrelated to porn (Alois 2014). In our interview, Angela White described being prevented from promoting sex education events or academic conferences on Facebook because she was known as a porn performer.

The danger here is that this discrimination is occurring not on the basis of behavior, but on the *status* of being a sex worker and that sex workers are being profiled—news sources even report porn stars being targeted by facial recognition software (Cuthbertson 2016). This means that corporations are discriminating not only on "immutable characteristics of individuals" but also now on the "algorithmically produced position of an individual" (boyd, Levy, and Marwick 2014). In response to the risk that one's online presence could be spontaneously deleted, sex workers around the globe have mobilized, sharing information and encouraging one another to take digital security steps: to back up their content; use encrypted software for emails; find privacy-aware domain registration services; switch content management systems; create alternative social media platforms; find adult-friendly hosting services; and adjust their vocabulary in order to circumvent algorithms and reduce the risk of detection. In 2020 members of the US Congress introduced the SAFE SEX Workers Study Act (HR 6928) specifically to examine the effects of FOSTA/SESTA on consensual adult sex work.

FOSTA represents another step toward sex exceptionalism, whereby sexual content is seen as warranting additional, specific treatment and penalties. The political impetus for FOSTA was an enforcement operation against Backpage.com, which was being investigated for knowingly facilitating the listing of underage girls in its classified advertisements. However, this new legislation was not necessary to indict Backpage.com: Charges were filed and the website was seized before SESTA/FOSTA had even come into effect. The introduction of these laws did nothing to improve the situation for people experiencing child sexual abuse or for migrant workers experiencing labor exploitation (such as providing safe housing, pathways for safe migration, translation of visa information, decriminalization of sex work, access to industrial rights mechanisms, or antidiscrimination protections). Instead, they sparked the shutting down of sites on which law enforcement could trace criminal activity, platforms on which survivors could speak out and seek assistance, and forums where sex workers could share safety information. Research demonstrates that sex workers use public forums for peer support and information sharing: a study of four thousand posts found that workers use them to seek advice around issues like housing instability and arrest (Barakat and Redmiles 2022, 20). Sex worker rights programs report that blanket bans affected the delivery of health promotion information and peer education (Theorizing the Web 2014). But the reputational pressure to be seen as proactive partners in anti-trafficking remains so significant that tech companies are willing to erase sex from their platforms completely and accept sex as a necessary casualty.

Online Gentrification

In her book, *The Gentrification of the Internet* (2021), Jessa Lingel describes how the commercialization of platforms has suppressed communities: "The biggest players have monopolized digital culture, pushing out smaller companies and

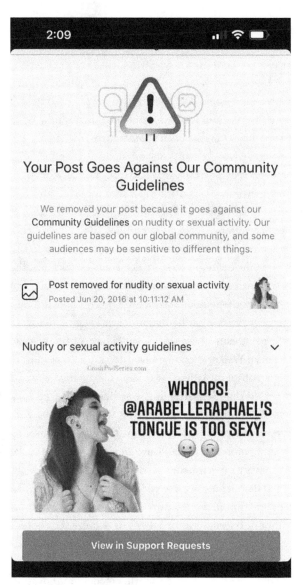

FIGURE 4.5. This image of Arabelle Raphael fully clothed with her tongue out, from the Crash Pad Series, was removed from Facebook in 2016 for nudity/sexual activity. Image by CrashPadSeries.com and Instagram.

older platforms" (3). Despite promises of democratization and equalization, since the early 1990s there has been a stark digital divide between who has benefited from communication technologies along socioeconomic, geographical, educational, racial, and gendered lines and who hasn't. As Terri Senft (2008) argues, "Unfortunately, the belief that everyone counts in a network society— or will, once they are given access—is a naïve one" (6). In pornography, there are inequalities in who is represented and who earns money in online commercial spaces—on OnlyFans, for example, the top 1 percent of accounts make 33 percent of the money (van der Nagel 2021, 401). Nancy K. Baym (2015b) writes that "the gross exacerbation of wealth inequality between site users and founders is one way 'social media' disempower the people they claim to empower." Even though marginalized communities and precarious laborers are creating the cultural products, and even if the means of *production* has been democratized, ownership and control of the infrastructure and wealth remain concentrated.

My participants reported increasing difficulty in earning a living from porn in a gig economy. Although their work had international presence and recognition, the solo subscription sites my participants ran had a small number of members (for example, one solo producer reported twenty-two members), whereas the male-run companies had sufficient members to allow them to run multiple sites, hire staff, and buy location property. For many performers, the small size of the industry and the lack of available work incentivized them toward producing their own content and maximizing work opportunities. Cat O'Nine Tails described her passion as the major driver keeping the work going: "If I wasn't so madly passionate about this, I would have given up years ago because it's so hard." Aeryn Walker didn't believe that any solo producers in Australia were "making an absolute killing" and hadn't "met anyone who's made bank." Gala Vanting said that Sensate Films was likely making a loss, but they positioned it as an "art project" and sustained it with other jobs. Kim Cums commented on receiving disproportionate stigma that was not offset by her income: "Nobody's making money off porn; leave us alone; we don't make enough money for you to harass us this much!"

In this light, the so-called democratization of porn begins to look more like the outsourcing of content creation in which individuals bear their own overhead expenses and corporations buy, license, or otherwise acquire the content under nonnegotiable terms of use for little to no remuneration. In our interview, Dinesh Wadiwel, a political philosopher researching human rights and pleasure at the University of Sydney, suggested that this model of innovative, creative, devolved start-ups making their way into an international market in fact "resonates with lots of new forms of dynamic capitalism." He proposed that this relationship actually resembled contract work, where the labor of production was contracted out, or even piecework, where people are paid by results, "which as we know leads to some of the most extortionate forms of labor (such as in the garment industry)." In his research on XTube, Mowlabocus (2010) also argued that the labor of amateur porn performers is piecework, "with no opportunity for wage negotiation, the price always being set by 'the company'" (84). Porn work is not always participatory and empowering—rather, like other cultural work, it can be "temporary and intermittent, work/play boundaries are collapsed, the pay is poor, and people must be mobile" (Baym 2015a, 15). New technologies have not only been enabling for users. Certainly they have "accelerated the speed and dispersed the space of production to unprecedented levels" (Hennessey 2000, 6). But the economic downturn in porn production means that performers need to establish diverse alternative income streams and are often engaged in temporary, contractual, short-term, and freelance labor with few protections. The decentralization of production across continents, the proliferation of temporary work in a gig economy, and the jurisdictional complexities of negotiating working conditions in a global marketplace mean that the labor force of porn workers is more dispersed than ever.

If this is the economic context in which pornography is being produced, distributed, and consumed, then it poses ongoing dilemmas about the value marginalized groups offer to company branding and its resulting capacity to overshadow unequal capitalist distribution; the potential for containing our own decentralized movements through subsuming them as niche content that can be bought as part of corporate diversity strategies; how to build alternative platforms and avenues without defaulting back to the structures we are battling against; and how to create work with maximum impact while maintaining one's political vision.

Tech-Facilitated Sexual Violence

Corporations are not democracies or public services. As private companies, their accountabilities lie not with their users, but with their shareholders. However, social media platforms operate as the "shapers of sex" (Tiidenberg and van der Nagel 2020, 51). Their policies, practices, and decisions matter because of their size and their market dominance. Their social power and the lack of viable alternatives mean that their content moderation practices are effectively gatekeeping conversations that are in the public interest. Sexual content moderation is notably inconsistent, featuring arbitrary guidelines, impromptu policy changes, and selective enforcement. Most dominant social media platforms engage in what Susanna Paasonen, Kylie Jarrett, and Ben Light (2019) describe as an "unspecified sense of risk" whereby they treat "sexuality, pornography and a range of bodily displays as lacking in safety in a markedly abstract, and hence obscure, vein" (1). One review of the policies and practices of Instagram, YouTube, Twitter, Reddit, and Tumblr found that their approaches to sexual content moderation were so incoherent that "the rules are in doctrinal chaos" (Peters 2020, 486). However, sexual content moderation practices can also be seen as a deliberate design decision: They intentionally reinforce a particular heteronormative and cisnormative sexual social order. Ysabel Gerrard and Helen Thornham (2020) conceptualize online sexual content moderation through the framework of "sexist assemblages" as a way to describe how both human and mechanical moderation "assemble to perpetuate normative gender roles, particularly white femininities, and to police content related to women and their bodies" (1266).

We ought to be concerned with how these political actors—tech companies and governments—are working in tandem to create a specific digital sexual landscape—one that devalues sexual content creators and that does not see us as part of the response to addressing sexual harassment, content theft, or image-based abuse, and appears disinterested in our active experiences of discrimination, violence, shadowbanning, demotion, demonetization, suspension, or deplatforming. Internet lawyer Daphne Keller (2019) argues that we should pay attention to this interrelationship, especially how government regulation drives and motivates the development of platform policies designed to avoid risk: "On the one hand, governments can bypass constitutional limits by deputizing private platforms as censors. On the other, platforms can take on and displace traditional state functions, operating the modern equivalent of the public square or the post office, without assuming state responsibilities" (2–3).

Recent regulation, such as the Online Safety Acts in Australia and the United Kingdom and the Kids Safety Online Act in the United States, incentivizes platforms to upscale their automation and surveillance to detect sexual content in ways that impact sex education, harm reduction, and health promotion information but does not provide the accountability structures necessary to deter them from designing, procuring, or deploying discriminatory algorithms.

What does all of this mean, then, for indie producers and their strategies of resistance? Some legal and financial avenues exist: In 2022 Tumblr settled discrimination complaints alleged by the New York City Commission on Human Rights after its members implemented an automated sexual content takedown system that disproportionately impacted LGBTIQA+ users. In countries like Australia where antidiscrimination protections are being developed to protect sex workers, it may be possible to bring actions for discrimination in accessing goods and services. But if we accept that the violent laws and policies documented in the previous two chapters simply represent the state and big tech doing exactly what they are designed to do (rather than an otherwise effective system that is flawed, broken, outdated, or confused), then attempts at lobbying and reform will likely only result in incremental change. Why would a white supremacist, sexist, ableist government or a heteronormative, transphobic, capitalist tech company support indie porn? Why would a politician stand up to decriminalize depictions of fisting? This situation leaves performers and producers wondering what forms of pressure might have purchase in these contexts and what kinds of resistance tactics would be most effective. The next half of this book (comprising "Part III: The Hustle" and "Part IV: Tensions") discusses how performers are strategically navigating these environments, the kinds of ethical and political conundrums they face in their resistance, and what coalitional work holds the most promise for getting indie producers the regulatory environments we need.

Part III

the
hustle

SuicideGirls

It's 2016. We are in a light-filled Airbnb in Sydney's inner-city suburb of Redfern on Gadigal Land. It's midwinter, about 5 degrees, and I have visible goose bumps up and down my legs. I run my fingers through my long pink hair extensions, hold in my stomach, point my toes, and look over my shoulder at Jasmine. I'm excited about finally shooting for SuicideGirls, which has long been a dream of mine. After having my piercings removed from the cover of *Penthouse*, my armpit hair edited out of *Picture* magazine, and my labia airbrushed in *People* magazine, I'm excited to shoot for a site that claims to celebrate alternative beauty. My broken bleached hair couldn't take much more peroxide, and I take the opportunity to go back to my rainbow roots.

It feels good to be shooting with another SuicideGirl. This is my third out of four shoots in four days. In one shoot, I won't see the pictures until they go online and have no say over the editing process. In this one, Jas will send me proofs so I can select my favorite forty to sixty among them for a complete set. Working with a fellow model feels collaborative since we both have an interest in the set selling so that we can recoup our costs. I trust her to use flattering angles to get shots that she herself would want as a model.

The poses are familiar to me from glamour modeling. Some are replicas of mainstream magazine poses: on my knees, arching my back, resting my index finger on my bottom lip, pulling my bra strap over my shoulder. But the positions are slightly less brash—there are fewer doggy style and open leg shots and more peripheral shots of body parts: feet, hands, faces. The poses are more subtle, sleepy, modest. I turn my shoulder forward to protrude my collarbone. I bring my hand lightly up to my neck. I look at the camera seductively and then stare off into the distance. It's what we call in mainstream magazine work "shy nude."

It is a similar repertoire to what I perform for Feck's alt-erotica site I Shot Myself, which also prides itself on its alleged distance from mainstream porn. The same way I learned to perform "sex eyes" and bold, dynamic poses from stripping, I learn to perform a doe-eyed, girl-next-door sex-kitten for these purportedly amateur sites. The pose is less-overt porn star but definitely borrows from and utilizes pornographic conventions, even if I am pretending not to be a professional. We run through a standard formula that we know constitutes a sellable set—in fact, we bring up a set from one of the most popular SuicideGirls and adapt each pose.

The model guidelines are prescriptive and titled "How to look good in photos, without (looking like you are) really trying." They provide instructions on facial expressions (parted lips, smiling eyes, three-quarter profiles, tilted chins, and no duck face), posing (keep it "classy," avoiding spread shots and positions that exaggerate rolls), hair (washed and lightly styled, no wigs), makeup (thin black eyeliner on the top lid only) and wardrobe (cotton tanks, tall socks, denim shorts, and sundresses). The guidelines include photo examples of what not to do: no stripper heels or stripper attire, including neon fishnets, metallic, sparkles, or "anything crotchless." Damn.

The specificity reminds me of Australian amateur site Abby Winters, whose CEO had a pet hate for belly rings. Their guidelines instructed models to cover hair regrowth and not to shoot if we had pimples, scratches, or mosquito bites in order that we appear "healthy." When shooting for Feck, I was told to stop wearing frills, to "tone down the eye makeup," and "maybe don't talk about politics." Similar instructions were given to me in a shoot for *Hustler* magazine: "The model shouldn't look too tacky, like a stripper, but like a woman with mainstream tastes." I had become suspicious of "redefined beauty" and "being yourself" as code for a specific class-based aesthetic, positioned against the mainstream but, in reality, equally conventionalized.

I am conscious of my age. My body has changed a lot in the past few years since retiring from pole instructing and as a result of recent IVF treatments. Jas tells me that, at twenty-nine, she is one of the older SuicideGirls in Australia, who are mostly between eighteen and twenty-two. I laugh and say, "I'm thirty-three" and joke that we are both veterans. I am competing with thousands of other "Suicide Hopefuls" all ten to fifteen years my junior and hoping that theirs will be selected as set of the day (SOTD). When our set is edited, it goes into a four-month queue, after which it is posted in "Member Review," where site members can comment and "like" it. Each day the company chooses a SOTD, which means the girl moves from being a "Suicide Hopeful" to an official "SuicideGirl" and receives a $500 prize.

Jas tells me that a new set goes live into member review every two hours, so my chance of actually becoming a SuicideGirl and being paid for my set is one in twelve. It's hard not to be disheartened by these terrible odds. Some models have been hopefuls for years. There are no clear criteria for what the company picks. Jas shows me sets in member review with thousands of likes that have never been chosen and other sets that were selected despite far fewer likes. The process appears to be less about the quality of the set and more like a mixture of popularity, taste, and company discretion. It's a system that encourages competition between models and, in doing so, extracts more labor from us.

SuicideGirls encourages hopefuls to keep submitting until one of their sets is chosen. This means that the site gains a constant stream of free content for their subscribers. The $500 payment is pitched as a reward rather than remuneration. I have paid $330 for my shoot and location, so after recouping that cost, a sixty-picture, full-nude SOTD feature would pay me $170, and this doesn't include the costs of my wardrobe, transport, or the labor to promote my set. To boost my chances of being picked, I should promote my profile, interact with members, encourage comments, write a blog, and post teasers in special groups interested in feet, arses, or breasts. In the early stages of my career, I might have found this fun. After thirteen years, having done my share of eight-hour shifts in six-inch heels and cold air-conditioning, I'm tired. I have to embark upon the emotional and relational labor of being personable, sexy, and available, of convincing members that I am likable and SuicideGirls that I am marketable.

Regardless of whether you get SOTD, Jas tells me, it's a great way to "build and promote your brand." With more than four million followers on Instagram, Jas tells me the hashtags to use to increase my visibility. Some girls have a hundred thousand followers, Jas tells me, and have been offered paid modeling jobs or have companies sending them free merchandise. It's something I have heard repeatedly as a live performer and artist—perform for free in return for mass exposure, which rarely (but sometimes) translates into paid work. However, with the dim likelihood of actually being paid for my set, it seems silly not to make the most of this endeavor. Being a SuicideGirl would permit me to tour and diversify my income stream. Reluctantly, I reactivate my Instagram account. As I fill out my bio on the SuicideGirls site, I produce a version of myself that seems creative, convincing, and noncontroversial. I select from the drop-down menu "artsy," "homebody," and "tree hugger."

5

Manufacturing Authenticity

Expression, Identity, and Labor

Given that private platforms require content that is safe, sanitized, and risk-averse, these standards filter down to production, prompting shifts in the ways performers speak about their labor and themselves. Dissatisfied with mass-produced pornography and tired of prescriptive formulas, consumers are seeking content they perceive as "authentic" and "real." In 2022 Pornhub reported that "Reality" was its highest trending category, growing by 169 percent, with searches for "real amateur homemade" growing by 310 percent in the United States (Pornhub Insights 2022). Authenticity thus emerges as what Dylan Ryan (2013) has called "the Holy Grail" in feminist pornographies (121). In alternative pornographies, Feona Attwood (2012) writes, the pornographic body is reconfigured "through retro glamour, alternative style and a contemporary ideal of sexual authenticity" (42). Performers emphasize their genuine pleasure, real orgasms, and love of sex and share intimate moments with audiences. Madison Young (2014a) argues, "The facilitation of creating space for the expression of authentic self in relation to our sexual desires has the ability to radically change pornography" (186).

FIGURE 5.1. Madison Young's performance piece *Self Care for the Limit/Less*, presented at Grace Exhibition Space in Brooklyn. Photo courtesy of Grace Exhibition Space and Madison Young.

In this chapter, I consider how discourses of authenticity, while offering some affordances to performers, are also deployed to justify labor extraction and naturalize specific representations of the body. Performers report that producers pursue a particular aesthetic premised on an imaginary natural-ness shaped by class, race, and gender, which they perform convincingly. Bod-ies and pleasures that are not intelligible as authentic—to either directors or consumers—risk incoherence and erasure. In having to repeatedly demonstrate that they are real, willing, genuine, and natural exhibitionists (positioning pornography not just as work but also as identity), discourses of authenticity, fantasies of community, and investments in loving one's work can function to obscure the emotional and relational labor of porn. The commodification of *realness*, alongside consumer entitlement to a freely available and constantly updated self, can dismiss queer, femme, and playful ways of exploring sexual identity, imagery, and iconography.

Documentary Realness

For some, a focus on authenticity provides opportunities to participate in the gig economy in innovative and experimental ways. As I demonstrated in chapter 1, a significant motivator for indie performers is the ability to represent, express, and document themselves. In Aeryn Walker's view, porn could be a medium through which to explore herself: "It's definitely an extension of who I am outside of porn and parts of me that I just want to explore more." Sexual expression was a recurring narrative for the performers I interviewed, who at times felt antagonistic toward performing a particular, predictable set of sexual practices. Instead of being instructed *how* to have sex in a way that felt staged or contrived, performers wanted to determine their own scripts and use porn to explore their own desires.

In aspiring to be read as authentic, indie pornographies have begun using many of the codes and conventions of documentary cinema: interviews, voiceovers, behind-the-scenes footage, and raw unscripted footage. Some performers describe their work in porn as documentary projects through which they charter their sexual journeys. For example, Kim Cums described being in a 24/7 BDSM relationship, "so filming those things just seems quite natural to us rather than trying to create something that isn't part of our natural flow anyway." Angela White recounted experiencing "firsts" on set (such as her first anal, first squirting, or first threesome) and valued capturing these live on camera. She described pornography as having a documentary function in which she could trace her sexual experiences over the course of her career. At the Second Annual Feminist Porn Conference in Toronto in 2014, Madison Young (2014b) spoke about navigating her romantic relationships on camera and collecting visual evidence across the span of a decade, tracing her pregnancy (during which she also performed) and sexual experiences as a first-time mother. The act of filming here provides a vehicle for performers not only to capture but also to cultivate their selves.

But documentary cinema itself is not an objective account of reality. Documentary theorists have illustrated the enmeshment of fiction and nonfiction through the use of particular editing techniques to shape material (Bonner 2013, 64). Michael Renov (2012) writes that "nonfiction" actually involves elements of "creative intervention" (2), including the construction of a character, the use of narrative, musical accompaniment, and camera angles to create meaning, sustain rhythm, and heighten emotional impact. At the same time, Bill Nichols (2017) argues that the use of certain techniques in documentary films (voiceover commentary, using nonactors, shooting daily life) can "give the *impression* of authenticity to what has actually been fabricated or constructed" (xii).

Indeed, investments in so-called realness are used to signal to viewers. In a session at the 2014 Feminist Porn Conference, academic Amy Jamgochian and Pink and White Productions owner Shine Louise Houston discussed the use of *real* as a "valuable term for search engine optimization." They argued that authenticity emerged in a context where "a strong demand has arisen for a distinction between 'gay for pay' performers of queer sex and performers whose sex on screen more closely represents their non-screen sex." Although these distinctions between on-screen and off-screen sex are often blurred, realness and authenticity still operate as effective "keywords" and "efficient codes" for specific genres and preferences (Jamgochian and Houston 2014). Shine has written explicitly about their decision to avoid terms like "realistic," "natural," and "true" on PinkLabel.tv and noted that claims of authenticity, which have appeared historically in their own promotion materials, in fact "go against the understandings of sexuality, queerness, and radicalism that lie beneath our work" (Houston 2015).

This drive to capture real sexual expressions is a legacy of the quest for maximum visibility, the impetus to show the "truth" of sex (Williams [1989] 1999), one of the hallmarks of "scientia sexualis," described by Foucault (1998) as the modern Western approach to sex. Authenticity is a response to readings of pornography as "fake" and "plastic." It is a result of pornography's incompleteness as an arbiter of truth, its positioning as something both *too real* and yet *not real enough* (Dennis 2009, 5). However, history reminds us that, as Catriona Mortimer-Sandilands and Bruce Erickson (2010) write, "there is nothing especially 'natural' about the ways Euro-western societies generally understand sex" (6–7). The focus on realness among queer and feminist producers sits in direct contrast to the ways in which discourses of naturalness have been mobilized *against* and in opposition to the *deviance* of LGBTIQA+ people and women (literally labeled as crimes against nature). On the mobilization of discourses of realness in queer pornography, Julie Levin Russo (2007, 240) writes,

> The idea that porn has a special capacity to transparently reflect the real, one of the most common aspects of this discourse, is necessarily problematic in its erasure of mediation. But it becomes increasingly untenable as porn encounters first video and then the Internet, moving further and further from the specifically visual and indexical particulars of its cinematic roots. If the celebration of referentiality is in tension with the digital pixels of the net, it is equally antithetical to the ideal project of queer porn, which is anything but reflecting an established, static "real" sexuality.

The use of authenticity to refer to a kind of genuineness and truthfulness in porn sits in contrast to theorizations of gender. Judith Butler (1996) describes gender itself as a form of mimicry, a pattern and repetition without an original referent: "Gender is a kind of imitation for which there is no original; in fact, it is a kind of imitation that produces the very notion of the original as an effect and consequence of the imitation itself" (378). If there is no inherent essence of gender or of sexuality, and if sexuality and gender are both culturally produced, then narratives of authenticity have, through their continual repetition, created an imaginary original as a referent through which to hold up particular expressions, activities, and aesthetics as natural and real (and, in turn, to produce other iterations as fake).

The concept of authenticity has a long history as part of colonial projects to police Indigenous peoples. Michelle Harris, Bronwyn Carlson, and Evan Poata-Smith (2013) describe how concepts of biological and cultural authenticity have been used to create concrete racial categories to which Indigenous people are expected to perform in order to access citizenship, services, and resources or to be politically recognized. These knowledges implore us to consider how authenticity discourses also serve to invalidate, questioning who is left out from the politicized boundaries of the authentic and at what cost.

Constructing the Mainstream

The paradigm of authenticity constructs an imaginary of naturalness but also of artifice. Authenticity is positioned as a radical, avant-garde alternative in direct opposition to an imagined, homogenous, mainstream pornography, which is constructed as commercial, performative, and fake. For example, Howard set up an alternative erotica website because "we reasoned that the problem with mainstream porn is that it's all faked, and that makes it really of limited interest to a lot of people, and we were very skeptical about its ability to actually turn people on." This notion of fakeness is echoed in Violet Blue's book, *The Smart Girl's Guide to Porn* (2006): "Remember, porn actors are up there because they look different to everyone else and are willing to change their bodies (sometimes frightfully radically) to fit a fantasy 'ideal.' However, I think that precisely because it's so far away from reality, most of the industry's purported 'ideal' that stars embody isn't what actually turns most of us on" (23–24).

Interestingly, pornography producers' readings of mainstream porn here are similar to those of anti-pornography feminists who seek to eliminate pornography in favor of returning to some nostalgic notion of an authentic sexual self. The strategy is different (abolition of pornography compared to the proliferation of alternative pornographic interventions), but there is both a shared

FIGURE 5.2. Award-winning porn performers Jiz Lee and Vanniall are known for their community activism. Jiz writes about online piracy, paying for porn, consent, and ethics, and Vanniall is a U+ advocate writing on sex work politics, HIV+ health, and social justice. Image by Ashley Lake.

investment in the existence of an authentic sexuality coupled with an active devaluing of femininity. In critiquing pornographic cultures, many popular "anti-porn" feminists refer to "excessive" femininity—acrylic nails, high-heeled shoes, large breasts, heavy makeup—as evidence of gender conformity: "polyester underplants and implants" (Levy 2010, 198) or the "bleached, waxed, tinted look of a Bratz or Barbie Doll" (Walter 2011, 2). Even in the discourses of the sex-positive writers described above, androgynous embodiment is positioned as real, neutral, or natural, and expressions of femininity (from lipstick to fingernails to glitter and heels) are represented as superficial, trite, and fake; its wearers are viewed as dupes who cannot be considered serious feminist or queer subjects. Linda M. Scott (2005) notes that contemporary feminism's "anti-beauty ideology" is founded on a period where "women with more education, more leisure, and more connections to institutions of power—from the church, to the press, to the university—have been the ones who tried to tell other women what they must wear in order to be liberated" (2).

Mainstream porn here is set up as the antithesis to "natural," "real" bodies and sex acts, but the term also reflects particular aesthetic conventions. Howard described how "we looked for ways of filming that tastefully so that it didn't look like mainstream porn, the way that that's usually produced . . . on cheap sets with the crew and in hotel rooms and where the performers are dressed and styled in a certain way to meet a certain stereotype." Feona Attwood (2007) writes that during the process of repudiating the mainstream, alternative pornographies established their own aesthetic conventions: "New sex taste cultures attempt to define themselves through a variety of oppositions to mainstream culture—and especially mainstream porn—as creative, vibrant, classy, intelligent, glamorous, erotic, radical, varied, original, unique, exceptional and sincere compared to the unimaginative, dull, tasteless, stupid, sleazy, ugly, hackneyed, standardized, commonplace, trite, mediocre, superficial and artificial. In the process, a system of aesthetics is evoked as a form of ethics" (449–50).

The active construction of the so-called mainstream allows producers to differentiate their products in opposition to it—to position their work as distinct, exceptional, and transgressive. Citing a world of Viagra, acrylic nails, silicone breasts, hair extensions, and embellished moans, Madison Young (2014a) argues that in the context of this formula of "fast food" sex, and "in an industry built on filming the glamorous performance of sex, the concept of authenticity is an anomaly" (186). The authenticity narrative therefore holds an economic function for producers in allowing them to situate their content as outside of pornography—as authentic erotica. Cindy Gallop's site Make Love Not Porn, for example, is marketable because it does not define itself as porn. Performer Vex Ashley (2016) writes that the title itself "demonstrates a wider misconception that 'real' sex is not and cannot be performative" (187).

The conceptual distinction between pornography and erotica was made by Audre Lorde ([1978] 1997), who positioned the erotic as a source of power, "creative energy," and "lifeforce" (55) that has been "misnamed by men and used against women" (54). Her comment that pornography "emphasizes sensation without feeling" (54) was taken up by white antipornography feminists such as Gloria Steinem (1980), who argued that erotica was about "sensuality and touch and warmth" while pornography was "about power and sex-as-weapon" (37–38). Subsequently, the use of the word *erotica* to differentiate from *porn* has been taken up by some as a matter of aesthetics: As Annie Sprinkle said in her film *Herstory of Porn* (2002), the difference "is all in the lighting!" Authenticity narratives have become commercially useful, setting up alternative pornographies as tasteful, boutique, and artistic and renouncing the stigma of pornography. Some scholars have interrogated this distinction between erotica and pornography: moses moon (2021) advocates for "proheauxism," an approach that does not "juxtapose the erotic and pornography, and recognize[s] that nonexploitative pleasure comes in varied forms" (58).

For the performers I interviewed, the challenge was describing content without further stigmatizing porn, or as Lucie Bee put it, "throw[ing] mainstream porn under the bus." In her experience working across both mainstream and alternative companies, Angela White reported more similarities than differences among ethical, feminist, and mainstream producers. Helen Corday commented, "I think it can be very problematic to do the distancing of like this is good porn and that is bad porn." Angela suggested that the way forward may be for mainstream and alternative producers to share strategies and processes: "I think a challenge is to try and produce different visions without shaming the mainstream industry, without Othering other parts of the industry."

Staging Authenticity

The valorization of amateur porn risks reifying a particular iteration of naturalness that is actually highly constructed. Porn sites that purport to depict "real," "alternative," or "redefined beauty" are often just as conventionalized as

FIGURE 5.3. The author during a photo shoot for SuicideGirls. Image by ShotbyAsh.

the mainstream genres they criticize. For example, while SuicideGirls pitches itself as alternative, they give calculated instructions about the kinds of aesthetic sets they accept: "tasteful," "picture perfect" shoots with "a little bit of face powder and mascara and freshly dyed hair" but specifically *not* "cheap wig[s]," "top hats," "stripper shoes," "food," or anything that looks "cheesy," "gross," or "creepy" (SuicideGirls, n.d.). In producing measurable indicators of acceptable gendered presentation, these sites produce bodies of a particular class, size, and appropriate femininity. "Authenticity" then becomes, as Giovanna Maina (2014) writes, "a quality that also has to be achieved through particular aesthetic techniques" (183).

In my interviews, performers spoke about the ways they were expected to reproduce conventions that would be intelligible to audiences as authentic. In these instances, it was not enough to replicate a performer's real-life desires and activities; their performances had to be understood as authentic to both the viewer and producer. Producers urged performers to do what they would at home but then proceeded to give detailed instructions that reflected the iconography of their brand or their own fantasies about what performers might be doing at home. In her paper "Manufacturing Realness," presented at the 2014 Feminist Porn Conference, Gala Vanting outlined what she thinks are "the more common characteristics of the 'real girl'" from her experience working for Australian companies.

She

- wears button-down dresses, striped socks, cotton full-brief underwear, little or no makeup; rejects "glamour";
- self-pleasures without accessories, unless she is appropriating household items; does not use sex toys; has multiple orgasms in a single session; has orgasms that are not "too loud" or "performed"; is "observed" or "documented" in states of arousal;
- is white or exoticized Other; is a size 8–14; is between eighteen and thirty years of age;
- is not a sex worker, and if she is, she trades in her sexual performativity for the welcome chance to have a "real" experience and be "herself"; is not motivated solely by money;
- does not have or effectively disguises bruises, shaving rash, ingrown hairs, tattoos, piercings; prefers to keep her pubic hair "natural";
- is heterosexual or bi-curious and cisgendered;
- prefers domestic settings, fields of long grass, or scenes of urban decay in which to engage in sexual activity.

In my interview with him, CEO Garion Hall describes this quite literally in relation to Abby Winters, a site that represents an alternative to glamour photography by featuring makeup-less, "amateur" models. Rather than being an expression of their authentic selves, model applications are assessed on such brand qualities as "wholesomeness and personality and enthusiasm" on a scale of one to five. Camera staff and post-producers are required to watch a twenty-two-minute corporate branding video about "wholesomeness," and models undergo two full days of training before they can shoot. Garion told me: "It refers to ten or twelve traits that our customers like to believe our models engender and things like having family values and that she's a homebody, that she likes to do things like cook and have a nice home. That she's not so much about going out to nightclubs as often as she can and getting pissed and falling over; she's more, you know, go out and have a good time with her friends, but she wouldn't go to a nightclub to find a new boyfriend, for example."

Rather than depict women's authentic pleasures, desires, and images, these aspects are tailored to a palatable girl-next-door paradigm at every step, from recruitment, training, shooting, and marketing. Performers who strategically navigate this path and answer the questions correctly receive financial reward (in the form of work), but if they describe hobbies that do not fit with the image, they are edited out. As Garion said, "If they start talking about their drug-taking habits, you know, we'd say, 'Yeah, look, we're not that interested,' and we'd certainly edit it out; it's just not what our customers want to pay us for." The "wholesome" paradigm is built on slut shaming: It requires models who are slutty enough to make pornography but not too slutty that they threaten consumer and producer fantasies.

Despite professing to celebrate the diversity of all women, some sites are exclusionary in terms of which women are permitted to participate. Howard described how he decided to exclude trans women from his site because he perceived them as presenting a market risk.

> The issue of queer and transgender and so on didn't come up until we had some people wanting to participate, and at some point I had to, at one point I did have to make a business decision. Once we had some level of participation from transgender people then we were starting to get flooded with other, with their friends; they put the word out, and we were starting to get quite inundated with people wanting to be involved, and I could see that the nature of the website was going to take a turn where it wouldn't be financially sustainable, so that's one of those decisions that was made really based on the sustainability of the website.

Instead of understanding trans women as women, and standing for women in all their diversity, Howard decided that trans women and nonbinary people presented a risk to the sensibility of his viewership. His initial solution—to create a separate, distinct website—would literally segregate trans and gender diverse models to a different space. But even then, he reported, "I looked at what else was around on the market, and I didn't think that it was a safe enough bet to put a lot of money and resources into." Although such companies like to see themselves as diverse and inclusive, their investment in diversity is limited by their own short-sighted, transphobic anticipation that those models will not be desirable, marketable, or financially viable.

Amateur Aesthetics

Despite the commercial context in which content can be produced, an aesthetic of authenticity can require a sense of amateurism and ordinariness, denoted by shooting in natural light and wearing everyday clothes. The construction of an ordinary aesthetic is not unique to film. Ruth Barcan documents how this same "staged authenticity" appears in the popular Australian adult magazines *The Picture* and *People*, where readers send in raw, untouched, naked photographs of themselves. These magazines produce an aesthetic of "ordinariness" that is in fact highly crafted: "The Home pages do not simply reproduce 'ordinariness'; they *produce* 'the ordinary' as a category. Many photos are in fact taken in the home—and thus the floral curtains and textured carpet of the living room, the cotton-print sheets, the rock posters on the bedroom wall and so on are important features of the genre" (Barcan 2000, 150).

Barcan situates this phenomenon within an Australian "legacy of anti-authoritarianism and anti-elitism" that celebrates and *mobilizes* ordinariness and demonstrates "a deep ambivalence to celebrity and glamour culture" (150). Performers reported to me that some producers were reluctant to hire women who had had plastic surgeries or were professional porn performers, assuming that they have internalized the aesthetic and gendered conventions of mainstream production. In its mission statement, one company specifically aspires to "value the beauty of natural mind and body above glamour and cosmetic enhancement." While this aspiration may seek to capture "real" women, in practice performers strategically navigate criteria for realness. Performers who have breast implants, who wear lingerie, who squirt, or who orgasm too loudly (in a way that appears too dramatized or, as Howard called it, "Americanized")—who are *real* in the sense that they *exist* in the world—do not always embody the right *kind* of realness. As Madison Missina reflected in our interview:

> Whenever I work with them they want me in particular daggy cotton underwear that I don't own because that's not my sexuality. They talk to me about how they want to produce this authentic porn, but they don't want me to wear makeup, and they don't want me to do my hair, and I've got to actually go out and buy [cotton] underwear because I'm a lingerie person and that's how I feel sexy. And then when it comes to having sex, because I've got implants they want me to do all these things to conceal my boobs, because "real women" don't have implants. And I've even been told, because I do female ejaculation, one feminist porn producer told me that that's not something that anyone would be interested in so we're not going to show that. She'd rather just a normal orgasm but no ejaculation.

In this environment, porn performers learn the language of authenticity and strategically manifest it in order to earn money. As Barcan (2000) writes: "Ordinariness becomes something to be imitated by professionals" (151). Websites, bios, and interviews in which performers detail their hobbies and interests are less likely to be honest declarations but, rather, as Hugo Liu (2007) calls them, "taste performances." Onscreen personalities are curated to enhance activities performers already enjoy, based on what will be popular or profitable, while being emotionally sustainable with the least risk of burnout. Here, authenticity does not refer to visible evidence of truth. Rather, we can understand authenticity as Heather Berg (2017) does, as "a performance of being oneself and wanting to be there—and, emphatically, being there not just for the money" (671).

Sex worker Mikey Way, who shot for an Australian porn company, blogged about how the required aesthetic standard was to look effortlessly beautiful, in a way that erased the labor not only of sex work but of gender performance as well. In the article "Fuck Your Feminist Porn" posted on the sex work journalism site *Tits and Sass*, Mikey Way (2015) writes: "Their insistence on natural, 'alternative' beauty excludes those who cannot attain white beauty ideals or at least have to work to reach them. At these porn companies, makeup is frowned upon, plastic surgery is a hell no, and fatness is as shunned as ever. While the image isn't one of people actively working to meet fashion industry perfection, it instead enters around only those who can achieve it without effort. Ultimately, their 'feminist' message is: 'don't work to be beautiful, but fuck you if you're not *effortlessly* beautiful.'"

The authenticity narrative (or what we might instead call the authenticity delusion) undoes a lot of advocacy sex workers have done in illuminating the labor involved in gendered performance and sexual interactions. Sex workers have denied that sex for free is necessarily more liberated and argued that demanding payment (for sexuality and gendered performance) challenges expectations of constant availability.

Intelligible Orgasms

The authenticity delusion impacts not only aesthetics but also sexual practices. As I argue in chapter 7, in moving away from activities seen as stereotypical (the male come shot, loud moaning, girl-girl scenes for the male gaze), the "female orgasm" has become the elusive moment some producers seek to portray in order to document pleasure. Madison Young (2014a) argues that feminists can navigate "the artificial environment of mainstream pornography" by "expressing pleasure (and orgasm) in a way that is authentic to the individual"— through communicating with their partners rather than merely "to pretend or perform one's pleasure" (186–87). Young argues for a greater variety of orgasms making it on-screen—bodies that "shake, tremble, contort," with "guttural screams or deep belly moans, or primal animal-like sounds" or a "flushed face and warm smile" rather than only those orgasms that look "pretty" (187).

However, in our interviews, performers reported that producers still expected a certain type of orgasmic performance. In their reaction to mainstream representations, producers were weary of orgasms that appeared embellished or exaggerated. One producer, for example, described the difference between the orgasms had by a mainstream performer when she performed on his site compared to a US site as evidence of the way his site apparently provided a platform for a more genuine unveiling of her true unmediated self. Howard recalled: "She came to us, and she made very mainstream porn, very stylized American-style porn, and when I explained what we were all about she listened and she said I understand and I like those values. And when you look at what . . . when you look at her masturbating to orgasm on our website and then look at her performing in American porn or other mainstream sites in Australia it's completely different, and so I think that's . . . that really underscores the difference."

Although Howard uses this as an indication that the performance on his site is more "real" or "truthful," this instance could also be an example of a professional performer identifying the requirements of the employer and performing accordingly. To pitch this as any more real than mainstream porn ignores the reality that the content is produced in a staged environment: Their movements are restricted by camera angles, someone may be holding operating equipment, they are expected to orgasm at least once. Solo masturbation scenes have their own conventions, expected to continue for approximately ten minutes to allow time for sufficient wide angles and close-ups, and performers are expected to make enough noise to reassure viewers about their internal process. This could be merely an instance of professionalism: being versatile, identifying what is needed to complete the job, and executing it convincingly.

Producer expectations of how an orgasm might look have led to some interesting experiences for performers where their orgasms were disbelieved. Angela White recalls having an orgasm that a company did not believe was really an orgasm because it didn't reach the requisite audio levels.

> I had an incident where I had an orgasm, and I was told that I "needed to have an orgasm now," and I said that I had. Obviously, it didn't conform to what they believed an orgasm should look like, so there can be those awkward moments. I mean, it's not just an issue in pornography, but even how orgasm is represented in mainstream film; it's always the head thrown back and loud orgasms, and many people have—myself included—varied orgasms. Sometimes my orgasms are silent, and other times they're screaming. There's not just one way to have an orgasm.

Authenticity here is dependent on what Gala Vanting (2014) has described as the circumstance in which "the performer embodies 'realness' which is aesthetically, aurally, and sexually consistent with the realness currently valued by those in control of the means of production, or is able to reproduce it based on cues given by the producer." In one particularly stark example, Gala recalls working for a company and being tasked with the job of identifying whether an orgasm was real. In her conference presentation "Manufacturing Realness" (2014), she describes the process as follows:

> During my employment behind-the-scenes, one of my responsibilities was the review of submissions. . . . Most performers created their submissions at home using cameras they loaned from the company. When they returned their work, it was my job to review their films for technical specifics (exposure, framing) and authenticity of performance. This required me to maintain that I could tell the difference between a "real" orgasm and a "performed" one by reading the cues of facial expression. Whether I actually could, or whether I just learned to internalize the cues of the company's brand of "realness" for the sake of functioning in my role, I remain uncertain. It is a fine art to confront another person on your evaluation of their sexual authenticity based on a few minutes' footage taken in what is unlikely to be a habitual situation for them.

Here it is a particular arrangement of expressions that is deemed recognizable, or "intelligible" in the sense that Judith Butler (2004) describes it, "produced as a consequence of recognition according to prevailing social norms" (3). Writing on visual representations of orgasm, Hannah Frith (2015) argues that this process of viewers recognizing orgasm relies on shared understandings of sexual conventions: "To recognise a bodily experience *as* an orgasm . . . requires considerable interpretative work as we draw on cultural scripts to interpret the bodily sensations provided by our senses. Orgasm does not just happen; it must be learned by developing an understanding of cultural conventions and symbolic systems" (387).

Indeed, consumers themselves make their own determinations. In her focus groups, Emily E. Crutcher (2015) found that viewers paid attention to vocal expression in combination with pace, timing, and type of activity to assess the authenticity of a performance (325–28). But these readings still assume that pleasure is evoked from specific alignments of sensation and desire that may not be universal. Trans women have spoken out about their orgasms not being recognizable to producers who are expecting erection and ejaculation. Producer and consumer expectations about orgasmic appearance do not necessarily reflect the realities for women who may be taking estrogen and androgen blockers. The art of orgasm intelligibility depends on assumptions about people's physiological and emotional relationships with their bodies.

In her book *Orgasmology* (2013), Annamarie Jagose reminds us that orgasm is no teller of truth and that looking to visual and audible cues for evidence of genuine pleasure can mislead us. Cisgender male performers such as Tyler Knight (2016) and Danny Wylde (Zeischegg 2018) have written about their experiences navigating erectile issues and taking Viagra on sets that demand both authenticity *and* performance. Making a Foucauldian argument, Jagose (2013, 2) writes that "arguing against a liberationist tradition that privileges sex as a resource for getting out from under the repressive operations of power, and therefore as a potential zone of freedom, Foucault makes it clear that orgasm must not be misrecognized as the truthful confession of bodily pleasure."

Queers have deliberately sought out nonorgasmic pleasures as disruptive— gender-expansive practices like fisting focus on duration and intensity of pleasure rather than climax. Other theorists have identified the potential for orgasms to be commodified: Paul Preciado (2013) argues that late capitalism seeks to take "orgasmic force" and transform it "into abstraction and digital data—into capital" (46). Unlike those who call on women to stop faking orgasm as a feminist issue, Jagose (2013) suggests that the practice of faking orgasms "is consistent with a queer theoretical approach that testifies to the potential of the unintelligible, the unproductive, and the wasteful" (xv). In this sense, every orgasm that goes unrecognized, remains unintelligible, is useless to capitalism, or disrupts what we think we know about the truth of sex may be performing a queer function of "undoing" authenticity.

Labors of Love

The authenticity delusion is situated among a wider cultural imperative for sex workers to describe their work as a kind of personal identity, a form of self-expression, a gratifying, rewarding, fulfilling experience or an altruistic endeavor with worthwhile social benefit. In part, this is a response to porn stigma: In reacting to readings of pornography as violence, exploitation, and abuse, performers have emphasized their positive experiences. However, the constant justification, defensive rebuttals, and incessant celebration have been mistaken as stating that pornography is always empowering and rarely work. The more that anti-porn advocates speak of porn's misogynistic and capitalistic tendencies, the greater the push among producers to position alternative pornography as *outside* work: as documentary, as archive, as reality, as natural, as love.

But this fantasy of genuine sexuality and the expectation that performers act out of love and not money is also driven by consumer demand for personalized intimacy. In seeking authentic depictions, customers and producers are both asking for *more* than they might ordinarily receive from a performer for the same price. It becomes part of the entitlement to performers' bodies and intimacies (noncommercial iterations that performers might otherwise keep for themselves to spend where they please). In our interview, Kim Cums discussed the lack of recognition among consumers about the administrative and financial investment involved in porn production. As a performer, consumers expected her to be a natural exhibitionist who loves sex and desires to share it freely with strangers for fun. Although many porn performers, including Kim, do find pleasure in exhibitionism (Ruberg 2016), they also put boundaries (and prices) on where, when, and how it can be accessed.

> People ask for free content all the time—like "toss me a free video or something?" and I'm like, "No." It takes so much time to produce any of these things; no you just can't have one for free, no way, like it's a business; there's not an appreciation, it's actually a business behind it, it's not just about producing free content. There's quite a backlash I find when you do try and do any sort of funding for it. There's an expectation of "Oh you should be doing it because you enjoy it" . . . [it's] a combination of yes personal enjoyment but also professional goals.

Porn performance here involves the labor of communicating enjoyment as well as managing audience access. In coining the term *emotional labor*, Arlie Russell Hochschild ([1983] 2012) writes, "Being friendly or enjoying your work is one thing, but having your enjoyment advertised, promised—in essence, sold—is quite another" (331). Hochschild contextualizes these forms of labor exploitation in light of the shift from an industrial to a service economy. Capitalist, postindustrial forms of labor exploitation rely on the "commercial logic of the managed heart" whereby emotional labor is employed toward the pursuit of profits, and as a result, "a commercial logic will penetrate deeper and deeper into what we used to think of as a private, psychological, sacred part of a person's self and soul" (333). Airline hostesses are required to smile and porn performers are expected to profess love for their work, and yet neither are explicitly remunerated for this labor.

In her article "Business as Usual" (2015a), Heather Berg analyzes advice from Los Angeles producers on casting. Their "key piece of advice" was to "hire for attitude." Directors describe mining potential performers' social media to ascertain their eagerness. One alt-porn producer Berg documents goes on to say, "When you do contact them, if the first thing they say is, 'How much do I get paid?' we usually stop talking to them after that . . . we know that that kind of girl, there's going to be a problem somewhere down the line." The work of porn performance goes beyond the life of the scene they are paid for—performers are hired for their commitment to the brand and their capacity to promote it.

Like other artists expected to work for exposure, this model increases competition, instills a culture in which performers are expected to be grateful for opportunities, and outsources the labor of marketing to performers. Similar examples exist in other parts of the sex industry—at the time of writing, Australian *Penthouse* magazine was no longer paying a set fee to centerfold models but instead was offering them magazines, which they could sell at venues to recoup their costs. In addition to this brand advertising role, performers often act as scriptwriters, directors, and editors: practices that increase performers' control but which are also cost-cutting measures for producers. We can see an example of this in the experiences of Mikey Way (2015) while performing for one site in Australia.

> Let's stop and do the math: I spent about two hours shaving, waxing, washing, and getting made up for the shoot. I spent about an hour on the setup, getting the lighting right, and cleaning the area I wanted to photograph in. Three hours in front of the camera. Another hour going through the footage, editing and color grading it. For about seven hours work in total, that's less than $30 an hour. Which is decent pay and all. Until you remember, this is porn. . . . That isn't feminist. That is exploitative, and it distracts from real solutions to issues in the industry, steering us away from discussions about labor rights and conditional consent and working conditions. That's right, working conditions—because this is work, not a hobby.

By making their labor visible and emphasizing their status as workers, performers denaturalize the performance and remind producers that this is capital-generating labor. This is not to say that performers do not find pleasure in the work, but they resist the naturalization of sex work in similar ways to the naturalization of much domestic, feminized, caring, and reproductive labor that makes it possible for others to profit.

Investments in authenticity have emerged from a broader cultural impetus for individuals to earn a living by doing what they love. The idea that anyone can build a career that is both income-generating and personally meaningful is no doubt a projection of privilege that ignores the fundamentally unequal division of labor. In her book *(Not) Getting Paid to Do What You Love* (2017),

Brooke Erin Duffy interviews social media producers involved in passion projects and finds that "the narrative of creative self-expression . . . conceals the unrelenting work (much of it unpaid) that takes place behind the screens" (ix–x). Building on Gina Neff's concept of venture labor and Kathleen Kuehn and Thomas F. Corrigan's concept of hope labor, Duffy calls these workers "aspirational labourers" because their work is mostly uncompensated in the expectation that "they will *one day* be compensated for their productivity" (5–6, emphasis in original). The seductive promise of future compensation effectively keeps them in a state of perpetual productivity, and yet they operate in an increasingly precarious gig economy in which paid work is sporadic, laborers are mobile, competition is high, and protections are lacking.

Porn performers are under similar expectations to foster relationships with consumers, recruit and maintain a membership base, attract clicks that can be converted into royalties, and gain social media followers in the hope of building an identifiable brand that is easily searchable and can be booked for upcoming gigs. There are similarities here between the labor performed by porn performers and musicians. Nancy K. Baym, in her book *Playing to the Crowd: Musicians, Audiences, and the Intimate Work of Connection* (2018), writes that, like porn performers, musicians had previously been distant to fans but are now expected to be relentlessly accessible: "maintaining a never-ending, always-engaging, continuously innovative conversation with their audience, one self-promotional enough to remind people that they have something to sell, yet interpersonal enough to make listeners feel connected and eager to spend money on them" (5–6).

Just as musicians engage in this *relational labor*, a term Baym uses to describe the communicative work of creating structures that support continued work (19), porn performers must build relationships to secure diverse income streams and multiple channels of potential work opportunities to survive in the context of major industry upheavals. One Australian company, from which performers receive royalties depending on scene clicks, contains a contractual clause stating that a performer forfeits all future royalties if they speak out publicly against the company. Performers must then maintain an ongoing positive relationship or face financial sanctions for speaking about poor work experiences. If this is the financial context in which authenticity and realness are being sold, it casts serious doubt over the authenticity of expressions of the self. In the gig economy, Baym writes, "the threat of poverty is ever-present" (8). Performers' language of realness and their cultivations of intimacy should be understood in the context of fostering relationships with both consumers and producers to keep potential work opportunities alive.

Mobilizing Community

Like authenticity, a sense of community can be mobilized to extract labor. Some performers were expected to contribute to site bulletin boards, online journals, blogs, and discussion forums for free under the guise of community. As described in "The Hustle" interlude, SuicideGirls, who pitch themselves as an online alternative community, use a business model whereby thousands of contributors submit nude photographs to be used on the site but are only paid if they are picked as "set of the day." In 2005 nearly forty models left Suicide-Girls citing poor pay and restrictive contracts (Osgerby 2014, 50). Bill Osgerby (2014, 52) argues that subcultural erotica sites like this mobilize a feeling of community that can obscure the commercial imperatives central to operation.

These dynamics can operate in smaller-scale DIY projects as well. DIY porn may not necessarily be a transcendence of capitalism—it is also entrepreneurial and small business–oriented and still involves the sale of a commodity. In porn, what works for a producer—minimal budgets, cost-cutting, model releases for unfettered use, or shooting an entire film in a single day—does not necessarily benefit the worker. In DIY porn, performers can end up taking on more unpaid tasks—holding the camera, supplying the wardrobe, doing the makeup, writing the script, or promoting the scene—but the revenue may still be concentrated in the hands of the producer. DIY porn is often low-budget (Dick Savvy even labeled his work "no-budget porn"), relying on friends and community to donate or trade for skills, labor, locations, or equipment. This is one of the benefits of DIY culture generally: What producers lack in funds they can make up for in the resourcefulness of artists and creatives. The appeal of DIY is about creating a culture of self-sufficiency (think dumpster diving, bicycle workshops, or community gardens) that doesn't rely on professionals, corporate infrastructure, or expensive equipment. But framing projects within a language of community building can also serve to extract more labor from performers; as Berg (2015a) argues, it "encourages all sorts of workers to give more for less, or for no pay at all."

In online discussions about queer porn in the United States, some have been suspicious of where profits were accumulating, critiquing public figureheads for using their social capital, status, and fans to accumulate what they saw as community money through crowdfunding campaigns. They emphasized the disjuncture between calling pornography revolutionary and then not paying performers sufficiently for their labor. On my social media threads some critiqued producers as profiting from the inclusion of marginalized performers without actively pushing for their rights or making space for them, as a means to look edgy and make money. They referred to feminist pornography as simply porn where you are paid less. These examples remind us to look deeper into the economic structures of indie pornographies from the lens of private property, ownership, and wealth accumulation. The risk more generally is that *community* can become a convenient front for the outsourcing of cheap labor to those who have creative but not financial resources.

Berg reminds us to be suspicious of claims to community and to take a closer look at who profits most. She compares porn to other sharing economies whereby performers are encouraged to share their sexuality with the camera, management, and the market. Sharing economies sound friendly, generous, and community-spirited, but as we see from examples like Airbnb and Uber, these economies are not simply about friends sharing hospitality or lifts with one another. Rather, the owners are buying property and monopolizing markets. Similarly, in his research into gay media sites and their promises of safer space, Joshua Gamson reminds us that such sites function primarily "to deliver a market share to corporations" (quoted in Dean 2005, 63). Gamson writes that, in these contexts, "community needs are conflated with consumption desires, and community equated with market" (65). In his analysis of porn Paul Preciado (2013) argues that "we are being confronted with a new kind of hot, psychotropic, punk capitalism" (33), one that wants to put our orgasmic potential to work by transforming it into private property (43). When DIY porn becomes about profit making or generating capital (not only financial but also social capital) and about using skill sharing, bartering, and trading as means of extracting labor, then DIY porn is no longer anti-capitalist; it becomes a technique of capitalist production.

This creates a pressing tension for indie pornography. These mediums *do* build communities, support alternative sexual cultures, and foster public political discussions—and often are created among small groups of friends, lovers, and peers. But at what point and to what extent is this sense of connectedness (which provides affirmation, belonging, and life-saving support for some) mobilized or exploited toward goals that serve individuals or corporations *under the guise* of community? Here we can see conflation not only between community and market but also between culture and industry.

Reinscription and Artifice

As authenticity becomes an aesthetic in itself, with signifiers to be mimicked, bodies risk *incoherence* where they do not meet these prescriptive formulas, where they are not intelligible to producers and cannot be consumed into the circuits of capital. However, claims to authentic truth or essence, positioned against pornography's supposed falsity, presume that pornography is not already a valuable cultural medium in itself. Pornography is *already* documentary, *already* an archive. It provides an enormous repository to trace back cultural pre-occupations, fashion trends, political moments, and sexual cultures. Archives themselves are never complete and always involve selective memory. Lauren Berlant and Michael Warner (1998) remind us that memory involves aspects of "amnesia" (549). But in the coedited book *Porn Archives*, Tim Dean writes that "pornography does not need to adhere to the criteria of documentary realism in order to furnish vital evidence about human sexuality" (Dean, Ruszczycky, and Squires 2014, 5). Regardless of whether pornography is authentic, it still has value. As Dean writes, "porn is itself an archive—of fantasy, of desire, of bodies and their actions, and of pleasure. Pornography, at least in its photographic forms, preserves evidence of something that is otherwise transient and ephemeral. It enables intimacy to enter the archive, and it is valuable for that reason alone . . . pornography need not be realistic to furnish valuable evidence" (9–10).

Some performers voiced resentment toward the pretense of authenticity and felt that at least mainstream porn was honest or *genuine* in its artifice. Madison Missina, for example, questioned why performers should have to experience real orgasms on set at all, noting that sexual pleasure exists beyond clitoral stimulation. She said that performers often found pleasure in "stunt sex"—in the nonorgasmic pleasures of exhibitionism, performativity, and acrobatic displays; in color coordination, set composition, and costuming; in the elements of stagecraft, sexual excessiveness, and theatricality. Kim Cums said something similar: "The same way with my personal life, I might not always get off every single time, right? But it's still a job that I enjoy doing, and I think there's authenticity in that. There's different types of pleasure that I think we should be able to recognize within the porn community."

Porn performers spoke about authenticity quite differently from producers. Rather than hold on to a static sense of their own sexuality, performers reported that performing gave them opportunities to try a plethora of activities, scenarios, sensations, dynamics, and aesthetics. What was important to them was having choice over their bodies and representations. From a performer's perspective, they may have represented themselves authentically not because they revealed their innate sexuality, but because their performance reflected whatever they genuinely desired to do on set on that particular day. Instead, they took issue with what they saw as hypocrisy of producers. Kim Cums told me that

I don't actually have an issue with when I'm on a set, and it's less authentic to my own sexuality. I have an issue when that conflicts with how the company sells itself to performers. . . . I don't mind going onto the set and saying, "Hey, I'm here as a performer and as an actor and as a professional, and I'm happy to pretend that I like this thing if that is your company's shooting style and you're up-front about the fact that that's your company's shooting style and that's the type of stuff that you like to do."

But if you come to me as a company, and say "Hey, performers, we want you to be your authentic self" and then you come back and say "Don't do any of the things that you actually like because what we actually want is for your authentic sexuality to fit into our niche of what our consumers think female authentic sexuality looks like." And so that's an issue that I have.

Performers described authenticity as something involving transparency about the commercial context, consumer expectations, technical requirements, and agency for performers to articulate their own desires and fantasies. In the view of Gala Vanting (2014), producers need to be prepared for what performers can offer and to hold space for that:

When we invite performers to be real, we need to be prepared for whatever form that realness may take, lest we fail to create a leak-proof container for their performance and whatever emotions and analyses may result from it. As producers we gravitate towards the creation of representations of the real which are legible to us. Because we're often working within our own communities, representing the folks we know or the desires that make sense to us, we may be less likely to come into contact with "realnesses" that don't. This is what happens, though, when you open up the possibility of representation to the general populace, which is what the "real amateur" producers have to do in order to find their non–sex worker, non–porn performer subjects.

Shine Louise Houston (2015) makes a similar point:

If "authentic" means "it really happened," then it is as true for the sex that we film as it is for any porno. Or to give us a little more credit, if "authentic" means "these people have sex this way," then it is true that at least on the day we shot, the models were having the sex of their choosing. The "authenticity" we do not truck in is the idea that there is a truth of every person's sexuality and gender that we can all find if we search hard enough. This would be the same "authenticity" that would pretend that the sex viewers can watch on our site is a mirror of some sort of "real" or "true" queer sexuality. We are not taking part in a race to realness, as if queers need to occupy the land of the real that heteros have possessed for so long.

Some projects reflected more complex understandings of representation, deliberately contesting the binary between artifice and reality. *Slit* magazine's themes have been playful and creative, including issues on tools, clowns, and weird science. *Slit*'s final issue explored how we understand our lives through the medium of representation. The magazine used French philosopher Jean Baudrillard's concept of "simulacra," a term he uses to describe the ways in which we experience the world through signs and symbols, which circulate and take on meaning and reference each other but do not reflect reality. Instead of distinguishing between artifice and authenticity, Baudrillard (1983) writes that "artifice is at the very heart of reality. . . . [R]eality itself, entirely impregnated by an aesthetic which is inseparable from its own structure, has been confused with its own image" (151–52). This issue of *Slit* (2012) is replete with sexual representations featuring repetition, mirror images, and media mash-ups as means of exploring how queer communities understand their selves. In their editorial, Meredith and Domino write, "*Simulacra* goes to the heart of some key debates in queer communities—such as whether sexuality and gender are caused or constituted by biology or socialisation." This sophisticated understanding of sexuality reflects a broader queer project that plays with performativity to disrupt the codes of what constitutes authenticity and exposes it as an imitation with no original.

These approaches reflect the post-pornographic philosophy described by the late Tim Stüttgen, who writes that post-pornography uses "performative excessiveness" and camp in order to contest the regimes of sexual representation. Post-pornography uses both "critical denaturalizing performance and glamorous affirmation," as Stüttgen (2009) writes. "Every gesture, subject—and gender—position, sex-practice, erogenous zone, camera perspective and value of affect and code can be profaned or appropriated, deconstructed and queered, reworked and genderfucked; it can get territorialized and deterritorialized. Welcome to the post-pornographic world of political perversion(s)" (10).

Post-porn, then, does not claim stakes in any fixed notion of what pornography is or does, and it looks beyond explicit sex. These approaches complicate binary readings of pornographies as fake/real, and instead of seeking to represent the authentic truth of sex, they take pleasure in its undoing, contestation, and incoherence.

Green, Organic Porn

I'm up late online browsing through news articles on indie pornographies. The header image in a *Guardian* article features a cover of Blake's DVD *Dreams of Spanking*. Blake is an advocate for ethical kink porn. Their tag line is, "When all you want is to be punished, ethically." It's a neat slogan. But there is something in the *Guardian* article (Williams 2014) that gives me pause. Graphic designers have lined up Blake's DVD on a shelf amid a row of boxes that read "fairtrade muesli" and cans labeled "organic chickpeas." The article is titled "Is There Such a Thing as Ethical Porn?," but it is clearly about more than ethics. The subhead reads: "The actors say they're happy, the makers say it's guilt-free—but what exactly is 'fair trade' porn? We find out." I'm confused by this point what the article is actually about. Is it ethical porn, fair trade porn, organic porn, or guilt-free porn?

Curious, I type "organic porn" into Google. I keep hearing the term repeated in media. An article for Australian *Cleo* magazine titled "100% Organic Porn" describes Erika Lust's film *Xconfessions* as "new wave organic porn." But apart from the subject matter exploring "a food fetish with a bearded hipster," the focus is on the film being "beautifully shot" and "based on sexual confessions submitted from fans around the world" (Gebilagin, n.d.). It's unclear what makes this organic. One user on Ask MetaFilter, under the heading "Shade grown organic porn?," seeks "organic kinky porn"; from the description, though, it appears that what they really want to know is that the models are not being exploited (Anonymous 2010).

The slippage and conflation between this terminology leaves me wondering if this is lazy journalism, a marketing strategy, or just poor porn literacy. On the one hand, as someone interested in environmental activism, animal liberation, and food security, I'm curious. On the other hand, their lack of substantiation makes them read like empty buzzwords.

I look further. A *Huffington Post* article reads, "Artisanal, Locally Grown, Free Range Porn for Women" (Nagy 2013). I have no doubt come up with some innovative marketing slogans in the past, but what on earth is free-range porn? Animal rights activists criticize free-range labels as not going far enough and having particularly low standards that still permit exploitation. What is locally grown? Does that mean that producers don't hire migrant workers? I'm not sure if this language is coming from producers or media, but in at least one article I find a small disclaimer at the bottom noting that one producer's reference to "fair trade" had inadvertently been editorialized as "free trade."

I open up a new tab and this time look for definitions of *organic*. In the context of certified produce, *organic* is generally used to describe products derived from organic farming methods. Organic food or clothing uses less water, produces fewer carbon dioxide emissions, is not exposed to pesticides, and avoids synthetic chemicals or genetically modified seeds. To be fair, there has certainly been a renewed interest in environmental sustainability, ethical manufacture, and cruelty-free products within the sex industry. Producers have found intersections with social and ecological justice movements, with the manufacture of environmentally conscious sex toys (such as solar-powered bullet vibrators) and the production of eco-sexual porn (Stephens and Sprinkle 2013). One European group, Fuck for Forests, creates porn to fundraise for environmental projects including seed exchange, permaculture, and rainforest preservation (Măntescu 2016).

Conversations about green, organic, and cruelty-free porn may be in their infancy, but they draw upon long-term claims by ecofeminists about connections between the rights of nonhuman animal and women, the burden of feminized and reproductive labor, and the struggle for bodily autonomy. Ecofeminists have interrogated the use of animal products in makeup, product testing, and clothing as well as the positioning of women and nonhuman animals as consumable. Can we really call our porn ethical or feminist if we exploit animal products in the process?

I have been vegan for over a decade but am still struggling to see how our porn—as a product—would meet the criteria for being organic. Some sex toys are still made with phthalates—chemicals linked to reproductive health and environmental problems—or from polyvinyl chloride (pvc), often produced in factories that employ a workforce of low-paid, minority communities exposed to physical dangers like dioxin. Even if one were to conduct an examination of whether porn workers consumed chemical-free diets, plant-based medications, or non-synthetic body products, or whether all of our equipment was organic, recycled, or biodegradable, it would be a fanciful claim.

I take a different angle. Perhaps I shouldn't have been so literal. *Organic* is also applied to porn in a way that suggests that the content is naturally evolving. Scenes that develop organically may be scenes that are unscripted, with little intervention from the producer and with a trajectory determined by performers as they go. Maybe organic porn develops from relationships, friendships, collaborations in a way that is spontaneous rather than from performers being formally recruited. Is it a stretch to describe porn as having an organic process because the scene develops or grows organically, with reduced intervention or modification? As we saw in chapter 5, claims to naturalness and authenticity are particularly fraught in a commercial environment that is heavily mediated. Even without the formality of a script, we are still drawing upon social cues, sexual scripts, and cultural references for coherence and understanding. I wait to see if the next thing I read will be about "non-GMO porn."

6

Fair Trade Porn

Marketing, Respectability, and Ethical Consumption

"If you care about the conditions under which your food was made," says feminist porn producer Tristan Taormino, "and the conditions under which your jeans were made, then you should care about the conditions under which your pornography is made. You should be willing to pay a little more" (quoted in Bussel 2013). Taormino calls feminist porn "organic, fair trade porn" and encourages people to "put their money where their politics are to support local, artisanal, and independent small businesses" (quoted in Breslaw 2013). Porn producers now use descriptors for their work that reference quality certification or labeling processes for food, clothing, agriculture, and consumables and that draw connections between labor production practices across industries. From San Francisco, one of the graphics used to promote PinkLabel.tv is a milk carton reading "Grade A" and "porn with good taste," referencing certification standards for milk. From the United Kingdom, Dreams of Spanking founder Blake describes their work as "fair trade" as a way to signal "complete respect for performers, for their boundaries and consent" (quoted in Williams 2014). The United Kingdom's Ethical Porn Partnership has promoted responsibly made

FIGURE 6.1. Faerie Willow performing in *Venus Chastising Cupid* for BDSM subscription site Dreams of Spanking, which promises "severe spanking fantasies produced with enthusiastic consent." Image by Dreams of Spanking.

porn that can broaden consumer choice, and former director Nichi Hodgson has argued for a code of conduct in pornography similar to "food or fashion," which prioritizes the welfare, autonomy, and decision-making of performers as well as their physical and psychological health (BBC Radio 4 2015). Many conversations about ethical production have been consumer-focused, seeking to broaden consumer choice and showcase the work of independent producers.

These provocations are notable because they implore regulators to think beyond media classification and instead about the *political economy* of pornography. They position pornography as part of broader systems of globalization and economic inequality. When we compare pornography to other production industries, we make visible its status as work and underscore the material conditions of its frontline workers. Taking pornography seriously as a creative transnational industry is essential because it compels us to consider trade relationships and inequalities without exceptionalizing pornography as distinct from other work or cultural products. As considered in the vignette "Green, Organic Porn," taking this approach implores producers to consider how their practices sit within the context of global inequality, labor migration, environmental destruction, and animal exploitation.

At the same time, the marketing of "fair trade pornography" reflects a broader trend toward ethical consumption where consumers seek to vote with their dollars and producers attempt to carve out a market for customized, limited-edition content. These strategies draw attention to the economic environment in which porn is distributed—the context of film piracy, tube monopolies, keyword cannibalization, and an unwillingness among consumers to pay for their porn. There remain inherent tensions in these endeavors because producers face the inevitable challenge of seeking to intervene in the systems of the market while also trying to exist as viable businesses within it. In some cases, this kind of marketing positions ethics as a commodity to be consumed, rather than an ongoing work in progress and practice.

Performers have questioned what it means to call pornography "fair trade," "ethical," "organic," or "cruelty-free" and what obligations, responsibilities, and accountabilities accompany these labels. Some sex workers have argued that feminist and ethical porn producers are enjoying privileges associated with the gentrification of the sex industry by emphasizing their distance from the mainstream. Just as food labeling practices have come under the fire of regulators (for example, for the misleading and deceptive labeling of "free-range" eggs), porn distributors must carefully consider how they represent their goods. The subsequent conversations highlight an ongoing tension between those who see an indie porn agenda as part of a politics of inclusion (to protect an industry and livelihood) or as a politics of resistance (about decriminalization, decentralization, and deprofessionalization). They put consumers on notice to look beyond marketing language and inquire further into the material conditions of production.

Custom Content and Commercial Opportunities

In response to content piracy, a saturated market, and the general unwillingness of consumers to pay for porn, niche markets for specialized content have emerged. Producers have begun fighting back against piracy by filing motions under the US Digital Millennium Copyright Act requesting that stolen content be taken down. They are urging their consumers to pay for their porn as a means of supporting workers' rights. The "Pay For Your Porn" campaign, backed by LA porn studios, sells merchandise and features performer videos urging consumers to support their working conditions. As San Francisco–based queer performer Jiz Lee (2015a) writes, "Fiscal compensation defines porn performance as labour, qualifies the value of the work, and validates the ownership of the image." Porn performer Siri has appealed to consumers by emphasizing the personal economic impact piracy has on her own membership site and her ability to earn a living. From Spain, María Bala's film *Support Your Local Pornographers* urges viewers to support locals who are producing content with few resources. Performers ask audiences to subscribe to their independent sites rather than download their pirated scenes. These initiatives are necessary in the shadow of big tech platforms; indie porn performers are required to repeatedly reiterate the labor involved in sex work and demand it be valued.

Producers have thus begun cultivating a pool of ethical porn consumers. Marketing porn as "fair trade," "organic," or "ethical" encourages consumers to think about the costs and labors of production—and it also provides a justification for its retail price. Jiz Lee (2015c) urges consumers to vote with their wallet as a form of ethical porn consumption, where consumers can directly support producers whose values and decisions they like. For many indie producers, getting paid is an issue of survival. But for more commercial operators across the adult industry, this kind of brand-building represents a business opportunity. In their research into the regulation of sex shops in Australia, Paul Maginn and Christine Steinmetz (2011) trace the "changing face of adult retailing," arguing that retailers have moved from appearing "seedy and sleazy" to taking a "corporate approach" to branding (with female staff and sexual health products) and now toward offering consumers "high-end, bespoke" products and positioning themselves as "erotic emporia" or "sensuality boutiques." Similarly, Lynn Comella (2008) describes the marketing of pornography and sex toys to women in the United States with sleek designs and "lifestyle branding" as part of the attempt to make porn and adult products more respectable: "Sultry images of porn starlets [have] been replaced with softer and more sanitized iconography; discourses of sexual health and education, as opposed to titillation, are increasingly used as marketing platforms" (63). In my interview with Howard, who ran his own erotica company, he described seeing a commercial opportunity in socially responsible porn. "The socially responsible porn movement has a much brighter future than the mainstream porn movement. I can see it becoming more and more publicized, and I can see more and more people making a conscious choice just in the same way they have about the food they eat, the appliances they buy, the transport they use, and all of those other decisions that affect the whole world."

These marketing shifts in the adult industry mirror similar marketing shifts among big business. Documenting her visit to the AVN awards, industry insiders repeatedly reported to Lynn Comella (2008) that "the hottest growth market in the adult industry is the women's market" (62). Following the spike in giant global brands in the nineties, Naomi Klein (2010, xv) argues that big businesses then began trying to *escape* their brands, emphasizing the notion of community over chain companies with no label, producing one-of-a-kind products linked to social causes: Absolut Vodka launched its limited edition Absolut No Label line while Starbucks opened unbranded coffee shops. To distinguish themselves from mass-produced and pirated porn, indie producers are doing something similar, now marketing their work as artisanal and niche (Nagy 2013). Madison Young even says of her work, "It's the difference between eating at McDonalds, or at a local restaurant that makes everything from scratch with local produce" (quoted in Martin 2012). As smaller scale pornography emerges as an artisanal product made by local indie artists and sold as a kind of handicraft (Sensate Films actually home-printed and hand-stitched individual wrapping), these products, as boutique, customized and rare, are positioned against an onslaught of ubiquitous and free content.

To survive in the marketplace, indie producers are diversifying their income streams, revenue models, and products. In her qualitative interviews with producers, Kate Darling (2013) found that because copyright infringement is so widespread and enforcement is not cost-effective, producers have turned to the production of "experience" goods (for example, live camera and chat) that cannot easily be copied. With little money to be had in pornographic scenes, producers turned to ancillary materials: Young, for instance, creates her own autographed original anus prints with archival ink and watercolor paper and uses these as handmade packaging for her DVDs, which she sells along with her memoir at festivals. A Four Chambered Heart in the United Kingdom (whose producers have an art background in analog photography) sell tote bags, T-shirts, prints, badges, sketchbooks, and vinyl records. Performer April Flores and her late husband Carlos Batts would wrap their DVDs in April's fishnet stockings (I was a lucky owner of April's *Voluptuous Cyberskin Pussy*, which was admired by many lovers as a coffee table feature). Producers have turned back to grassroots channels of distribution—hand packaging, hard copy DVDs, USBs, or prints for sale at festivals and educational workshops. Many have moved from subscription models, to pay-per-view, crowdfunding, wish lists, donations, and patronage.

As generative AI and intimate messaging chatbots become more available, and consumers can design their own porn star avatars, customization and personalization have become a central focus of online porn work. Consumers can now request tailored sexual experiences, and porn sites are emerging built on non-fungible tokens (NFTS), unique digital assets that accrue value in a similar way to hard copy visual art. In a context of mass digital availability, part of the value in indie porn may be found in its analog appeal and human touch: live interactions, limited-edition prints, the screening of privately curated porn collections, and porno memorabilia in pop-up galleries.

Building a Base of Ethical Consumers

The emergence of fair trade, green, and artisanal porn resembles a broader trend in food and fashion toward a new consumer-citizen who seeks to avoid mass-produced, corporatized products and instead seeks out localized content.

Ethical consumption is an important part of porn literacy; it equips consumers with a vocabulary and criteria through which to navigate online content and participate in political activism. Understanding the production values is just as important as knowing what kinds of activities are represented in the content itself. At the same time, ethical consumption is a way for consumers, via their commitments to or boycotts of certain producers/distributors, to produce their identities via the products they buy (Adams and Raisborough 2008, 1166). As a result, what emerges is a "citizen-consumer" hybrid, someone who can "satisfy competing ideologies of consumerism (an ideal rooted in individual self-interest) and citizenship (an ideal rooted in collective responsibility to a social and ecological commons)" (Johnston 2008, 229). This discerning consumer not only seeks informed product choice but also has an investment in creating a new subjectivity whose responsible shopping, taste, and lifestyle choices produce their identity.

Ethical consumption also performs a unique role in regard to pornography. It often relies upon, rather than dismantles, porn stigma. The promise of ethical consumption provides a relief from what Alan McKee (2017) describes as "the insistent Othering of porn consumers" (390). Despite research suggesting that a significant proportion of porn consumers are now women, and that people watch porn for a variety of reasons, including boredom, release, pleasure, leisure, relationship building, and identity exploration (Smith, Barker, and Attwood 2015), pornography consumers have been overwhelmingly depicted as "pimply teenagers, furtive perverts in raincoats, and asocial compulsively masturbating misfits" (Kipnis 1996, 161). Jeff Sparrow (2012), for example, describes his experiences inside an Australian sex cinema as "strange and unpleasant" and "disengaged from humanity" and describes patrons as "a small congregation of the old, the mad, and the lost" (1–8).

Ethical labels appeal to those who feel otherwise alienated from pornography, as they position porn consumers not as tragic media victims, but as discerning and critical consumers, distanced from the derided stereotype of "lecherous grandfathers" (7). In doing so, they do not necessarily lift the stigma attached to mainstream porn consumers, but rather reinforce it. One feminist producer explicitly recognized this. "There is that idea that we're just exploiters, that we're all dirty raincoat people, or something like that. I think this is actually where feminist porn is useful because feminist porn does give us a certain respectability. You're able to stand up and go, 'No, I'm . . .' whereas people who are making fairly standard porn . . . they don't get to do that as such. They're sort of lower down on the heap as it were. They're probably more stigmatized than us."

In their studies on fair trade and feminist pornographies, both Alessandra Mondin and Rachael Liberman identify the impact of these labels in making pornography accessible to some consumers. Mondin (2014) argues that such labels are "intended to build consumer confidence . . . for those consumers who feel uneasy at the perceived lack of ethics in mainstream productions, and for those who might be sceptical of porn altogether" (190). As Mondin writes, "They are supporting the development of a new consumer base that perhaps stayed away from porn because of worries about harms to its performers, but who may now feel more comfortable with the possibilities of ethical productions" (190).

In her interviews with feminist porn consumers, Liberman (2015) similarly found that audiences arrive at feminist pornography "based on both distaste for mainstream depictions of female sexuality and an interest in diversifying their pornography diet; these orientations have led them to develop a 'taste' for ethically produced, or 'feminist,' pornography content" (174).

As such, when porn websites position themselves as "alternative," they offer to make viewers feel comfortable and guilt-free in their consumerism. Garion Hall, who runs the "natural amateurs" site Abby Winters, confirmed in our interview, "People who pay for porn these days are probably more concerned about performers' rights than they were in the past, because everyone can just go to a cheap site and get so much free porn, like why would anyone bother paying for it? . . . We ask customers, 'Well, why do you pay for porn?' And they say, 'Well, I believe what you guys are doing is good and I want to look after the models and the producers and stuff.' And that's nice to know."

The political impact of citizen-consumers is, as Josée Johnston (2008) describes, at once "hopeful" and full of "tensions and contradictions" (229). In her examination of Whole Foods Market, Johnston explores the success of ethical consumption in a "growth-oriented corporate setting" and finds that this model "provides relatively superficial attention to citizenship goals in order better to serve three key elements of consumerist ideology: consumer choice, status distinction, and ecological cornucopianism" (262). In other words, these initiatives place too much faith in the marketplace to progress toward meaningful social interventions, and the prioritizing of consumption can eclipse the impact of activism. Gala Vanting was suspicious of the language used in marketing. "So we have this whole greenwashing thing with feminist porn, where you know as the consumer that the performer was paid properly and that they got lots of bananas on set, and you know—this word 'free range' which I find quite garish because it makes me think about farming meat."

FIGURE 6.2. Papi Coxxx featured in a flyer for Courtney Trouble's site Indie Porn Revolution, formerly No Fauxxx, established in 2002. Image by Courtney Trouble.

Heather Berg makes a similar point in her comparison with the way multinational corporations like Starbucks have promoted their coffee as fair trade. "Artisanal" is a term that, as Berg (2015b) explains, connotes "an 'upmarket' product for which capitalists can command a higher price" (28). She draws from Slavoj Žižek, who argues that when purchasing from Starbucks' Fairtrade line, consumers' need to do something meaningful is not necessarily connected to the collective project that benefits those who pick the coffee beans. When we look closer, we can see that this "collective project" is in fact "imaginary" and "asymmetrical" (28), Berg argues. In 2020 Starbucks staff reported that they had been banned from wearing Black Lives Matter material in the workplace because it might be deemed divisive, and in 2023 workers in the United States were striking after the company prohibited the display of LGBTQ flags during Pride month.

If we are invested in more equitable collective conditions for porn workers, consumer choice will only take us so far. Corporations frequently co-opt the language of ethics and fair trade without changing their operating processes. A diverse marketplace does not let governments off the hook for failing to address the conditions in which porn is produced and distributed.

Signposting, Buzzwords, and Search Engine Optimization

Porn marketing terminology is used to position a brand in the market, signal to consumers about the content, and categorize the work for optimal online reach. Search technology, write Ken Hillis, Michael Petit, and Kylie Jarrett (2012), is "a site of knowledge and power" (i), and our increasing reliance on search engines, in particular Google, impacts how we think about ourselves. Choosing slogans, tags, and descriptors was complicated by considerations about search optimization and signposting to guide consumers. As one feminist producer described her situation, "I still use 'porn for women' because it's very handy with Google. And you know, actually I should say that the monster that is Google makes a big difference as to what things get called because it's how you get your traffic."

Producers need to be strategic in their marketing terms because it affects whether or not their intended audiences can find the work. Aeryn Walker, for example, used "feminist porn" even though she didn't like it because it was a term that others had used to describe her work: "I used to use it for advertising simply because a lot of people call [me] that." Another producer refrained from using "feminist" at times, even though she felt her work fit within that ambit, because she thought the term "feminist porn can attract people, but I think it can also repel people." Producers shifted through different labels over time. As Anna Brownfield explained to me, "At first when I started, I called it 'chick porn,' but everyone just assumed I was making lesbian films for a hetero male market, and then for a while I was using 'new wave erotica.' So it's been difficult to find a term. Also when I started there weren't as many people making it as there are now—feminist porn has become a bit more of a blanket term."

Content signposting is important in helping individuals navigate mass amounts of online material. Just as producers include descriptors of the sexual activities a viewer can expect to see, they also convey information about behind-the-scenes production values. But self-regulatory practices such as tagging are political and contested. Although it may seem straightforward to tag a sexual practice (e.g., squirting, pegging, fisting), performers uploading their content to streaming sites have critiqued the imposition of top-down tagging systems and argued for the ability to articulate their own descriptions of practice as well as identity (race, gender, sexuality, neurotype, etc.). This is especially the case where racialized categories like "ebony" and "interracial" are often the only available tags for BIPOC performers to appear in search results and earn income (Egwuatu et al. 2024). On major tube sites, tagging is usually limited to content rather than production ethics. But a concern for the political economy of pornography calls for a more sophisticated vocabulary of tagging. Such an approach could support consumers to search content based on production ethics, pay rates, collaborative process, solidarity work, performer testimonials, or accountability practices.

Discrepancies between the experiences of workers and the expectations of consumers have prompted increasing calls for transparency and accountability in the marketing of pornography. As Kim Cums noted in our interview, what a consumer expects from feminist pornography (representational deliverables, such as a focus on women's pleasure) may be different from what a performer expects (fair pay and the ability to approve content). In Fulden Ergen's (2018) review of thirty-three ethical porn websites, producers communicated about their labor practices in different ways, predominantly under the logic of "fair trade"; however, some sites used the discourse of ethical pornography "superficially . . . without revealing the actual practice of production" (1). In our interviews, porn performers (rather than producers) tended to be more critical about the descriptors used to market their work, particularly if the production process did not meet up to the branding. As Kim Cums suggested during our interview,

> I don't want feminist porn to kind of become a label that's only on the surface so that it looks nice, it looks like there's female pleasure, it looks like all these really good things are happening, but behind-the-scenes that's not the actual reality. I'd much rather have a porn company that maybe does do a lot of great scenes but behind-the-scenes performers are getting paid well and there is consent and everyone's happy with their jobs. . . . I think that's a lot more important that on the back end things are solid and ethical.

While producers have taken steps to reveal their production practices to verify their ethical claims, they can also fall into documentary tropes that do not necessarily attest to the experiences of performers. In her research, Karly-Lynne Scott (2016) found that ethical porn production is often signaled to consumers by specific conventions, including "interviews with performers, behind-the-scenes material, as well as outtakes and other instances of failed labour" (120). Scott suggests that rather than being read as "documentary evi-

FIGURE 6.3. Still from *Touch* (Sensate Films, 2013), starring Hyperballad. A partnership between Gala Vanting and Aven Frey, Sensate Films describe their approach as "slow porn," focusing on presence, process, and attention to detail, in contrast to the "more, faster!" mindset within mass production. Image by Sensate Films.

dence," we should be less naïve and more skeptical in understanding these as "elements of pornographic performance," remembering how performers strategically navigate such conventions in order to get paid: "As such, ethical spectatorship cannot arise simply from consuming pornography that claims to be ethically produced, but requires critical engagement that stands in opposition to the rhetoric produced by conventions that purport to reveal the hidden labour of pornography" (120).

What might this critical spectatorship look like? As I argued in chapter 5, performers themselves may be under financial pressure to give enthusiastic reports of their work, so the kinds of critical feedback they have may only be articulated in peer spaces. It then becomes even more crucial to listen to the public demands coming from sex worker–led movements.

Global Inequalities in Trade Relationships

There has been limited academic work applying the concept of fair trade to pornography, but what exists has predominantly focused on labor standards rather than trade relationships. Alessandra Mondin classifies the work of Pink and White Productions' Crash Pad Series site in San Francisco as fair trade because of its focus on labor conditions and nonexploitative business practices.

Mondin (2014) identifies how the site prioritizes and cares for performers' well-being and agency: Performers discuss their sexual preferences before scenes, provide after-care for one another, have a say in their scene partner, receive fair compensation, and participate in interviews where they speak for themselves. In addition, the company also operates a streaming network, Pink-Label.tv, which grants profits directly to the directors of the films (190). The fair trade movement is indeed about promoting fair labor standards. When applied to field, farm, or factory work (such as cotton, cocoa, coffee, or garments), fair trade is concerned with the conditions of the work—minimum wages, sick leave and superannuation, industrial rights, work health and safety—as well as the frameworks that surround it: immigration scrutiny, insecure housing, criminalization. Thinking about fair trade in the context of porn production therefore means considering how social, legal, and economic factors impact performers, including barriers to accessing rights, standards and fair pay, obstacles to finding affordable housing, and options for safe, legal migration.

But fair trade is not only about working conditions. The fair trade movement emerged in the mid-twentieth century in the face of imperialism to address the role of multinational corporations in generating wealth inequalities between countries, extracting the minerals and resources of low-income countries, and exploiting the labor of Black, Brown, and impoverished communities. It advocates a form of trade designed to help independent producers and cooperatives achieve better trading conditions to promote sustainability instead of charity or aid. In the global supply chain, fair trade can include paying higher prices to independents who are exporting their products as well as promoting better labor standards in the country of manufacture. Fair trade is particularly important when the goods are produced in lower income countries because it seeks to address wealth disparities between nations and recognizes that conventional exploitative trading relationships keep nations in poverty.

Reflecting on the use of fair trade marketing among indie producers, Gala said: "I find it pretty wild that feminist porn has chosen to align its brand with the fair trade movement, given its whiteness. It feels like a comical oversight. . . . I feel like we completely whitewash the origins and actuality of fair trade by drawing this comparison, which is something we need to be extra careful about."

In a domestic setting, we ought to be concerned about the dynamics of tech platforms or white, wealthy, cis producers and distributors accumulating the content of racialized performers as a source of diversity and profit without contributing to broader movements for their survival, liberation, and justice. We ought to be concerned about platform ranking and tagging systems that

fetishize racialized performers while contributing to their invisibility and reduced income without the requisite solidarity work to address the urgent context
of police brutality, mass incarceration, or deaths in custody. Like small countries
that export precious stones, textiles, and minerals internationally, indie performers bring rich and unique perspectives, identities, and cultures that are of value
to mainstream industries. But without fair trade, the wealth, livelihood, and opportunity discrepancies between performers, producers, and distributors will
persist, perpetuating divergences in health outcomes and life expectancy.

This is the case globally where porn is sold via large distribution platforms in
the United States or Europe. In her documentary *Pornocracy* (2017), Ovidie reveals that webcamming company LiveJasmin—headquartered in Amsterdam—
has an annual turnover of US$305 million. It considers itself to be merely a tech
company, providing a platform on which members and models meet. And yet
the site hosts two million models worldwide, based predominantly in Romania and Colombia, who have an average monthly income of US$1,400 (Ovidie
2017). Small producers cannot always make their way through major marketing channels and instead must rely on global distributors for visibility and
exposure. The unequal power in trading relationships brings exploitation in
negotiating licensing terms and conditions and means that wealth remains
with the global distributors rather than the local producers.

In their examination of pornography as a global creative industry, Rebecca
Sullivan and Alan McKee (2015) note that the globalization of the production,
distribution, and consumption of pornography now poses challenges for workplace health and safety. Noting that existing production hubs in Montreal, Los
Angeles, and Amsterdam are now being rivaled by emerging centers such as in
Budapest, where the cost of production is cheaper, Sullivan and McKee argue
that concerns over exploitation in the supply chain are being met in part by
the unionizing and collectivizing of sex workers throughout the world advocating for rights, freedom from discrimination, and access to services. Notably,
they call for governments and international NGOs to support both sex worker
rights and fair trade pornographies (39–43).

If porn producers and distributors are invested in fair trade, it requires
more than ensuring fair labor practices and paying a fair price to license the
content. Greater equity in trading relationships and power dynamics is necessary. A fair trade approach might include agreed-on minimum prices that
cover a "living wage" for workers, a "social premium" to cover community
projects (governed by democratic cooperatives of workers), direct purchasing
to cut out the middlemen, terms and conditions set by local producers and
performers, or the signing of long-term partnerships for improved income

FIGURE 6.4. In 2021 the BIPOC Adult Industry Collective ran a microgrant program to provide monetary aid to performers impacted by the COVID-19 pandemic. The collective takes a holistic approach to their work that includes performer advocacy, education, mental health programming, financial assistance, and mutual aid. Image by BIPOC Adult Industry Collective.

security. It must also include addressing the underlying structural issues—white supremacy, imperialism, colonization—that cause these axes of marginalization to begin with.

Conflating Ethics and Legality

To complicate the existing linguistic slippage in descriptions of green, organic, and fair trade content, popular discourse frequently conflates ethics and legality. At their most rudimentary, some marketing descriptors assume that ethical pornography must be legally produced and that legally produced pornography must be ethical. Yet neither of these things is true. As I demonstrated in chapter 2, performers have developed comprehensive ethical standards in contexts where production remains criminalized. Because legal frameworks are usually out of touch with performer needs, pornography can be produced in accordance with the law but remain unethical (performers can experience racist taglines, poor pay, or transphobic sets with no legal recourse). Law is rarely synonymous with ethics.

In some cases, platforms make simplistic claims about legality that are hard to substantiate. For example, PiggyBankGirls, a crowdfunding site launched in 2014 where sex workers could post erotic photos for donations, committed to operating in a way where there were "fair and legal work conditions for everybody involved" (Tarrant 2016, 166–67). But it is unclear how such platforms determine whether their users' content is produced legally, considering that the legality of an image may differ according to who produced it and the jurisdiction in which it was filmed, distributed, and downloaded. PiggyBankGirls promoted their concept of "fair trade pornography" as being "against child pornography, sodomy, [and] violence" (PiggyBankGirls, n.d.), although it is unclear what prohibiting anal sex has to do with fair trade. The former tube site Ethixxx.com marketed "licensed, ethically produced adult content" and promoted itself as "Pro-Porn. Anti-Exploitation." These labels define fair trade and ethical pornographies by what they are *not*.

While these slogans may be well intentioned, they present a simplistic understanding of legality, exploitation, and consent. Consent is not as simple as filling out a model release form (2257 Form), checking performer ID, or shooting a behind-the-scenes interview. Whether content is consensual could depend on the specific labor conditions, pay rates, and agreements of each performer. It is not something that is static or transactional, but a dynamic process that can change and move. Whether content is legal could depend on country-specific case law and legislation that fluctuates over time with changing community standards (for example, around BDSM); in some places, ensuring legal working conditions would necessitate significant law reform among right-wing governments. What constitutes exploitation (aside from the fact that all work under capitalism is inherently exploitative) could depend on housing and health care policies that impact the safety and well-being of performers. Are performers facing a rental crisis? Can they access free health care? Can they afford their medication? These sorts of social factors impact people's decisions around work. Platforms' claims that they are fair, legal, or nonexploitative therefore depend on multiple factors outside their control, factors that require political action and attention.

When they define themselves by what they are *not*, some platforms reinforce false binaries between force and choice, victimhood and empowerment, trafficking and freedom. Some overcompensate for porn stigma by donating to various causes that "legitimize" them. For example, the UK Ethical Porn Partnership (2015, n.p.) claimed it would "channel funds to anti-trafficking, anti-sexual violence and sex education initiatives, as well as taking an unequivocal stand on condemning child abuse imagery, and all non-consensual sexually explicit material." However, racialized and migrant sex workers have documented ongoing problems with the anti-trafficking movement. They have argued that current responses to slavery and trafficking work to strengthen a criminal justice system and a carceral state but do not actually improve their lives, agency, or options (Kim and Jeffreys 2013; Butterfly Asian and Migrant Sex Workers Support Network 2018). Organizations such as the National Center on Sexual Exploitation (NCOSE, formerly called Morality in Media) claims that it is fighting sex trafficking and sexual exploitation but frequently advocates against porn, sex work, same-sex marriage, and sex education.

Elizabeth Bernstein (2010) refers to anti-trafficking campaigns as a form of "militarized humanitarianism" and "carceral feminism" (45). Through targeted policing, immigration raids, and deportation, anti-trafficking interventions often disadvantage the people they espouse to protect, leaving them with debt and no means to repay it (Global Alliance against Trafficking in Women 2007; Kempadoo and Doezema 1998, 46–47). "Rescue" programs relocate sex workers to lower paid feminized work (such as sewing) for their supposed rehabilitation—as part of what Elena Shih (2023) calls "a moral economy of low-wage women's work" (82). Migrant sex workers have argued that their working conditions would instead be improved by safe, legal pathways to migrate for sex work, translated visa materials, and equitable access to industrial rights protections without threat of arrest or deportation.

Loose concepts of what constitutes ethical porn further gatekeep *who* can participate instead of looking at the structural conditions in which it is produced. One comedy video on YouTube suggests that *organic porn* means using "well adjusted" performers from "solid homes" who have not experienced childhood trauma (Cauvin 2016). The presumption that cruelty-free pornography would source performers with no histories of abuse or mental health issues is a problematic one given that, globally, one in three women experience violence in their lifetime and the global prevalence of anxiety and depression is increasing. Such puritan approaches blame individuals for structural oppressions and make paternalistic assumptions about who has agency and capacity to make decisions over their own bodies. Sex work can be survival work, an alternative to straight work, and a way for people to reclaim their body, decisions, narratives, and boundaries, including after assault, abuse, or violence. This urge, as Gala Vanting put it, to "stamp our porn performers as 100 percent not trafficked so that we can feel like ethical consumers" alleviates the conscience of distributors instead of equipping them to challenge the underlying factors—economic inequality, racist border policies, criminalization of sex work, gendered violence, or lack of social support. What does this do to our sexual imaginary if there is no room for the intimacies of people who live in the gray areas, who have sexual stories to tell from their axes of marginalization? Instead of distancing themselves from the people trying to survive criminalization and late-stage capitalism, platforms could be fighting the carceral, violent structures that create their precarity.

Rubber Stamps

One of the challenges of indie pornographies is that they seek to intervene in the market (transforming its value system) while simultaneously participating in it. This is the tension of fair trade generally. Fair trade coffee seeks to modify trade relationships as well as place certified coffee in mainstream retail outlets (Taylor 2005, 129–30). The risk for porn producers is that the marketing of indie porn, while it simplifies consumer choice, does not necessarily change the regulatory frameworks. Market-based interventions and proactive initiatives like voluntary industry codes do not absolve the need to repeal state criminal laws, a task that is largely left to sex worker rights organizations. Unless they also compel consumers to mobilize and engage in political advocacy, market initiatives can act as a means for consumer self-actualization and identity making at the expense of material change.

There have been international attempts to establish formally codified criteria for ethical pornography through a literal stamping of approved products, registering of businesses, and creating of oversight bodies. In the United States, the Adult Performer Advocacy Committee (APAC), a California body established in 2014 and made up of porn performers, launched an APAC Stamp, which they described in 2018 as "an approval system which gives performers guidance on the companies, agents, and outside professionals who follow guidelines in order to maintain ethical work practices that protect the rights and safety of performers in the adult entertainment industry" (Adult Performer Advocacy Committee, n.d.a). At the time, the website included a reporting form whereby the committee confidentially documented any reported issues or concerns with APAC Stamp holders with the aim of addressing violations of performer rights. They continue to provide organized representation for performers as well as resources and referrals to adult-friendly therapy and banking services. In the United Kingdom, the Ethical Porn Partnership (EPP) was a coalition of producers and performers seeking better working conditions, fair pay, and greater transparency in contracts for porn performers. When first established, the partnership's primary goals were to create a regulatory body and stamp certifying best practices for consumer confidence and to produce a concrete register of approved sites.

The journey of the EPP shows how the development of ethical codes involves political contestation and nuanced deliberation. While their draft goals have been refined over time, the first iteration circulated among stakeholders in 2015 included clear and accurate labeling of content, transparency around distribution, good working conditions, and performer choice on safer sex—all aspects that align with the ethic of care approach voiced by my participants in chapter 2. However, they also included criteria that content must be of good quality, with good production values, as well as innovative when it comes to scripting, design, or casting. In cases like this, ethics can easily become confused with aesthetics, becoming about high-quality casting, scripting, and camera skills. Subsequent draft goals of the EPP were amended to remove the requirement for legality and to include royalties paid to performers and psychological/emotional support for performers. While the partnership paused operations in 2018, their process illustrates how conversations about ethics remain ongoing.

Of course, performers ought to be leading discussions and setting industry standards about what constitute best-practice ethical sets. This becomes more complicated if they decide to become an accreditation or certification body, making decisions about monitoring, enforcement, licensing, and compliance. The codification process, as well as the certification process, becomes a process of inclusion and exclusion. Gala Vanting commented to me: "I think that there is just no possibility of creating a standardized ethical code for feminist porn, or ethical porn, because ethics and feminism are locally based, locally variant. What I value in my intersection of identities as a feminist and a whole bunch of other things isn't going to be what is valued by the next person. . . . As soon as you create a code like this, identities and performances start to drop through it because it is full of holes; it's always going to be full of holes."

While chapters 1 and 2 demonstrated the value of generating localized ethical codes, the process of certifying them brings additional considerations. Naomi Klein's work on the ethics of consumption reminds us that we should be cautious in letting businesses drive this movement rather than focusing on government responsibility to decriminalize production. We should be careful that our discussions about ethics in pornography do not become, per Klein (2010), "glorified ethical shopping guides: how-to's on saving the world through boycotts and personal lifestyle choices. Are your sneakers 'No Sweat'? Your rugs 'Rugmark'? Your soccer balls 'Child Free'? Is your moisturizer 'Cruelty Free'? Your coffee 'Fair Trade'?" (428). Is your pornography ethical?

This is not to say that there is no people power in boycott. Consumers ought to support their local indie producers directly and get involved in their political campaigns. Similarly, it is not to say that there is no room for ethical codes—industry workers are usually better placed to develop internal standards than governments. However, none of this supplants the need for infrastructural change. The risk of displacing this responsibility on the consumer is that governments never actually decriminalize, put worker protections into place, or introduce antidiscrimination laws because they assume that the market will simply regulate itself via its own internal industry codes of conduct.

In this scenario, basic labor rights then become something to capitalize on and profit from—a marker to distinguish one's brand. Decriminalization falls off the policy agenda, and attention is diverted from industrial rights toward consumer lifestyle choice. The movement becomes ethical porn (a market-based mechanism) rather than a series of political demands: decriminalizing sex work (a call for legislative change), strengthening antitrust laws (to limit the market power of big tech), cracking down on monopolies (by penalizing practices of buying up competitors), requiring tube sites to compensate content producers (to create a more level playing field), or providing adequate social support (to reduce worker exploitation).

Brand or Movement?

References to pornography as green, organic, cruelty-free, and fair trade can be useful signals to discerning consumers. The trend reflects a broader awareness of how media products sit within global economic infrastructures as well as a desire to improve the material conditions of production. These marketing strategies ensure that indie pornographies do not drop off the consumer radar altogether and that indie content remains visible. They are fruitful because they compel us to consider the next question: If we are thinking about labor, we need to be thinking about transnational trade relationships and distribution power. If we are thinking about cruelty-free production, we need to be thinking about our use of nonhuman animal products and environmental justice. If we are thinking about fair wages and sustainability, we need to consider how our toys, equipment, and materials are being made, and by whom.

But while such labels might be useful to producers in reaching their consumer base, differentiating their product, carving out a niche, or justifying a premium, the real test is in the experiences of performers. In chapter 5 I detailed the gap between performer experiences and producer expectations in authentic content. Regardless, an obligation still remains on governments to radically reform the legal, economic, and technical environments that shape production. An ethical rubber stamp does not solve the problems associated with criminalization, discrimination, or stigma. At worst, it risks producing a hierarchy between those who receive a tick of approval and those who cannot afford to comply with the criteria. People who can already afford media exposure, who work in legal jurisdictions, who are citizens rather than migrants or temporary visa holders, who own registered companies, who are willing to record their identification on file, who perform vanilla sex acts or who have access to quality production equipment that makes their content appear professional and palatable: They are the ones who overwhelmingly receive public acclaim, accreditation, work opportunities, and the protective factors of mainstream approval. They are the ones who occupy the public space, set the ethical boundaries, and attract the revenue. We ought to consider who is left out by these projects and what perspectives and experiences we miss.

In our interview, Gala Vanting reported that although she appreciated these initiatives "because it speaks to the fact that this movement is gaining momentum," she did not feel hopeful about the thought of codifying ethics. Rather, she felt that this push toward standardization threatened a movement that ought to have its strength in differences: "I am also quite concerned about and fascinated by the tendency to greenwash the industry and produce this sort of uncomplicated 'It's very simple: I will just tell you that it's ethical, and you will buy it and know that it's ethical.' I'm concerned about this, and the ways in which ethics are marketed, and I think that we can look to other industries like food to get some clues about how this might go awry."

Although there can be value in the development of a shared, normative ethics (which I identified in chapters 1 and 2, for example), when we look to other social movements an effective aspect of resistance is that they are nonbranded and decentralized. In writing about Reclaim the Streets, a movement for community ownership of public space, Richard J. F. Day (2005) describes the tactics used as being open to everybody, this being one of the key factors in their efficacy: "They tend to spread in a viral way, with no one taking ownership or attempting to exercise control over how they are implemented" (19). The

FIGURE 6.5. Annie Sprinkle and Beth Stephens's eco-sexual banner for Pride 2015. Annie and Beth have created multimedia art projects about love, sex, and queer ecologies together since 2002, including their *Wedding to the Earth* and the Ecosex Manifesto in 2008. Image courtesy of Annie Sprinkle and Beth Stephens.

movement Food Not Bombs offers another example of the benefits of decentralization. Instead of a centralized organization, the movement comprises an international network with multiple collectives operating autonomously. As Ben Holtzman, Craig Hughes, and Kevin Van Meter (2007) describe it, "The decentralized nature of FNB has also been fundamental to its continued importance. Each chapter (of which there are currently over two hundred internationally) is guided by the basic ideas of the group—non-violence, vegetarianism, direct action, and direct democracy—but functions autonomously" (50).

This model offers local communities avenues for direct participation rather than concentrating control in one chapter. When movements become centralized and incorporated as NGOs, they can lose their original impetus. In the documentary *How to Change the World: The Revolution Will Not Be Organised* (2015), the original Greenpeace founders speak about how ego, fame, administration, and incorporation diluted their original goals of bearing witness and direct action. Instead of a proliferation of decentralized offices around the world operating independently, they document how Greenpeace established a central headquarters and funds came to be spent on CEO salary and administration to keep personnel in employment. Disputes about who owned the name, chapters suing one another, and original activists wanting credit meant that the movement was then destabilized by investments in ego, fame, and the job market: "Our goal was not to make the organization famous; our goal was to make nature famous" (Rothwell 2015).

Indie pornography has more to gain as a from-the-ground-up, grassroots, nonbranded movement than as an exclusive, avant-garde club. The ongoing industry debates around what constitutes fair trade, organic, and ethical porn are instructive in that they build a more comprehensive vocabulary for both consumers and regulators to understand porn production. But achieving these political aspirations requires something more than self-congratulatory status distinction. The use of fair trade terminology—and its co-optation by white filmmakers and larger companies—has an obvious class dimension. One Twitter user, for example, made fun of this trend by using the hashtag #wholefaps, a play on whole foods, tweeting, "I'm so bougie that my porn gotta be ethical, locally sourced and fair trade before I think about masturbating to it." This tweet recognizes that for many, porn's appeal may be in its dirt, its cheapness, and its taboo status. Some producers insist that they would never call their work *feminist porn* because the term presumes there is a correct way for women to enjoy it (DeGenevieve 2014, 194). The next chapter turns to consider how this push toward recognition manifests in the path toward identifying the nebulous category of "good" pornography.

Part IV

tensions

Your Stigma, Your Labor

The space is buzzing, the lights are dim, and a life-size image of Jiz Lee climbing out from inside a giant pink vulva is projected onto the wall. It's the cover of their edited anthology *Coming Out Like a Porn Star*, and we are holding two book launches in Gadigal Country (Sydney) and Naarm (Melbourne). There are three Australian essays included, and I am chairing a panel of porn performers to discuss the book's themes: pornography, protection, and privacy.

The contents of the book are heavy. Coming out is not new for porn performers—so many of us have come out at various stages of our lives as queer, trans, neurodivergent, mad, disabled, kinky, HIV positive, or polyamorous. The risks are not unknown to us—the threat of eviction, sexual assault, barriers to employment, custody battles, discrimination, service denial, and prohibitions on migration—and provide real incentives to stay in the closet.

Visibility is associated with both privilege and risk, and this event is not immune. People are live tweeting the Naarm launch, and though we film the panel discussion, we decide not to film the Q and A to avoid any impromptu discussion of legalities being caught on public record.

The whole conversation feels emotional. It's personal. We make our way through muddy terrain, discussing the privacy implications of increased surveillance and the strain of coming out on familial and interpersonal relationships. An audience member asks what happens when coming out goes wrong. Gala talks about a former partner who didn't want the mother of his child to be a sex worker. I speak about my dad's comment that no parent in the history of the world would be happy, much less proud, if their child had done what I had. The most heartbreaking realization for many of us has been when our loved ones just don't have the investment in that process of "undoing" what they think they know about porn. Even though we can provide the resources, the patience, and the destigmatizing language, it is of little use if a person is not engaged in their own process of unpacking stigma. It stings to find out we aren't worth the effort.

We all have misgivings and regrets about the mistakes we have each made in coming out. In their essay, Jiz reflects that when they first came out to their family, they tried to play up what they understood to be more socially acceptable porn performances. They were too insistent on making comparisons to independent films like *Shortbus* that seemed more respectable. Gala similarly describes how internalized stigma manifested in the ways she described her work. Performing in "alternative porn," the presence of body hair and not looking like a "porn star" offered a virtue that mainstream sites did not. It attracted curiosity, marvel, and even congratulations, "allowing some of their core stigmas to perpetuate." I think back to my own experience of media and how the labels of *feminist porn* and *queer porn* offered me a protective buffer, making my work seem more palatable and giving me a platform in the media. On these occasions, our tactics risked furthering stigma rather than dismantling it, reproducing stereotypes rather than challenging them, and not doing enough to unpack the stratification of stigma across pornography and sex work more generally.

As our language and politics evolved, the labor continued. Passing the microphone between us, it is evident how much work sex workers do in other people's emotional regulation. We grapple with the question of how to allow people time and space to grow while also looking after ourselves and still earning enough to live. Coming out involves added emotional and educative labor on top of the labor of sex work. It often means managing other people's immediate gut responses, deescalating their anger, and quelling their greatest fears about pornography. It's confronting.

Gala has a solution. Instead of spending her energy educating others, she chooses to invest it in "coming in," in cultivating her own communities of care, reframing her whore family as central rather than peripheral, and choosing not to own other people's discomforts. It's straightforward, she says. "Your stigma, your labor." That process of undoing, unlearning, and unpacking is not ours to repeatedly facilitate. Whorephobia is not ours to apologize for, or cower from, or compromise on. Our communities do not require external approval. Your stigma, your labor. I wish someone would put this on a T-shirt.

7

Good Porn

Stigma, Respectability, and Diversity Politics

What constitutes *good* porn? This was the question I asked students at a porn masterclass at the University of Western Australia in 2019. I had flown to Perth to hold a lecture and workshop with fellow porn scholars Alan McKee and Paul Maginn. It was a genuine question and one that took its cue from Annie Sprinkle's 1999 film *Herstory of Porn*, where she famously declared that the answer to bad porn was simply to make better porn. More recently, producers, consumers, and regulators are calling for the production of better porn as a solution to the supposed problem of pornography. Feminist filmmaker Erika Lust even titled her book *Good Porn: A Woman's Guide* (2010), in which she provides alternative depictions to the "diminished, impoverished vision of sexuality" she perceived in pornography (11). Violet Blue's *Smart Girl's Guide to Porn* (2006) aims to assist women "interested in finding good porn" (xiii). Even governments are searching for criteria on what kind of content ought to be permissible.

In this chapter I argue that the focus on *good* porn and *better* porn can become a red herring when deployed in conversations about regulation. I argue this for three reasons. First, creating distinctions between good porn and bad porn inevitably reinforces porn stigma and creates new hierarchies and regimes of criminalization. The politics of who gets to define good content is heavily contested, especially in law reform contexts. Too often, the aesthetics of good porn is based on middle-class notions of taste, cisnormative conceptualizations of naturalness, and regulators' sense of disgust. Second, the project of creating good porn in a neoliberal marketplace lends itself to all kinds of diversity washing, the expectation being that visibility is sufficient, resulting in an overemphasis on content regulation at the expense of labor rights. Third, placing the onus on producers to create better content distracts regulators from large-scale, infrastructural changes they could be making to prompt legal, social, and cultural change toward a more just and equitable sexual society.

This is not to say that normative projects to improve pornography are not valid—we should strive for queer, feminist, anti-racist, disability justice, and worker-centered approaches to porn production. But this generative and critical work has been underway within the industry for at least fifty years. And these reflexive works in progress should not be mistaken for simplified codified standards. Instead of erasing the long and sophisticated history of indie porn and viewing heteronormative and misogynistic pornography as representative, governments could be amplifying the rich independent content already being produced and facilitating the conditions for it to flourish. They could be producing comprehensive sex and relationship education, repealing criminal laws on production, and addressing inequitable distribution. If regulators, parents, and consumers want *good* porn, then they ought to invest in equitable production and distribution environments.

Good, Bad, and Disgusting

In our porn class, we asked participants what they thought constituted good, bad, and disgusting pornography. Our motivation was not to produce concrete categories, but to elicit how people's personal and visceral responses impacted their values. Our theory was that, in evaluating pornography, personal taste is often conflated with value and ethics. If a person thinks something is disgusting, they are more likely to think it is bad and that perhaps that it should be illegal. (As discussed in the vignette "What Happened to Our Squirt?," when politicians held a private screening of BDSM pornography in the Australian Parliament, their reaction of revulsion was precisely how fetish material became prohibited.) Further, we thought that a key problem in discussions on good porn and bad porn was the assumption that everyone is using the same criteria. But what constitutes good porn might differ dramatically depending on whom you ask.

In deciding whether pornography is good or bad, does one distinguish by virtue of representation, aesthetics, production values, educative function, or visceral response? Is it enough that the participants consent? Is it relevant whether the content is lawful? Does it matter how it is consumed? We wanted to make transparent the value systems that lie behind these terms. Further, we wanted to consider who was at the forefront of people's minds when they were deliberating. What is good involves different considerations for producers, performers, consumers, and regulators. Producers may be concerned with narratives and representation; performers may be concerned with contractual expectations and workplace conditions; consumers may be concerned with the accessibility of content that affirms their bodies and desires; regulators may be concerned with classifying content, minimizing risk, and reducing liability.

When one begins to unpack the term *good porn*, it is easy to run into trouble. Some might suggest that good porn includes content that has an educative function or eroticizes safer sex. But arguably it is the government's role to roll out population-level sexual health programming, and pornography—a medium that both produces and reflects culture—ought to reflect the real, messy ways that human beings interact instead of being held to higher standards than other media. Does it make porn less good if its function is purely arousal? This assumption highlights how debates on pornography routinely devalue pleasure. It is easy to see here how a compulsion to find good porn can replicate key stigmas about pornography that have been driven by regulators— that sexually explicit material lacks artistic, cultural, scientific, or literary merit and that eliciting arousal renders it dirt-for-dirt's sake and nothing more. A further expectation about what constitutes good porn is that the performers ought to be enjoying themselves. Although this fantasy might relieve consumer guilt, as we saw in the chapter on authenticity, it makes unrealistic assumptions about the experiences of laborers under capitalism.

My concern is that the discursive category of good porn is fundamentally concerned with respectability. It is a means by which predominantly middle-class, cisgender, white women are marketing their products through a language of repudiation: We are not *that*. The movement for better porn risks unwittingly accepting regulatory hang-ups about porn's lack of value. If not unpacked, *good porn* becomes shorthand for high-brow stylistic conventions. In turn, shorthand use of *good porn* can be disciplinary in itself, stigmatizing pornographies that fall outside it. While we ought to interrogate the ethics of cultural production (especially the gendered, racialized, and classed aspects of how desire is produced and reflected), crude definitions of good porn have the potential to become regulatory weapons used to set legal parameters that gatekeep who can create porn. Historically, the removal of transgressive material from pornography has resulted in the loss of much queer material from porn archives (Strub 2019). Also: Aren't there surprising and unexpected pleasures to be found in *bad* porn?

Porn Stigma and Respectability Politics

As indie pornographers venture toward better porn, it is instructive to turn to the relationship between porn stigma and respectability politics. The term "politics of respectability" was coined by Evelyn Brookes Higginbotham in her book *Righteous Discontent* (1993) to describe how some African American women in the United States appealed to white society to demonstrate their respectability and refute stereotypes in order to access services, resources, education, and social mobility. In employing a politics of respectability, members of marginalized communities attempt to gain acceptance from the mainstream by illustrating their compatibility and sameness rather than challenging mainstream values for their failure to accept or embrace difference. Respectability politics has been employed by many social groups, including in gay and lesbian politics, in an attempt to repudiate sexual shame and has been critiqued for the way it privileges an elite few, maintains social hierarchies, and further stigmatizes those who do not, will not, or cannot assimilate. Respectability—a tool by which to renounce or distance oneself from stigma—has a long history in debates around pornography and sexuality. In her book *Formations of Class and Gender: Becoming Respectable* (2002), Beverly Skeggs describes respectability as "a property of the middle-class individuals defined against the masses" (3), a mechanism by which to identify those in need of control, to intervene in the lives of the working class, and to justify attempts to supposedly rescue women from professions with little social legitimacy or deviant sexuality.

Historically sex work has been viewed as a kind of dirty work, which "a significant portion of society as distasteful, disgusting, dangerous, demeaning, immoral, or contemptible" (Ashforth and Kreiner 2014, 82). In her in-depth study of porn stigma, Georgina Voss (2015) argues that stigma shapes every aspect of the pornography industry, from pejorative stereotypes to the use of 2257 forms and obscenity laws. It is in this context that projects to identify and defend good porn emerge. In an attempt to distance themselves from the stigma of pornography, some producers have turned to professionalization. Voss writes that "the promise of 'mainstreaming' is threaded through the pornography industry's history" relayed through hopeful stories that industry members would one day "become socially legitimate and escape stigma related sanctions" (59). The project of mainstreaming is a project of legitimization, offering producers business success and social reward rather than censure. Current investments in finding good porn and better porn should be situated in light of porn's sizable history of stigma.

The irony is that this push toward respectability and professionalization sits in direct contrast to a history of pornography that is characterized by rebellious, seditious content and regulatory contest. Pornography is not meant to be respectable. Part of its appeal is its challenge to boundaries of acceptability and decency. Its history is characterized by the ruling class wanting to keep corruptive content out of the hands of the masses. In Lynn Hunt's (1993) history of pornography, she describes how regulators were preoccupied with heresy and iconoclasm. As she writes, pornography "was defined over time by the conflicts between writers, artists and engravers on the one side and spies, policemen, clergymen and state officials on the other" (11). Throughout modernity in Europe, pornography came into being as a regulatory category out of the boldness of artists to "test the boundaries of the 'decent' and the aim of the ecclesiastical and secular police to regulate it" (10).

The kinds of cultural erasure we are witnessing now with the sanitizing of online pornography can be seen as a shortcoming of mainstreaming. Pornography has historically been a means to mock the middle and upper classes: Laura Kipnis (1992) describes how *Hustler* magazine emerged in 1974 as a working-class alternative to the classier gentleman's magazine *Playboy* established in 1953. Constance Penley (2004) fondly describes *Hustler*'s "white trash sensibilities . . . deliberately stupid humour, savaging of the middle-class and professional codes of decorum, raunchiness and sluttiness" (313). Penley points out that during what's called the golden era of pornography in the 1970s, when big-budget feature-length films were released in cinemas, the bawdy humor, lewd language, and antiestablishment sentiment that was so renowned in pornographies of the 1960s and earlier stag film era tend to "drop out" of porn (320). As films sought to reach a broader demographic, they lost this quality, becoming more technically produced and socially conservative.

However, the advent of home video technology in the 1980s began to again democratize the content. As Penley describes that period, "Fortunately, in the eighties and nineties, porn films got trashy. . . . [M]any more people could produce it, even those who lacked money, technical training, or a sense of cinema aesthetics." But as pornography became mass produced throughout the 1990s and 2000s, it began to lose its "historical continuity with avant-garde

FIGURE 7.1. *Hole Theory*, produced by Aorta Films and starring "hole expert" Ashley Paige and "expert hole" Corey More, explores the depth and magnificence of holes. Aorta Films describes itself as "LUSTY, OPULENT, ETHICAL FUCKERY." Image by Aorta Films.

revolutionary art, populist struggles, or any kind of counter-cultural impulses" (312). Although the advent of digital technologies has brought the potential for diverse content, the regulatory, economic, and technological environment has encouraged the dominance of sanitized, risk-averse, respectable porn.

Good Porn / Bad Porn

Producers who have an investment in distinguishing themselves from bad porn have widely disparate interpretations of what constitutes it. In my interviews, producers described different aspects they sought to resist in rejecting what they view as mainstream pornography. Some critiques related to cinematography and visual language. For example, rejections of pornography that prioritized cisgender male heterosexual fantasies, a focus on fellatio at the expense of cunnilingus, and a failure to explore women's subjectivities. Others related to the idealization of particular body types, narrow beauty norms, body hair trends, and cosmetic surgeries. Some producers took issue with performative scripting, repetitive formulas, and unrealistic scenarios, referring to mainstream pornography as "fake." Conversely, others saw it as too real, concerned that it was increasingly degrading and "getting more and more violent." Some objections were related to a producer's personal taste in production quality, including poor lighting or sets that looked "cheap" or "tacky." Lastly, some critiques referred to mainstream content as "clinical" or missing "passion and anticipation."

Some of these sentiments reflect an Australian cultural ambivalence toward glamour, commerce, and celebrity culture, which is unimpressed by fame and stardom and more likely to celebrate amateur, local, and homegrown content. Producers were skeptical of the exportation, saturation, and centering of American conventions and style. In part, they reflect feminist desires to rewrite and reinscribe sexual scripts and subjectivities and broaden the repetitive gender and racial narratives in previous content. But they also represent the influence of anti-pornography and anti-trans feminisms in their understanding of gender presentations and relationship to surgeries, advocating for middle-class, white, and cisgendered ideals of what natural sex and natural bodies look like.

In contrast to producers, the performers I interviewed spoke less about good porn and bad porn and more about concerns about working conditions, labor exploitation, or the ability to be included in contract negotiations. Performers were often critical of the term *mainstream pornography*. Because they often work as freelancers across multiple productions, they have more nuanced understandings about the different set values and production ethics. When Courtney Trouble appeared at the Perv Queerotic Film Festival in Sydney, they spoke instead about "corporate porn," reflecting the business structures behind production. When Jiz Lee spoke the following year, they referred to resources, budget, and distribution networks as being material factors distinguishing mainstream from indie porn.

Performers I spoke to used more specific phrases, such as "heteronormative porn," to describe their work in large commercial contexts. They pointed out that a number of feminist directors have now infiltrated mainstream production, noting Dana Vespoli's work at Evil Angel and Tristan Taormino's work at Vivid. Some performers were eager to emphasize the similarities rather than the differences between mainstream and independent pornographies and were dubious about empty rhetoric that promised good porn but did not deliver. Angela White, who works across a range of indie and corporate spaces, called the distinction "counterproductive" and pointed out that "just because it's a female director or producer doesn't necessarily make it feminist. And just because it's a male director or producer doesn't necessarily make it, you know, misogynistic or patriarchal."

These conversations about what constitutes good porn also have potential policy implications. For example, a 2016 Australian Senate report (following a committee inquiry into online pornography access) discussed the option of legalizing "ethical pornography," providing a preliminary definition of what might be included in such a category: "This pornography would be produced with consent and have content that depicts respectful relationships and does not include violence" (43). This framing of ethical pornography as something distinct from mainstream pornography (as if mainstream pornography does not involve consent) is clearly problematic. Should all pornography be required to depict respectful relationships, and what would that look like? Would this be interpreted to mean romantically involved couples? Would a prohibition on violence still permit consensual BDSM, rough sex, or dirty talk? If this version of ethical pornography becomes a special category that can be legally produced, what then happens to content (including content produced within ethics of care, participation, and accountability) that features BDSM practices, casual relationships, sex with multiple partners or in groups, differently abled sex using various body parts and orifices, serodiscordant or raw sex, all of which could suddenly fall outside the legal definition?

By contrast, some producers deliberately seek to capture the full, messy complexity of human sexuality. Aorta Films and the A. O. Movement Collective (2019), for example, describe how porn work involves both risk and care: they describe their film (W/HOLE) as an exploration of how "queer porn can evolve trauma into orgasm, and grief into politically radical, transformative, body-based joy." This unsanitized approach is unafraid to honestly address how grief, trauma, sex, and joy often converge in unpredictable ways.

My concern with the haste to find good porn is not to stifle consumers' navigation of online content. In an information age, a key skill is sifting through content, part of which involves developing a vocabulary for discerning between sexual media based on different ethics and values. A key task for producers is enhancing their search engine optimization so that their content is searchable for their intended audiences. My concern, rather, is the slippage between "good," "better," "ethical," and "legal," understanding who and what is excluded (and subsequently stigmatized or even criminalized). This is not hyperbole: Attempts to introduce legislation in California that would allow consumers to sue performers who do not use condoms and legislation in the United Kingdom that interpreted BDSM as "injury" are forewarnings for the future.

The preoccupation with good, better, and ethical pornography operates as a respectability bid to regulators by appealing to common stereotypes. It erases a vibrant political history of provocative pornography and detracts from actual steps parliaments could take to decriminalize production, improve work health and safety, or provide relevant sex education. My participants generally agreed that the production and sale of pornography should be decriminalized, but beyond that, some questioned why porn should be available only to those aged eighteen and not those aged sixteen, who can legally consent to sex. Others questioned why sexually explicit media was situated as its own specific classification category when it could simply be integrated into other forms of media (pointing out that violence appears throughout media and does not have its own special category). The good/bad porn binary ultimately risks creating a new version of Gayle Rubin's ([1984] 2011) charmed circle, with good porn in the inner circle (coupled, condomed, authentic, vanilla, heteronormative) and bad porn in the outer (gang bangs, raw, performative, kinky, queer sex)—differentiated not only on the basis of content but also on who participates. Expecting producers to make better porn operates as a diversion tactic that lets governments off the hook.

Diversity Politics

As this chapter's vignette demonstrates, good porn is sometimes described as content that includes a greater diversity of genders, sexualities, races, bodies, abilities, and ages. This investment in inclusion and diversity reflects a twentieth-century focus on identity politics and an emphasis on representation as a political strategy. In her early writing on the politics of visibility, Lisa M. Walker (1993) describes how "participants often symbolize their demands for social justice by celebrating visible signifiers of difference that have historically targeted them for discrimination" (868)—queer haircuts, for example. As a result, indie pornographies, especially queer pornographies, are often invested in representing underrepresented or misrepresented identities to provide moments of affirmation and validation. In her doctoral thesis on queer pornography, Grace Sharkey (2018) analyzes the content moderation practices of Pink and White Productions' site Crash Pad and found that identity categories were a "major organising tool" (89).

In my interviews, queer and feminist producers also described an investment in visibility and representation. Nic Holas, a queer, HIV-positive porn performer, spoke about the importance of representing HIV-positive sex on screen: "It's a basic act of queer rebellion in just putting those bodies into porn." Cat O'Nine Tails described being "really dissatisfied with the porn and the adult material and the erotica out there" and wanting to reimagine women's sexuality on screen. Morgana Muses, who began her porn career at the age of forty-seven, actively fought to recognize the agency and sexual subjectivity of mature women in pornography. In each of these instances, visibility matters—both to the performers and to the audiences.

However, performers said they were sometimes suspicious of being used for the purposes of diversity signaling. Critical race scholars have written about the limitations of diversity-and-inclusion approaches, arguing that they are an inadequate substitute for responding to structural oppressions. In her book *A Taste for Brown Sugar: Black Women in Pornography* (2014), Mireille Miller-Young writes that Black women appear in interracial and white pornography only "to the extent that they are seen as marketable" (230). Diversity signaling itself is a liberal strategy that seeks to incorporate and assimilate rather than dismantle the structures that oppress marginalized groups. The enthusiasm for diversity and inclusion can be seen across workplaces, institutions, and governments. Sara Ahmed (2012) describes how diversity approaches operate merely as a "symbolic commitment" used to obscure racism and institutional whiteness. It takes significant energy to do what Ahmed (2017) calls "diversity work," that is, "when you have to try to make others comfortable with the fact of your own existence" (131). Diversity work—in which Ahmed includes various forms of passing, softening, comforting, being on guard, working to appear, explaining oneself, and minimizing difference—carries an emotional toll: "Your body becomes a performance indicator / You become a tick in a box" (126).

In a piece for the Swiss porn magazine POV, one of my interviewees, Gala Vanting (2015a), writes that some producers are not necessarily prepared for the accountability that comes with using "diversity" and "inclusivity" in their advertising, noting that inclusivity is "a massive responsibility" that goes far beyond "organic fruit and coconut water on set" (5). She continues:

> Queer/POC/disabled/trans and gender diverse folks, in addition to being babes capable of fiercely beautiful expressions of eroticism, can help a producer to look inclusive, which has become a saleable quality now that we've begun marketing ethical and diverse and real to feminist porn audiences. If a producer appears to be getting on board with inclusivity, whether they've adopted some affirmative action–style casting, or employed the current Hot Piece of queer porn for their new project, they can stand to get porno brownie points for representing bodies they didn't before. But unless this sits alongside some other, more contained, not publicly-visible actions, I'm not giving you any points, and neither are a lot of my colleagues and audience members.

Diversity may well constitute one aspect of good porn, but it can hardly stop there. The purpose of inclusion ought not to be appropriation and assimilation, but to actively listen and act upon new perspectives on how to change operational structures, visual conventions, and the machinery of the business itself. While the substitution of positive images for negative ones can form an attempt at "righting the balance," replacing dominant, abject, and reductionist representations with a more complex range of experiences, we also need to consider whether, as cultural theorist Stuart Hall (2013) asks, such images "simply *appropriate* 'difference' into a spectacle in order to sell a product?" (263). In her examination of alt erotica site SuicideGirls, Shoshana Magnet (2007) argues that the company still prioritizes profit rather than structural change and that the limited representations of tattooed, punk women merely reflect the fact that "content diversity is good for business" (577). As defined by the porn performers I interviewed, inclusion was not about tokenistic, but self-deterministic representation; as discussed in chapter 8, it was about having an active stake in the design, decisions, and ownership.

Pornography is often cited as being more diverse than mainstream media in terms of the bodies, genders, and sexualities it represents. Some turn to pornography as a site where their bodies are desired and celebrated as an escape from the stigmatized representations so prevalent in mainstream entertainment. But visibility is not enough here: Pornographies feature high visibility of trans performers, people with disabilities, and older performers but often via problematic tropes and stereotypes. Trans porn performers have repeatedly spoken about their misgendering, transphobic labeling, and unrealistic expectations of how they ought to perform or experience pleasure. People who are amputees have described the sting of desire that is marked by fetishization and titillation. To move beyond tokenism, diverse porn must honor what Mireille Miller-Young (2014) calls "black people's sustained battle for sexual subjectivity, agency and autonomy" and "aspirations for erotic sovereignty" (29). If we want pornography to be what Miller-Young calls "a site for progressive, antiracist, and antisexist politics" then we need both "multidimensional representations and fair work conditions" (261). Visibility, diversity, and inclusion are not enough.

In thinking about the limits of representation and identity categories, *Slit* magazine provides a useful example of a project that positions sexually explicit work as a *politics* rather than a *genre*. *Slit* is invested in remaining accountable to their communities. In the front editorial to the "Simulacra" issue (2012), the editors write, "*Slit* has always been troubled by the impossibility of being 'representative' of the communities that *Slit* envisages we are a part of. It strives to encourage contribution. But if the goal of representation is to counter the mainstream exclusion of voices, then identity-based inclusion is not enough. Regardless of who is featured in the mag, *Slit* strives to represent through politics and ethics more than identity" (3).

This building of affinity and community through politics is perhaps most evident in *Slit* magazine's title change from being a "dyke and trans" magazine to a "queer and feminist" magazine. Editors Meredith and Domino described how, for them, diverse representation meant being accountable to community, responding to criticism, and justifying their decision-making. The re-titling was a response to what Domino called "a changing way of communicating a politic." However, the process remains an adaptive one. Domino reflected:

> Even then we felt quite conflicted about the name change for the last issue—where did this leave our anti-racist politics, which is central to what motivates both of us? And our anti-capitalist politics? But at the same time we didn't want a shopping list of words. And so we wrote an editorial that explained a bit of our thought processes and our feelings about the limitations of language and labels. The process and practice of the magazine attempts to express these things, and simply adding a label that something is "feminist" doesn't make it so.

Part of approaching this as a work-in-progress is to ask self-reflexively, as Meredith and Domino do, "Why 'queer and feminist' and not 'queer and anti-racist?' A radical sex politics must be connected to a radical race, gender and class politics, and start by engaging with the responsibilities of making a magazine within the violence of ongoing colonisation within Australia" (*Slit* 2012, 3). This process of ongoing reflexivity about the connections, conditions, or experiences we might share (or not) in relation to power provides space for political actors to imagine broader alternatives than mere diversity and inclusion.

Inversion Practices

In reacting to the ambiguous and nebulous category of mainstream pornography, some producers have turned to practices of inversion and subversion as indicators of good porn. Feminist producers, for example, seek to reorient the "male gaze," a concept coined by Laura Mulvey (1975), who argued that "the determining male gaze projects its phantasy onto the female form which is styled accordingly" (11). Producers of porn for women are often concerned with reorienting this gaze, disrupting formulaic representations of women's sexuality, creating new sexual scripts through which to showcase women's points-of-view, and recognizing women as consumers (not just subjects) of erotic media. Cat

FIGURE 7.2. Glitta Supernova featured on the cover of the tenth issue of *Slit* magazine (2006). A community project focusing on local porn, politics, and culture, *Slit* is now archived at the Australian Queer Archives and the National Library of Australia. Image courtesy of *Slit* magazine. Original photograph by Cat O'Nine Tails.

O'Nine Tails said, "There's not many women shooting any erotica out there, particularly naked heterosexual men for women to look at." Another producer said, "I want to show women's pleasure. I want to show women's agency. . . . So much mainstream porn is focused on male desire, male fantasy." For her, a feminist approach meant "putting women at the forefront of my filmmaking" and including their personal fantasies, interests, and writings. In these investments we can see producers creating new visual languages, what Anne Sabo (2012) has called a "gender democratic gaze of devoted mutuality as opposed to the objectifying gaze" (53).

These practices of inversion are common cinematic techniques and can be powerful in rejecting cisgender, male-centered frameworks. Anna Brownfield, who produces feature porn films, reverses gendered and sexual scripts with the intent of exposing them. Her work depicts sexualized cis-heterosexual men, featuring extended scenes and close-ups of men masturbating, being expected to ingest their own body fluids, and having anally receptive strap-on sex with cisgender women. Other producers represented women in assertive positions to counter the sheer volume of images depicting women as submissive. Cat O'Nine Tails similarly describes her intention to subvert stereotypical roles and appeal to "the female viewer" by "trying to play around with roles [so] it's not always the same old submissive woman, master dominant man."

Although practices of inversion can be pleasurable for audiences, they are not necessarily radical reimaginings of sexual power and relations. Stuart Hall (2013) reminds us that "to reverse the stereotype is not necessarily to overturn or subvert it" (261). These counter-strategies for contesting the dominant regimes of representation can be reactionary and remain within the confines of binary structures (active/passive, top/bottom, male/female). Mulvey's conception of the male gaze continues to be a dominant (and blunt) frame for understanding gender on film, especially given that images are being produced, shared, interpreted, and interacted with in more dynamic ways. Repeated reference to the male gaze can obscure the operation of the colonial and imperialist gaze, the white gaze, cisgender gaze, heterosexual gaze, and ableist gaze. Some performer-producers I interviewed had begun to distinguish their work from "porn for women" because it relied upon fixed assumptions about the category of womanhood. Helen Corday rejected a monolithic category of women's experience: "I find it very interesting when people say they're making porn for women because it does seem to play into this stereotype often of what women would want to see. I think it generalizes women as heterosexual women for a start and also fairly vanilla. . . . I like rough sex, and I think that's not often depicted in porn for women."

These endeavors can fall into the trap of presenting only what Grace Sharkey (2018) calls the "*right* kind of woman" (114), acting to flatten out and eclipse the diversity of women's desires into one-dimensional tropes. Techniques aimed at foregrounding women's pleasure can easily fall into stereotypical signifiers. Linda Williams ([1989] 1999) describes how pornography has developed conventions that seek to show "maximum visibility" and "visual evidence of the mechanical 'truth' of bodily pleasure" (94, 101). In this quest to discover the truth of sex, the spectacle of penile ejaculation (in the form of the money shot) has emerged as demonstrable, visible proof of the body's involuntary confessions (119). Trans women have described being pressured to ejaculate in scenes in order to demonstrate a physical sexual response that is intelligible to this narrow pleasure vocabulary.

G-spot ejaculation, argues Ingrid Ryberg (2008), has now become "something of a lesbian pornographic trope" (74). The depiction of G-spot ejaculation as an equivalent spectacle, with tags for squirting and gushing, can become *the* representation of pleasure. Ryberg argues that G-spot ejaculation scenes seek to prove pleasure but still within the conventions of maximum visibility (74). There remains a risk that they replace tropes of conventional porn (the come shot and close-up graphics) with new ones (squirting and strap-ons). Yet ejaculation only speaks to one specific type of sexual response. Among feminist pornographers, some have veered away from representing essentialist tropes of "what women want," epitomized by narratives, cunnilingus, and soft lighting. Instead, they aim to represent different pathways to pleasure, varied relationships to bodies, an expanded suite of erogenous zones, and how to navigate trauma, grief, medication, chronic pain, flare-ups, capacity, hormonal shifts, pregnancy, menopause, surgery, and scar tissue.

Legal Distinctions

We can understand the dangers of investing in good porn/bad porn respectability projects by looking at how they have been taken up in legal arguments to defend pornography. One recurring theme among indie producers is an investment in the value of sexual material (whether documentary, artistic, or political) and its potential positive impact on consumers. Reiterating the positive aspects of pornography has been a common tactic to counter dominant narratives about pornography as inherently violent, degrading, and exploitative. In doing so, it is tempting to argue that some porn deserves greater legal protection than others.

This strategy was used in the famous Canadian Supreme Court case *Little Sisters v. Canada* ([2000] 2 S.C.R. 1120). In 2000, when Canadian customs targeted shipments to a gay and lesbian bookstore and attempted to prevent their entry into Canada on the basis that they were obscene, counsel for the Little Sisters Book and Art Emporium argued that previous case law (in particular, the infamous decision in *R. v. Butler* [1992], 1 S.C.R. 452, which interpreted pornography as harmful) did not apply to gay and lesbian pornography as *Butler* only addressed heterosexual pornography. In her analysis of this case, socio-legal scholar Lara Karaian (2009) argues that in separating out gay and lesbian pornography as *distinct from* heterosexual pornography, Little Sisters relied on arguments that lesbian pornography was emancipatory because sexually explicit materials were "important to *all* women and are *essential* to the emotional, social, sexual and political lives of lesbians" (quoting feminist advocacy group LEAF, 385). In doing so, the *Little Sisters* case consolidated the assumption that (heterosexual) pornography reflects domination and victimizes women (Cossman et al. 1997). The arguments explicitly note the "liberating effects" of gay and lesbian material, due to its "subverting [of] dominant constructs of masculinity and femininity" that operate to "challenge the sexism that is believed to be endorsed and reinforced by mainstream heterosexual pornography" (quoting legal advocacy group Egale, Karaian 2009, 385). In doing so it reinforced heterosexual pornography as harmful, regardless of its production or representations.

This line of thinking—the resistance to conflating queer sexualities with heterosexual sexualities as if they are the same—is not isolated or new, and it makes sense: Lesbian scholars have long criticized readings of lesbian sex from a heterosexual paradigm and problematized the anti-porn position as marginalizing lesbian, queer, and BDSM sexualities. This is a compelling argument— we shouldn't take cisnormative, heteronormative lenses and employ them to read queer texts built on different values, ethics, and frames of reference. However, this argument is different from situating lesbian or queer sexualities as deserving of better legal protections. Although lesbian pornographies may at times have liberating and emancipatory effects, if we rely on fixed concepts about what gay and lesbian pornography *is* (subversive, sex-positive, emancipatory, different from mainstream pornography) and argue definitively about what porn *does* (community building, affirmation, sex education), we risk producing a homogenous and monolithic category that does not accurately reflect the diversity and nuance with which gay and lesbian or queer pornographies are produced, consumed, and circulated. Will such categories then become like "porn for women"—a genre characterized by soft lighting, narrative arcs, or cunnilingus that distills a limited articulation of pleasure and desire? What happens to queer pornography that speaks to HIV (like Treasure Island's *Viral Loads*, which was targeted by stigmatizing media), chemsex (and the use of recreational drugs for party and play cultures), intergenerational sex, and less respectable, messy, and complicated understandings of sex?

There must be room for normative evaluations of pornography's processes and content. Our media content is desperately in need of material that is anti-racist, anti-sexist, anti-ableist, and we ought to be interrogating all of our media and cultural production through such lenses—not just pornography. But the *Little Sisters* case is a reminder that in advocating for the decriminalization or availability of pornographies, we need to be careful not to rely on the reification of identity categories or a mere reversal of good/bad sexual subjectivity. What I mean is this: Pornography is not necessarily good simply because it is gay or lesbian and bad if it is heterosexual. It is not necessarily better simply because it was produced by women instead of men. Pegging alone does not make porn revolutionary. The danger in advocating for some porn as better or more deserving, whether in case law or via attempts to certify ethical porn, is that we set up a model citizenship project by which independent pornographies are expected to be perpetually positive, celebratory, and responsible. As Gayle Rubin (2009) reminds us, "It should not be necessary to justify gay populations, or transgendered [sic] individuals, or movements for civil equality for all citizens regardless of whom and how they fuck by arguing that they possess some special quality and power to bring about economic utopia or re-create an earthly paradise" (370).

Such a project consolidates pornography as a thing rather than as a rhetorical tool used by regulators (to revisit Kendrick 1996) and ignores the function of the category of pornography as something which "sits at the limits of the social" (Sharkey 2018, 9). Following a radical reading of independent pornographies, the goal is not to seek legalized identities or certified products, but to transform power structures that position sex as outside culture and dismantle the existing systems of un/desirability and erotic stratification.

Appeals for Recognition

As regulators try to determine the limits of legal pornography, industry stakeholders can become embroiled in problematic political processes. Appeals for recognition and legalization of pornography (as opposed to decriminalization of pornography) have potential to result in worse conditions for more marginalized producers. We can see a useful example in Australia's classification law, which prohibits the depiction of any fetish content. The prohibition on fetish was not an original part of Australia's X18+ category; rather it eventuated as a result of political lobbying that backfired. In the late 1990s, following a long political campaign against pornography, Australia's prime minister had promised to ban the sale of X18+ federally. In response, the adult business lobbyist association Eros began a campaign to introduce a new federal classification category, one they called nonviolent erotica (NVE), in the hope that it could be legally sold. Eros had realized that their campaign to "Legalise X" was not gaining political traction, so the creation of a new category would allow adult retailers to sell explicit content. However, the new NVE category included a more restricted definition than that in the existing X18+ category.

As Eros cofounder Robbie Swan described it in our interview, their role was "putting forward all the time measures that are politically palatable for politicians and that we think maximizes our members' benefits." He recalled the point at which negotiations turned: "Basically, they said, 'Look, if we want to form this nonviolent erotica category that you are saying is the way to go to keep most X-rated material, you are going to have to offer something up. What is it going to be?'" While an NVE category may have been favorable for some Eros members in the short-term, their willingness to compromise backfired. As the "What Happened to Our Squirt?" vignette describes, Australian politicians held a screening of BDSM pornographies in Parliament, reported being subsequently offended, and as a result NVE was never introduced, the sale of X18+ content remained illegal, and the federal X18+ category was narrowed to exclude all depictions of fetish. The ban on fetish, which disadvantages anyone making or selling kink-related content, remains in place. In our interview, Robbie defended Eros's decision but also recognized the resulting community backlash. "I mean, over the years we have received a bit of grief from BDSM groups for what we did. . . . I mean, we are a lobby group who represented a whole bunch of X-rated traders. What were we meant to do? We could have turned our back on the whole thing and said, 'No, fuck you. We're just going to go ahead and go out on our own and try and save the lot.' Or we could have just gone in and negotiated with them, as we did."

This was not an example of evidence-based policy being codified into law or a meaningful consultation with stakeholders, but a moment of political expediency that accepted compromises based on short-term gains. Robbie described this as a win for Eros at the time, having staved off the threat of a total ban on X18+ content. But, as he recognizes, for people who practice BDSM, who produce fetish content, or who watch kinky material, this was really a loss: "I mean, as far as we were concerned as lobbyists for the industry, we had had a win. As lobbyists or as people with a civil libertarian viewpoint on material we probably had taken a small hit because material that we thought shouldn't be banned was being banned. What could we do? I mean, that's what politics is. That's politics."

Although Eros returned to subsequent law reform efforts, the ban on fetish has not gradually eroded over time—instead, it fell off the political agenda and, more than two decades later, remains in place. Eros's advocacy in the years after this incident focused not on coming back for other marginalized groups, but on reporting nonmember retailers to law enforcement agencies. In my archival research, I uncovered correspondence during the 2000–2003 Eros campaign to "Legalise X" wherein Eros specifically wrote to state attorneys general reporting other adult retailers selling unclassified or X18+ material.

This moment provides a striking example of the divergent stakes involved in law reform efforts and how appeals for recognition can function to criminalize marginalized groups. Governments rarely "come back for the rest" once small gains have been won for the most privileged. Tactical interventions that offer short-term concessions instead of prioritizing long-term visions are constrained by a compromised political environment that is more concerned with electoral power than evidence-based policy.

Creating Whorearchies

Appeals to the state can overshadow how stigma itself operates as a policing force. Campaigns for legal recognition reveal an experiential gap between porn performers and adult businesses, who do not always recognize their own role in perpetuating whorearchies. In my research, adult industry lobby groups were more likely to support market-based mechanisms and industry standards as determined, audited, and monitored by an industry body or government. One business owner I spoke to, Howard, even expressed pride in compliance in a way that distinguished his company from others, to the extent that he didn't want law reform to let in the "bottom feeders." In comparison, performers were more likely to take a radical approach; they had little faith in the likelihood of the state protecting sex workers, saw the state as primarily serving, protecting, and maintaining the interests of powerful groups, were skeptical of decision-making structures and processes that excluded them, and believed it was preferable to invest their energy in developing localized, community-based approaches. "Porn workers do not trust the state," writes Heather Berg (2021), because "porn workers tell a story of violent state neglect" (154). In my study, some performers described a defiant and willful disregard of laws, with a willingness to be arrested and test the laws in court, and a preference for generating ethical codes that sit entirely outside the state. Luna Trash stated, "Especially seeing as the law has done absolutely nothing for us as sex workers and as porn producers, it seems ridiculous that we should have to fit into their structure and still have the proper setup if they're going to keep us on the edge and could throw us in jail at any minute if they decided, [through] little loopholes in the law. I mean, really, anyone in porn I guess should be trying to keep outside it as much as possible."

Attempts to discern, identify, and even codify good porn risk creating hierarchies and regimes of stigma. As regulators draw boundaries between good and bad porn, they make moral judgments about who ought to be producing porn and what porn ought to look like. In our interview, Janelle Fawkes, former CEO of Scarlet Alliance, was concerned that such deliberations would lead to governments "trying to control or determine what's the right way of doing sex work and creating this hierarchy within or around sex work, on who's doing it right and who's not." This was something she felt was a danger as the industry moved forward in discussions of ethical porn. Janelle warned against "falling into that trap" where feminist or ethical porn erects a hierarchical divide between the kinds of porn or producers that are valued. She believed there were lessons to be learned from the sex worker rights movement and emphasized the importance of keeping discussions on pornography to a framework that prioritizes autonomy, agency, and health promotion: "I think that that approach can really; well it does develop hierarchies, it does exclude lots of people. . . . When I think about those divisions that often come up about feminist porn or ethical porn and how that also creates that divide and almost places any other kind of porn as lesser or less beneficial, or the people working within it as less valued, then I think about the other ways within the sex worker rights movement that we've really tried to avoid that stuff."

Kim Cums, a porn performer who wrote her master's thesis on escorting, noted in our interview that because "[sexual] identities are very closely tied with systems of legality" as sex workers fight for their rights, it is often the case that we can end up defending categories of legality instead and legitimizing some forms of sex work at the expense of others. As Kim told me: "So you're carving out a niche for yourself where you say, 'Oh, I'm not charging for the sex that you're having with me; I'm charging for the time that you're spending with me,' and you find those are loopholes to legitimize your own work and your own identity and to keep yourself on the right side of the law."

Although such tactics can be a vital means to protect oneself from criminalization, Kim was concerned that these distinctions could simultaneously operate as an example of "when sex workers use their own identity as a tactical advantage against other sex workers . . . [as a] social defense mechanism of where they are on the hierarchy." These tactics, Kim argued, can contribute to a "whorearchy"—the hierarchical systems within sex work that determine who is afforded privilege, social capital, and respectability. Sex work is stratified along social and legal lines, and the whorearchy is structured, as Belle Knox (2014) argues, "according to intimacy of contact with clients and police" and is maintained through the operation of disdain among sex workers. The whorearchy can be seen in many aspects of the sex industry, in distinctions between indoor/outdoor work, contact/online work, independent/contractual work, and in marketing language that emphasizes workers as "high class." Luna Trash noted that these debates about privilege and stratification impacted other parts of the sex industry: "I guess it's the same as what's happening with pole sports and pole dancing and stuff, where people are trying so hard to get it socially acceptable as an Olympic sport. At the same [time] they are throwing strippers under the bus because they're trying so hard not to be associated."

Lessons from sex worker rights organizing indicate that government approval for sex industry businesses—essentially licensing frameworks controlling who can sex work, where they can sex work, what kinds of sex work they can do—has created a two-tiered industry whereby the majority of workers are criminalized because they cannot comply with the onerous conditions, thereby becoming more vulnerable to exploitation, with less access to justice and support mechanisms. Instead of securing protections only for some porn workers (those who are tertiary educated, middle class, or engaging in porn for fun or self-expression) or some kinds of content (vanilla, coupled, hetero), sex workers bring a politics from below that centers on the structural forces that impact performers' agency and decision-making at work. These include the decriminalization of not only pornography but also sex work, HIV, and drug use more broadly. They include pushes to end border control policies that prevent people from traveling for sex work and the dismantling of criminal justice approaches to trafficking that disproportionately police and harass migrant sex workers. In taking on these lessons, indie porn movements can play an important role in decriminalization, destigmatization, decarceration, and decolonization.

At a time when gay and lesbian rights movements are adopting a homonormative agenda (Puar 2007; Ashford 2011), one that seeks legal recognition by distancing itself from the "bad queer" and "undesirable" sexual intimacies, such as public sex, kink, polyamory, and pornography (Stychin 1995; Adler 2018), Michael Warner's concept of a "queer ethic of dignity in shame" is instructive in recognizing the importance of social movements being led by the needs of those most abject, marginalized, and least reputable. Instead of appealing for recognition to be seen and validated by others, a politics of "dignity in shame" (where one "doesn't pretend to be *above* the indignity of sex") (Warner 2000, 35), as opposed to a politics of respectability (a process of normalization that reinforces stigma on others), can assist in fostering solidarity between all sex workers, not only privileged producers at the top, regardless of the type or legality of our work, to ensure that the rights won for some do not come at the expense of others.

FIGURE 7.3. *Stomping Pigs* by artist Tallulah's Rash from Decolonise Sex Work, a Blak sex work grassroots collective in so-called Australia that raises money for mutual aid. Image by Tallulah's Rash.

Enabling Regulatory Environments

What does all this mean for our resistance tactics? Holding on to an oppositional politics ("alternative to," "independent of") can be a means of maintaining critical thinking (always reassessing the next frontier or changing face of oppression). But in holding on to fixed ideas about what mainstream pornography is and does, and advocating for indie pornographies as inherently better, without constantly reassessing what is actually radical about them, we can forget to observe how the center shifts and how indie pornographies can create their own hierarchies, exclusions, and disciplinary codes. Although indie pornographies have been received with much enthusiasm, their revolutionary promises are constrained and shaped by a myriad of regulatory forces (economic, technological, legal, social, cultural, and political). In some cases, these revolutionary claims may become fantasies in themselves.

If we understand the movement for indie pornographies as simply a project to create and define good porn and better porn, we are doing a serious disservice to the spirit of the movement. The lack of transparency in the criteria by which good porn and bad porn are delineated and its constant slippage have led to this loose shorthand gaining regulatory traction. At times, these terms are guided more by the protection of middle-class tastes than by workers' needs and should be understood as respectability bids that repudiate (but reproduce) porn stigma. If we understand indie porn as being about independence from the oppressive structures that govern sexually explicit material, then we ought to be concerned more with how to dismantle those structures than seeking recognition within them.

Critical legal scholar Dean Spade, writing on intersectional resistance in the tradition of women-of-color feminism and transformative social justice theory, reminds us that rights-based projects for inclusion and equality often end up dividing communities and reproducing (instead of dismantling) the gendered and racialized violence of administrative systems. They do this, in part, "by mobilizing narratives of deservingness and undeservingness, by participating in the logics and structures that undergird relations of domination, and by becoming sites for the expansion of harmful systems and institutions" (Spade 2013, 1032). Instead of setting up hierarchies between which producers deserve rights and protection, indie porn producers could rather "seek material change" (1049). We see this approach from the BIPOC Adult Industry Collective (2021), who distribute mutual aid to sex workers in need of housing, food, personal protective equipment, work supplies, medical care, gender confirmation surgery, menstrual cups, and diapers. Their regular programming includes mental health support (facilitated by qualified sex workers), performer advocacy (including arranging mediation, safe housing, and contract negotiation), and education (webinars, information sessions, and a coworking café).

It is unrealistic to expect producers to just create better porn when production is criminalized, when tube sites dominate search engine results, and when algorithmic ranking systems favor white bodies. How are people expected to create better porn when producers have to censor body fluids, nonprocreative sex, and kinky intimacies? What use is better porn when indie producers cannot advertise on social media, when banks deny services to adult businesses, and when platforms take predatory commissions? Instead of setting up hierarchies about what constitutes good and bad porn, imagine if our interventions were focused on changing the systems that shape production, distribution, and performer welfare.

Imagine if the production, sale, screening, and advertising of pornography was decriminalized. Instead of policing and surveillance, imagine if resources went toward preventing and addressing the root causes of sexual stigma, violence, and image-based abuse. Imagine if governments offered grants, provided venues, and facilitated opportunities to screen experimental, community-created porn. Imagine if X18+ was not a classification category at all and that, instead of fixating on sex, classification scrutinized media for misogyny, racism, ableism, ageism, transphobia, homophobia, whorephobia, cissexism, colonization, and white supremacy. What if "safe for work" hashtags did not reproduce the crude assumption that sex is not part of the workplace? Instead of paternalizing young people, what if governments involved them in conversations with porn performers to create new syllabi for porn literacy? What if governments treated the lives, health, safety, industrial, and emotional needs of sex workers as if they mattered? Wouldn't it be *better* to build a world in which sex workers could migrate, co-operatize, and control their own image, one where whore stigma does not exist? Or, what if we organized against the glorification of the work ethic and distributed health care, food, shelter, and resources so that people did not live in poverty or have to work just to survive? If we want better porn, there is a lot to do to build the legal, economic, social, cultural, and infrastructural environments in which indie porn can thrive.

COVID-Safe Pornography

It's the inaugural San Francisco PornFilmFestival, but alas, I am not in San Francisco. It's the notorious year of 2020, and the world is in various states of lockdown due to the COVID-19 pandemic. Instead, I am virtually attending the festival from my couch in Sydney's inner west. It's less exciting, but there is still a stellar lineup of films on the bill. One in particular stands out. Titled *Sex in Times of Corona*, it is a comedic, entertaining, and lighthearted short made by sixteen erotic filmmakers under lockdown in their block of flats in Berlin. The PinkLabel.tv advertisement reads "Get your solidarity smut!"

Sex in Times of Corona positions sex workers as innovative public health leaders, pitched in the trailer as "11 bizarre ways to have sex—without getting too close." It's a lot sexier than the information coming out of the World Health Organization. Beginning with the public service announcement that "there's no need to be celibate these days," the film showcases varied ways in which people can still experience sexual connection at a time when physical distancing is mandatory. Throughout the film audiences see mutual masturbation, characters performing stripteases for one another, BDSM scenes featuring isolation in an underground dungeon, and kinky makeout sessions in hazmat suits and gas masks. In one scene, a performer is fucked by a dildo attached by gaffer tape to a long camera pole through the window of the adjacent flat. In another, a performer offers peepshows from her apartment to viewers in five opposite windows across the courtyard. It's fun, educational, and in an age of skin hunger and physical distancing, it assists audiences in reimaging what constitutes intimacy and connection.

But it's not just the content that is compelling. The film is a project to raise emergency funds for BesD e.V., the Professional Association of Erotic and Sexual Services, to support sex workers who cannot access government assistance

With contributions from sixteen erotic filmmakers, the short film *Sex in Times of Corona* raised emergency funds for BesD e.V., the Professional Association of Erotic and Sexual Services, during COVID-19 lockdown in Berlin. Image by Jo Pollux, courtesy of Candy Flip and San Francisco PornFilmFestival.

during the pandemic. As precarious laborers, sex workers may not have official documentation to prove their earnings; they may be working unlawfully or cannot afford for governments to connect their legal identity and type of work. While government responses to the pandemic were typically founded on assumptions of nuclear families, monogamous relationships, and heteronormative households, artists, sex workers, and queer communities pioneered innovative responses to the global pandemic, including sharing sex-positive public health messaging, mobilizing funds for mutual aid, and creating COVID-safe experiences of intimacy. It's a perfect example of how porn can be purposed toward solidarity projects—the filmmakers raised over €1,700 on their first day of fundraising alone.

8

Whore Data

Technology, Design, and Carceral Surveillance

During the COVID-19 pandemic, sex workers around the globe experienced an unprecedented loss of income due to the closure of businesses and workplaces. Many were unable to access formal financial support, especially those who were on temporary visas, ineligible for government payments, or sole traders who could not meet requirements to account for their prior earnings—either because they were not out about their sex work, they wanted to maintain privacy, or they needed to avoid discrimination, arrest, or deportation. The lack of support prompted economic and mental health challenges for sex workers, some of whom were experiencing homelessness and housing instability, an inability to pay bills, rent, food, or prescription medicines. As a result, many sex workers transitioned to online work, including producing their own sexual content for camming, subscription, and streaming sites. In Australia, this transition was supported by sex worker organizations, such as Scarlet Alliance, who developed a guide called "Getting started in online/non-contact work" alongside other translated harm-reduction resources and COVID-safe plans to assist people to return to work safely. The guide suggested how sex workers could continue as online pleasure providers through phone sex, live video bookings, text messaging sessions, camming, and selling video content with tips on digital privacy and security.

Coinciding with this rapid uptake of online work, the Australian government introduced its new Online Safety Act 2021, with a new framework for regulating platforms and electronic service providers—promoted as the first of its kind in the world. The act provided an avenue for internet users to complain about any sexual content online (actual, simulated, or implied) that was not subject to a restricted access scheme. It afforded the eSafety Commissioner—a public servant—the power to issue removal notices, require search engines to delete links, and require app stores to prevent downloads within twenty-four hours, with civil penalties for noncompliance. In a context where sex workers already face malicious and vexatious flagging, the commissioner could decide that content be removed without any criteria other than the fact that she thought it "fit," with no requirement to notify users, to provide reasons or an opportunity to respond, or to publish enforcement data about her decisions. The act came under public scrutiny from digital rights and sex worker organizations for the way it invited complaints about sexual content, reproduced the problematic classification framework discussed in chapter 3, and facilitated opaque decisions about online sexual content. Stakeholders were concerned about the act's chilling effect, particularly its incentives for platforms to use automated and biometric technologies to detect user age and to screen sexual content.

The coalescing of these two events—the introduction of the Online Safety Act during the advent of the COVID-19 pandemic—meant that the offline sex working environment became more heavily policed while the online sex working environment became even more surveilled. Asian massage parlors were the first businesses in Australia to be targeted by law enforcement for COVID public health compliance, and later, as the country began to ease restrictions, brothels and strip clubs were initially flagged for indefinite closure, despite other personal services businesses—waxing, tattooing, and saunas—being permitted to reopen. Facing a lack of government support, sex workers mobilized, creating the National Cabinet of Whores to align messages, resources, and responses among peer sex worker organizations. In addition, a sex worker started a crowdfunded national Emergency Support Fund, later coordinated by Scarlet Alliance and its members due to overwhelming response and need. The fund distributed 1,794 payments directly to sex workers, coming to a total of $317,978, with additional lump sums of $3,380 to sex work organizations (the Aboriginal and Torres Strait Islander Sex Worker Advisory Group, Vixen Collective, and Respect Inc.) for distribution to individual sex workers. Grassroots community groups such as Decolonise Sex Work, a Blak sex worker collective, were formed separately to share resources, supplies, and mutual aid.

The same month I received my PhD, I returned to complete my graduate diploma of legal practice to become admitted as a solicitor, taking up volunteer training at the Sex Worker Legal Service. The service would assist sex workers by recovering debts from clients, issuing takedown notices for copyright infringement, giving advice on sham contracts, and dealing with cases of stalking and assault. I returned to policy work at Scarlet Alliance at the time the Online Safety Act was still in draft form, writing submissions to government and contributing to a national COVID-safe plan that could be adapted for use by various sex industry businesses. At the same time, I had the opportunity to work alongside the New York City sex worker collectives Hacking//Hustling and Decoding Stigma, which work at the intersections of tech and social justice with the goals of abolishing carceral technologies and imagining liberatory futures for sex workers.

This final chapter is about the ingenuity and creativity of sex workers in designing our own futures in the face of regulatory, economic, and technical environments that are not built for us. It is about the turn—by both governments and platforms—to automated decision-making to govern sexual content at scale and the ways in which machine learning acts in tandem with whorephobic laws to exacerbate both online and offline inequalities. As more sex workers integrate online sexual content into their repertoire, the regressive regulation of pornography converges with an anti–sex work agenda. The impacts of both are now being widely felt in both digital and physical environments. Exorbitant amounts of money, time, and labor are being directed toward designing technological systems that alienate the very communities who could assist in designing better approaches. As a result, sex workers are in the practice of designing our own systems—hacking, repurposing, and re-jigging them to survive and thrive. Earlier in the book, in chapters 1 and 2, I demonstrated how porn performers were taking things into their own hands, establishing new ethical paradigms and bringing new values to production. In this chapter I showcase how sex workers are intervening in technology design to create new spaces, infrastructure, and systems.

Design Justice

Pornography itself is a contested category, invented by regulators to control the democratization of culture. This means that our current systems are neither natural nor ahistorical. They are definitely not inevitable. The comprehensive systems of surveillance that govern sex in online space, the practices of commercial extraction in pornography distribution, and the selective definitions of *harm* and *risk* that plague classification and criminal laws are neither desirable nor necessary. They certainly do not lead us to a more equitable sexual culture. The porn landscape is the outcome of a series of deliberate design decisions engineered by people who rarely have a stake in or knowledge of sexual economies—politicians, public servants, tech start-ups, celebrities, entrepreneurs, and nonprofits with motivations that have little to do with the liberation of sex workers. In emerging research, sex workers report how technology design negatively impacts their lives (Barwulor et al. 2021). In Hacking//Hustling's research report "Posting into the Void" (2020), 51 percent of sex worker activists reported that shadowbanning had interrupted their abilities to do movement organizing.

In her book *Design Justice: Community-Led Practices to Build the Worlds We Need* (2020), Sasha Costanza-Chock describes how design decisions operate to inequitably distribute the benefits and burdens of various technologies: "Design justice focuses explicitly on the ways that design reproduces and/or challenges the matrix of domination (white supremacy, heteropatriarchy, capitalism, ableism, settler colonialism, and other forms of structural inequality)" (23). This is a useful framework through which to assess pornography regulation because one can quickly see how the design of porn regulation reproduces whorephobia and disproportionately burdens sexual content creators while benefiting tech companies, governments, and law enforcement. Moreover, systems of content curation, legality, and enforcement disproportionately privilege white, middle-class, able-bodied, cisgender porn performers (through systems of content amplification) and disproportionately disadvantage Indigenous performers, Black performers, performers of color, disabled performers, and trans and gender-diverse performers (through blocking, removing, de-ranking, and suppressing content).

Throughout this book I have argued that porn stigma is at the heart of regulatory design. But porn stigma is bound up with a plethora of other colonial, white supremacist, capitalist, ableist, classist, and heteronormative projects. Porn regulation has been a component of colonization projects—as discussed in chapter 3, the criminalization of porn possession played a role in the Australian government's theft of Aboriginal land in the Northern Territory. The conflation of pornography with sexual abuse material and trafficking has fueled a criminal justice approach to anti-trafficking that has demanded more police power, state power, and surveillance and resulted in excessive policing, arrest, and deportation of Asian and migrant sex workers. At the same time, these carceral projects have ignored calls for land back, treaty, safe migration pathways, or industrial rights.

In responding to COVID-19, some governments used the pandemic to shut down sexual commerce, with a disproportionate impact on workers who are immunocompromised, chronically ill, or living with disability, for whom online pornography can be an accessible method of making money. As Emily Coombes and colleagues (2022) write, "There are deep links between whorephobia and ableism, both in how the communities are seen as disposable, incapable of making their own decisions, and needing to be saved or cured" (n.p.). In the United States, businesses and individuals were excluded from the Economic Injury Disaster Loan Program passed in 2020 if they derived income from a "prurient sexual nature." These deliberate decisions engineer a society that maintains an inequitable social order. Projects to abolish pornography further play a role in maintaining class hierarchies: They operate to mark out a rescue industry, providing jobs for middle-class "helping" professionals, setting up private NGOs, start-ups, and charities as social welfare providers, and funneling workers into more reputable forms of (lesser paid) labor. In singling out sexual labor, they fundamentally fail to address the structural regimes that keep people in poverty, deny people access to health or housing, address the exploitation of work under capitalism, or work toward a future where work, wealth, and resources are distributed more equitably.

Gabriella Garcia, a poetic technologist working in New York, argues that sex work stigma has been literally coded into technology design. Her thesis, "SHIFT+CONTROL+END+DELETE: Encoded Stigma" (2020), argues that to undo this we need the wisdom of sex workers, "the incredible breadth of knowledge each has to offer—as observers, laborers, artists, educators, entrepreneurs, targets, activists, partners and citizens" (2). When I met Gabriella, she had just begun fortnightly meetings for her new cross-institutional coalition Decoding Stigma, built from "laborers, futurists, advocates, artists, designers, technologists, researchers, teachers, and students" invested in conversations about sex at the tech school. Birthed as part of her residency at New York University's Interactive Telecommunications Program, Decoding Stigma calls for the inclusion of sex worker voices in all spaces designing the future. The need to involve sex workers in tech design ought to be self-evident. As Costanza-Chock (2020) writes, "The most valuable ingredient in design justice is the full inclusion of, accountability to, and control by people with direct lived experience of the conditions designers claim they are trying to change" (25). The leadership of whores may pave a future not limited to algorithmic fairness, transparency, or explainability, but toward algorithmic *reparations*.

Pornography and Nudity Classifiers

Many tech companies simply take it as a given that pornography does not belong on their platform and that they ought to create systems that detect, suppress, filter, or blacklist it. So deeply ingrained is this reputational and moral imperative that some do not even appear concerned about losing customers to maintain it; Steve Jobs's commitment to preventing pornography on the iPhone is one such example: "If you want porn, get an Android." The kinds of concerns identified in Part II ("Regulatory Fantasies") about how governments and technology companies regulate pornography (by distinguishing it from art or culture, by obsessing over nonnormative practices, and by preventing, removing, or destroying content) are now enhanced with the deployment of automation (that treats pornography as an aberration or error).

As discussed in chapter 4, machine learning is used to identify and flag pornography on social media platforms, screening for particular words, body parts, body fluids, and activities. Danielle Blunt and I (2021) refer to such technologies as "automated whorephobia" because in the same way that automation exacerbates other forms of gender inequity, racial oppression, and class disparity, such deployments of technology are founded upon and automate sex work stigma. They create a variety of problems, including contested definitions of what constitutes pornography, what assemblages make up sex, and what counts as nudity. Although it is professed to be inadvertent over-capture, they pick up sex education, harm reduction, and health promotion information as a matter of course. In Alice Witt's study of content moderation on Instagram, she found that 22 percent of removed images were actually false positives (Witt, Suzor, and Huggins 2019). Instagram formally apologized in 2019 for blocking pole dancing hashtags after receiving a petition from seventeen thousand users (Are and Paasonen 2021). When Tumblr implemented a machine learning approach as part of their ban on adult content in 2018, it was described as an example of "algorithmic failure" by picking up nipples, memes, and fully clothed selfies as well as whales and dolphins (Pilipets and Paasonen 2020).

Since its inception, Google has been concerned with censoring pornography, perceiving it as spam or a virus requiring detection and removal. Google's Safe Search has developed in sophistication over the years, beginning as a Boolean textual analysis, collating a set of words that would indicate the likelihood of content being pornography, then layering behavioral data from users (Monea 2022, 79). The pixel analysis of images increased around 2008 as graphics processing units became more powerful; then, in 2012, Google began using machine learning to train convolutional neural networks and, in 2016, released its Cloud Vision API. Cloud Vision features include "explicit content detection"—however, explicit content is far more expansive than particular body parts. As Alexander Monea explains, images may be considered explicit if they fall into the categories of "adult" or "racy." The "adult" category exemplifies the unimaginative cisnormative lens that conflates all nudity with sexuality and fixates on specific erogenous zones and anatomical configurations (genitals, female breasts, and sometimes buttocks). At its foundation, the cis-hetero obsession with explicitness is fundamentally about reinforcing a heteronormative public/public divide where sex does not belong in public space. The "racy" category, conversely, has the greatest potential for over-capture, as it includes "lewd or provocative poses, sheer or see-through clothing, closeups of sensitive regions" (Monea 2022, 81). Apart from the fraught task of identifying this borderline content, the "racy" category exemplifies the common heterosexual panic that nudity is so corruptive that anything mildly resembling or reminding users of their own—or other's—bodies must swiftly be removed.

These normative values then form the foundation for more technical problems, such as how computer vision systems become labeled with metadata. Google's Cloud Vision software is built on the large visual image database ImageNet, which is organized according to the lexical database WordNet. WordNet captures relationships between words by grouping English words into synsets, or synonyms, with parent, child, and sibling concepts. As Monea details, the child synsets for "sex" in WordNet connect terms like sodomy with bestiality and crossbreeding with miscegenation, translating "biological essentialism . . . [and] scientific racism in machine readable form" (86). Pornography detection is not a precise project: Classifiers generally detect pornography through an analysis of the percentage and distribution of skin pixels. But Skin Sheriff, one nudity classifier, reports that the process is both subjective and imprecise: "The task of deciding whether images contain pornography is still largely manual and tedious because existing automatic techniques deliver inexact results. Furthermore, the separation of pornographic and non-pornographic images is not always possible. Even for humans it can be a subjective decision" (Platzer, Stuetz, and Lindorfer 2014, 45).

Rather than design more efficient and accurate classifiers, we ought to pay more attention to the systematic theft of nude images used to build training data for these enforcement regimes. Livia Foldes, an artist, designer and cofounder of Decoding Stigma, draws connections between the colonial and carceral theft involved in both neural networks and art museums. Her work is prompted by the digitization of sexually suggestive museum collections. With machine classifiers now tasked with distinguishing between art and

FIGURE 8.1. An image from *NSFW Venus* by Livia Foldes, artist and designer from Decoding Stigma. Foldes has digitally removed nude bodies from GitHub images used to train the NudeNet classifier. Image by Livia Foldes.

pornography, the gatekeeping of acceptable content has moved "from cultural gatekeepers to libertarian technocrats" (Foldes, n.d., n.p.). In her artwork NSFW *Venus*, Livia takes open-source images from a GitHub repository used to train the NudeNet classifier. Noting that the images are stolen and uncredited, scraped without consent, she seeks to "acknowledge and address" the people in the images without "reinscribing the violence" that produced them (Foldes, n.d., n.p.). To do so, she borrows from Filipino artist Stephanie Syjuco, who uses Photoshop's "healing brush" to digitally remove subjects from prison mugshots in anthropological archives. Livia similarly removes nude bodies from the images, leaving a smudged gap where the subjects once were. If "repatriation and reparations" are the answers to addressing colonial violence of the museum, she asks what healing could mean for machine learning archives that are "endlessly copied and circulated" (Foldes, n.d., n.p.).

Scraping and Surveillance

Significant resources are now being diverted to the use of machine learning tools to screen content for the purposes of detecting child sexual abuse material (CSAM), potential trafficking victims, and nonconsensual intimate imagery as well as to create age-verification systems to restrict access. Some of these approaches rely on digital fingerprinting software that use image metadata (such as filenames or image hashes) to compare content with images that are already in a database of known, harmful, illegal, or nonconsensual content. For example, in 2021 Apple announced they would be scanning all US iPhones for images of CSAM before they were uploaded to the storage service iCloud. While they paused this move following critiques from digital privacy stakeholders, such initiatives form part of a broader push toward increased surveillance of devices, users, and their content. In 2022 the *New York Times* ran an article about a parent who took photos of his toddler's groin area and texted them to his wife and doctor to diagnose and treat a medical condition. Google detected this as child abuse material and disabled his account. Even after he requested a review of the system, Google would not reinstate the account, and he lost his emails, contact information, phone number, and email addresses as well as photos from the first few years of his son's life (Hill 2022).

Part of the problem is that engineering detection software inevitably requires trade-offs to be made about what constitutes an acceptable rate of false positives and false negatives. But further, such technologies are rarely assessed by the people most impacted by them. Porn performers' images and biometrics are being nonconsensually scraped, scanned, and used to train deep-learning algorithms that have potential to place them at further risk. Porn subscription websites, tube sites, and escort directories are often considered fair game by start-ups seeking to develop new regulatory technologies that do not necessarily support those workers themselves. For this reason, Garcia (2021) argues that "the sex worker has become an object model on which surveillance technologies are trained. These technologies parallel—and inform—technologies for predictive policing, protest surveillance and migration control" (n.p.).

A prominent example is the anti-trafficking organization Thorn, founded by celebrities Ashton Kutcher and Demi Moore, which uses a tool called Spotlight to detect child-trafficking victims. Thorn is part of what technology writer Violet Blue (2019) describes as the "lucrative growth market" of anti-trafficking, attracting millions of dollars in corporate donations from tech companies. Thorne has partnerships with tech giants such as Google, Microsoft, Meta, Twitter, and data-mining company Palantir, which developed mass surveillance technology for the US military. In her exposé of the software, Blue notes that, in its own materials, Spotlight describes itself as being "built on a data archive of millions of records of escort ads and forum data collected from various websites" which it "turns into an asset for law enforcement" (n.p.). Officers have access to escort emails, phone numbers, keywords, age, and location. Spotlight is an example of a suite of technologies that exploit sexual commerce to fuel a carceral surveillance society and, in doing so, place sex workers increasingly at risk. Governments and big tech appear far less invested in proven strategies to reduce poverty, worker exploitation, criminalization, or racist migration policies.

A further problem is that such technologies pit young people against sex workers, as if it is not possible to protect both simultaneously. And yet these are not mutually exclusive aims. In 2019 the child protection organization Prostasia developed its "Best Practice Principles for Sexual Content Moderation and Child Protection" following a multistakeholder consultation. They set out principles to assist platforms in adopting a more nuanced approach. They include restricting sexual content that causes direct harm to a child (rather than blanket restrictions that are not substantiated by evidence); evaluating the human rights impacts of restricting sexual content; transparent and detailed criteria for prohibiting or blocking sexual content (especially where the content is lawful); proportionality of response (including not referring lawful conduct to law enforcement or industry databases); consideration of the context in which material is posted; human review before adding content to hash databases or blocklists; providing users with notice whenever content is restricted or blocked; providing users with the means of filtering out unwanted sexual content; and prioritizing content-removal requests from people depicted in images.

Identity Verification and Age Estimation

As platforms and governments design strategies to prevent the dissemination of nonconsensual intimate images, many have prioritized identity verification and content takedowns. Frequently, performers are expected to sign up to subscription sites using their legal names and scan their faces in order to create user profiles for pay wallets. Both the development and deployment of digital identity verification raises serious privacy concerns for porn performers in contexts where stigma, discrimination, and criminalization remain unabated. Websites like namethatpornstar.com invite users to upload images of porn performers so that others can crowdsource their names. In 2017 the reverse image search web app Pornstar.id announced that they had developed a neural face recognition network that had been trained on six hundred and fifty thousand images of more than seven thousand adult performers. That same year, Pornhub announced it was using machine learning to automatically tag its millions of videos and facial recognition software to detect and tag thousands of individual porn stars, including the physical attributes of performers. Such technologies create databases of performers' faces, which could be used to cross-reference their identities with other government databases (such as credit cards, mobile phones, or driver's licenses). The Russian facial recognition service Find Face was used to match explicit photos with images posted to the social network vк (formerly Vkontakte), which outed porn performers to their families, friends, and acquaintances. Despite the often-transient nature of sex work, the use of what I call "whore data" risks fixing or freezing sex worker identities as if they are static.

While user verification has emerged as a response to nonconsensual content, the avenues for having nonconsensual content removed are often inaccessible to sex workers. For example, Australia's new Online Safety Act makes it an offense to post (or threaten to post) an intimate image, but this does not apply where the person has consented to the posting of the image (by someone, in some place, at some point). While this may sound straightforward, this framing excludes most sex workers from being able to take down their nonconsensually posted content. It denies the ability of sex workers to consent to specific uses of our sexual content. In 2023 Google changed their policy to make it easier to remove nonconsensual intimate imagery from search results; however, it relates only to personal, not commercial, content. Moreover, some platforms require that, in order to make a complaint about nonconsensual intimate imagery, the person must verify their identity by providing government-issued identification, presenting further risks by linking their legal and professional identities. The advent of new criminal laws for image-based abuse has limited use, given that sex workers experience systemic barriers to accessing police and the legal system. These kinds of barriers arise when systems are designed without the knowledge, experience, and leadership of affected communities.

On top of this, Western democracies such as France, Germany, Australia, and the United Kingdom are investigating or implementing mandatory age-verification systems to identify or estimate the age of porn consumers. Human classifiers already have difficulty identifying age accurately: If you recall from the chapter 3 vignette, Australia's Classification Board previously suggested that small breast size could be an indicator of a performer being underage, despite the measure being highly variable. In one study, pediatric endocrinologists in court misidentified adult women from legitimate pornographic sites as being under eighteen on the basis of their breast size and youthful appearance, erring two-thirds of the time (Rosenbloom 2013). Facial recognition software has been shown to have high rates of error when purporting to recognize age and gender. In their study "Gender Shades" (2018), Joy Buolamwini and Tinmit Gebru found that facial recognition technology was racially biased and had the highest error rates when used among women of color. Age-estimation software (where eighteen stands in as a proxy for developmental maturity) often relies on such markers as wrinkles and dispersion of facial hair to assess a person's age; however, these vary according to a range of factors, including race, hormone therapy, cosmetics, and styling. When we investigated this further, my colleague Abdul Obeid analyzed more than ten thousand images as part of the UTKFace dataset using a convolutional neural network and found a significant degree of racial bias, especially among the "Asian" and "African" racial categories. Some faces were misclassified by more than forty years, and, unsurprisingly, white faces ranked best overall (Stardust et al. 2024). Australia's eSafety Commissioner also considered using "behavioural signalling" to estimate age by collecting digital traces or gesture patterns. This is a data-heavy process that requires a multitude of data points, such as a person's IP address, search queries, username, and comments. Automated age estimation and restricted access will not guarantee the safety of young people (whose sexual development needs differ dramatically between the ages of twelve, sixteen, and eighteen), but it will collate extensive information about their browsing histories and online presence.

As governments and platforms invest in age and identity estimation systems, the expertise of porn performers is being wildly overlooked. We saw in chapter 1 that many porn performers are already working as sexperts. Performers are often first responders to audience questions about fantasy, reality, health, desire, and bodily diversity. A more sustainable and affordable approach would be to invest in porn literacy programs to equip young people with the knowledge and skills to comprehend and navigate content. Porn literacy is being taught at a handful of universities and high schools and includes content on sex and social media, sexting, consent, respectful relationships, body dissatisfaction, labor exploitation, obscenity law, sexual health, nonconsensual intimate imagery, sexual harassment, and talking with peers about porn. Performers are a missing piece of this puzzle.

Through our experiences on set, porn performers have much to offer about sex, health, intimacy, safety, and labor, and we can also embolden consumers to do more to support the rights of performers. With dedicated resourcing and investment, this knowledge could be harnessed and amplified by technology that is co-designed by sex workers and young people. Indeed, an International Delphi Panel brought together experts in media studies, adolescent sexual health, and reproductive health to review the content of independent porn sites. The projects Sex School, Make Love Not Porn, Pink Label, and Lust Cinema were all understood as websites with the potential to support healthy sexual development (McKee, Dawson, and Kang 2023).

Resistance Art

One of the generative things to emerge from the regulatory environment is an explosion of countercultural and resistance art. Because prohibition provokes transgression, and transgression brings pleasure, a proliferation of defiant, witty, and humorous queer and sex worker art, comics, GIFs, and memes now adorn the internet, shifting the top-down regulatory lens to offer a view from the margins. Jake Elwes's 2016 film *Machine Learning Porn* is one project that deliberately perverts the binary gender of porn classifiers and challenges the internal logics of machine learning. Elwes took a neural network that Yahoo had trained in 2016 to censor pornography and reverse-engineered it. By identifying what the network deciphers as explicit imagery, Elwes used it playfully to produce computer-generated pornography. Interestingly, the resulting images look pornographic in the sense that they feature flesh, crevices, folds, bulges, erectile tissues, openings, and cavities in dark browns, deep purples, and light pinks, but they do not necessarily make up human bodies. Like algorithms, like regulators, and like big tech, the film sees porn only in the abstract, as assortments of pixels devoid of context.

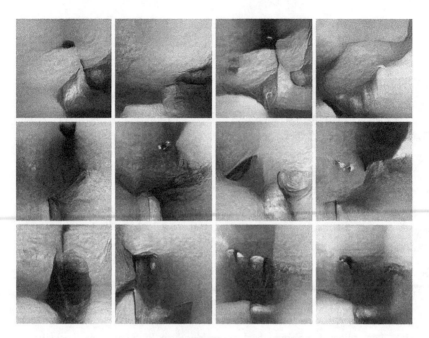

FIGURE 8.2. Jake Elwes reverse-engineered online porn detectors in order to create the film *Machine Learning Porn* (2016). Film stills copyright and courtesy of Jake Elwes.

In 2021 Lena Chen, Maggie Oates, and many other collaborators launched their innovative artwork OnlyBans (a riff off the subscription platform Only-Fans), an interactive game whereby players assume the role of a sex worker and attempt to establish and monetize an online profile through sharing sexy content. However, as Chen and Oates describe the game, "Players encounter content moderation algorithms, shadow-banning, 'real name' policies, facial recognition software, and other threats based on actual experiences of sex workers. As the player attempts to evade being censored by Instagram, flagged by PayPal, and watched by Microsoft, the game reveals just how 'free' the Internet is when one is engaged in stigmatized labor subject to policing and criminalization" (Chen, n.d.). As the player is interrupted by pop-ups and alerts about their content, the aim of the game is to encourage empathy from players about the surveillance, policing, and discrimination of sex workers in digital spaces. If only more politicians and tech bros would play OnlyBans!

Sex worker artworks have also sought to expose the liminality and temporality of online space for sexual subcultures. So often our relationships with platforms (and, by extension, our access to communities, economies, and information) are controlled by the whim of external parties. In 2020 the sex worker artist collective Veil Machine (made up of New York artists Niko Flux, Empress Wu, and Sybil Fury) hosted a protest project called E-Viction, a fictional listing site that resembled the (now defunct) Craigslist Personals section. The site eviction.net was live for twelve hours, showcasing eighteen sex workers and allied performers, and featuring live camming, private shows, riddles, rabbit holes, pop-ups, resources, and artwork for sale before self-destructing. The implosion of the site—which began to glitch, citing critical errors before shutting down completely—mirrored the transient presence of sexual subcultures in online space, appearing in effervescent bursts followed by swift evaporation. Because the internet infrastructures, servers, platforms, and networks we occupy are so often privately owned and our residence there is so conditional, claiming back this space can be a means for sexual subcultures to regain control over their content, work, and cultures.

In pursuit of archiving this kind of cultural material, Veil Machine have since been working with the collective Kink Out to create an online sex worker art gallery called Body of Workers. Kink educator Yin Q, a nonbinary first-generation Chinese American, describes this "virtual art salon" as being similar to a locker room where sex workers share stories, snacks, resources, and referrals. Through a self-sustaining revenue model, their concept is that workers can adjust their privacy settings when they want to be seen by customers, patrons, curators, or the public, who can engage with them through a virtual peepshow. In a panel discussion we held together in 2021, Yin explained their rationale to maintain control over the content: "So much sex worker art, culture and work has been put out there but then stolen, taken, doxed, whatever, and then appropriated and placed into the hands of Netflix producers as well as numerous movies about sex workers, and yet never have any benefits gone back into the community." Cooperative projects such as these are powerful because they acknowledge the value of sexual labor, refuse to be assimilated into dominant tech companies, and actively work toward the collective benefit of communities.

Collective Imagining

Because sex workers have historically found innovative ways to connect in the context of policing and surveillance, it makes sense that sex workers can offer vital contributions to the revisioning of internet governance. By moving out of a legal and policy space, where options are so narrowly configured, and into a space of speculative dreaming, science fiction, and imaginative design, sex workers are stepping outside the realms of logic, strategy, and pragmatism and opening up new possibilities.

FIGURE 8.3. In the interactive online game OnlyBans, created by Lena Chen and Maggie Oates with many collaborators, players take on the role of a sex worker and experience real-name policies, shadowbanning, demonetization, and deplatforming. Image by OnlyBans.

Gabriella Garcia's work is so necessary because it centers unapologetically on liberatory dreaming and radical futures. Throughout 2020–2023 Decoding Stigma ran a lively and interactive program of events that took a visionary approach to the question of how we decode sex work stigma. Their program included a workshop called "Freedom to F*cking Dream" that was facilitated by Sasha Costanza-Chock of the Design Justice Network and Joana Varon of Coding Rights. It had the aim of "healing the heteropatriarchal whorepho-bia that has been embedded into technology." In the workshop, we used the Oracle for Transfeminist Technologies, an exquisitely designed card deck that encourages users to collectively draw, discuss, map, envision, and reshape the future.

At a time when marginalized communities can easily be co-opted as glorified consultants to tick corporate boxes and solve the problems of big tech, to turn inward is an act of resistance. Decoding Stigma's events are meaningful because of their internal focus on healing and community. To direct our energies toward liberatory imaginaries and radical alternatives is to refuse extractive capitalism, step outside the terms of reference of regulators, and to set our own priorities. The Oracle cards are especially potent because they use what has historically been an analog, tangible form of divination and apply it toward solving new world technological problems. This mix of old school and new school reminds us of the importance of remembering and learning from history in advocating for different technological futures. Toward this end, Decoding Stigma and Hacking//Hustling's joint event "Browser Histories" invited participants to curate a temporary digital collection of such keepsakes as photos, artwork, screenshots, stories, tips, hacks, journals, and dead links—a nostalgic treasure chest of artifacts that had been lost in the war on pornography.

Cooperative Governance

While porn performers continue to fight against the community standards of dominant platforms, sex worker collectives are establishing alternative forums. What is notable about sex worker peer platforms—similar to what we saw among porn collectives in chapter 1—is that they often take cooperative approaches to their structure, policies, and decision-making and prioritize ways to meaningfully and materially benefit communities, including through mutual aid. In 2018 the Melbourne-based collective of sex workers and technologists Assembly Four pioneered the sex worker–friendly social platform Switter (an alternative to Twitter) that connects sex workers, clients, and allies. Switter was founded in response to the impact of FOSTA/SESTA (see chapter 4) and built on the open-source, decentralized microblogging network Mastodon. In its first ten months Switter amassed more than two hundred thousand users and over 5.5 million status updates. Assembly Four commit a portion of profits to fund sex worker projects and are actively involved in community development and advocacy to change internet governance.

Worker-owned porn platforms are emerging in other parts of the world. The cooperative Peep.Me was deliberately founded to be collectively owned and democratically governed by adult performers. On their website, Peep.Me describe their deliberate "purpose over profit" stance that involves profit sharing and donating 10 percent to sex worker–led organizations as part of their business model. Their governance model is based on the premise that "the path to economic liberation begins with community ownership and governance of our marketplaces." When I spoke to the founders, Jade Rulz and Donia Love, they described their excitement at the ideals of the site. Jade, a biracial, bisexual escort who was impacted by the closure of advertising sites, was motivated by "being able to offer [a platform] to other people who are marginalized and have had to deal with the same sort of hurdles and issues with consistent money, or being able to own their own image, or being able to make a profit."

However, independent platforms are founded at their own risk. In 2023–24 I interviewed eleven indie platforms that had been aspiring to create sex worker–friendly alternatives to sites like Pornhub, OnlyFans, and Twitter. Of those eleven platforms, five had shut down or paused their operations indefinitely, citing the difficulties of bringing their radical visions to life in the current regulatory environment. The platforms—Switter, Sex School, Body of Workers, and Peep.Me—expressed to me their deep sense of grief at losing such important political projects (worker cooperatives! live-action porn literacy! sex worker socials!) and their frustration in trying to foreground ethics, accountability, and justice in a climate that prioritized speed, scale, and surveillance. "It's an eternal struggle," said Lina Bembe, a queer feminine migrant of color and part of the core performer team at Sex School. "It just boils down to—there's no place for platforms to exist."

As Yin Q described of Body of Workers, "We were coming up against the constant speed at which AI and social media was going and the regulations around it that we had to pause." The emotional and financial toll of this work was evident—Donia, a white, nonbinary femme and cofounder of Peep.Me, reflected, "Honestly, if we had had a million dollars . . . we would've been able to pay people and build the necessary mental health infrastructure we needed." This reflection—that if they had more funding, they would have spent it on mental health support—should give us pause: This is the emotional climate facing indie producers in the wake of big tech.

In 2021 I interviewed Eliza Sorensen, one of Assembly Four's founders, as part of a workshop on online gendered harm. A Koori disabled sex worker and technologist, Eliza described how Australia's new Online Safety Act had the potential to make small, independent platforms more vulnerable by inviting vexatious complaints about sexual content and requiring platforms to respond to takedown notices within twenty-four hours. "There are some real risks, I think, for very small communities to run their own platforms," Eliza told me. The legislation is "actually preventing decentralization." Eliza continued, "One of the things that, as a platform, I know that I grapple with is that we still have to work within the confines of the law, and regardless of our personal opinion of actually wanting to tear those structures down, we can be held criminally liable. So I'm not entirely sure how we, as platform owners and things like that, actually even get to change anything until we can change the legislation in place." In 2022 Switter closed, citing the impossibility of ethically complying with increasing anti-LGBTQ and anti–sex work laws.

For Veil Machine, even the process of documenting sexual censorship placed the artists in precarious legal situations. When promoting their E-Viction event, Veil Machine reported that their first post was taken down within hours despite depicting no sexual content; their GoFundMe campaign was removed; their Twitch was temporarily suspended; they were banned from using Mailchimp; their Instagram account was regularly shadowbanned; and they consistently experienced log-in problems on Google (Cloud Salon 2021). In these instances, the design of the current regulatory framework disproportionately burdens sex worker artists who are critical of censorship and disincentivizes us from creating our own spaces. Indeed, simply the act of running that exhibition alone (by virtue of distributing money to sex workers and advertising sexual content) left the organizers at risk of prosecution for a range of offenses, from obscenity to prostitution, trafficking, racketeering, conspiracy, and money laundering.

Despite these projects being disbanded or suspended, the ideals behind them remain very much alive. Their legacies and provocations live on. Yin Q felt that Body of Workers was still inspiring change by offering important lessons, even if its future iterations may look different: "I think it's inspiring for the [younger] generation of sex workers . . . the techies who can really just get in there and really keep cultivating a queer online universe."

Dismantling Institutions

In this context, for communities to even engage in tech spaces is risky and requires surmounting significant barriers. I interviewed Danielle Blunt, cofounder of Hacking//Hustling and recipient of a Pioneer Award from the Electronic Frontiers Foundation, about their strategies for intervening in both tech and academic spaces. As a grassroots sex worker collective, Hacking//Hustling were often at the forefront of tech issues, mobilizing with the resources available to them. Two years before academic research emerged on the effects of FOSTA-SESTA, Hacking//Hustling had already published their report "Erased: The Impact of FOSTA-SESTA and the Removal of Backpage on Sex Workers" (Blunt and Wolf 2020), which Blunt described as "entirely funded by client donations and my human footstool." In 2020 Hacking//Hustling organized an

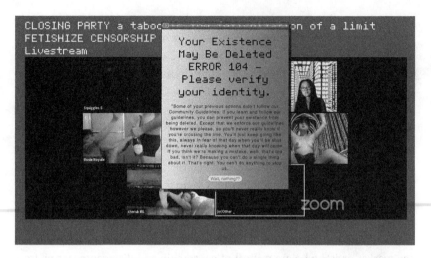

FIGURE 8.4. Veil Machine's 2020 pop-up event E-Viction was curated by Empress Wu, Sybil Fury, and Niko Flux. Veil Machine describes itself as "a sex worker art collective exploring: Intimacy through lies. Authenticity through commodification. The digital as the real." Image by Veil Machine.

event at Harvard Law School called "Big Tech Is Watching." Blunt described how this work involved identifying radical individuals within institutions, finding opportunities for sex workers to speak "in spaces where they have been historically denied access," and paying people in cash on the day of speaking, with the goal of diverting funds from institutions to communities. "We landed on the name Hacking//Hustling because that is what sex workers do to survive. We hack systems that were not built for us to get the shit we need. We hustle to survive and care for our community when the state fails to do so."

For those sex workers who enjoy institutional affiliations, access, and privilege, there are challenges to working within academic structures. In 2021 Lorelei Lee, a porn performer, sex worker activist, and organizer with the Disabled Sex Workers' Coalition, led the coordination of a conference called "Informal, Criminalized, Precarious: Sex Workers Organizing against Barriers." Lorelei was a Justice Catalyst Fellow at Cornell Law School, and the conference focused on structural barriers to labor rights, including what they described as "the difficulty of organizing with a cohort that is chronically deprived of financial and social support, making precarity and trauma the norm." Unsurprisingly, we struggled to find funding. The academic institutions we were working across—some of which had billions of dollars in endowments—came back to us repeatedly with similar messages that there was no budget for honoraria. Lorelei prepared an extensive budget justification, emphasizing "the expertise that sex worker organizers are being asked to share, expertise that has been acquired painstakingly and often at great cost." Eventually, thanks to donations from a range of groups including the Black Law Students Association, the Women's Law Coalition, and the Asian American Feminist Collective, supplemented by Hacking//Hustling, we were able to pay sex worker speakers. Notably, a number of those speakers chose to donate their honoraria to grassroots sex worker mutual aid fundraisers.

As part of the conference, I moderated a panel at the Berkman Klein Center at Harvard. In our discussion, Chibundo Egwuatu, an organizer who researches Black sex worker activism as part of Black liberatory futures, noted that if we want sex workers to be part of the conversations on platforms, tech, and regulation, then we need to think about material concerns: "If we wanna get people to the table to talk about tech, specifically sex workers, they need to be housed; so they need to be paid, they need to have money, disposable income with which to take care of themselves, and then, of course, surplus energy and attention to give to projects."

How else can we expect sex workers to be part of the conversation if we don't provide the material means? As Egwuatu argues, building liberatory futures involves significant changes to institutional practice and social infrastructure. Following the conference, Lorelei and Rachel Kuo, a scholar of race and social movements, produced a "non-comprehensive community toolkit and report" called "Dis/Organizing Toolkit: How We Build Collectives beyond Institutions." The toolkit identifies the dual tension for sex workers when working with institutions. On the one hand, informal political collectives work to "disorganize exclusive and formal institutions, systems, and structures" (Kuo and Lee 2021, 2); that is, they interrogate their modus operandi and expose their internal hierarchies. On the other hand, institutional systems threaten to disorganize collectives themselves, swallowing or breaking them up.

Reinvesting Energies

The material situation in which many porn performers find ourselves means that we are repeatedly confronted with design injustice. The prevalence of sex work stigma in legislation, policy, and media directly affects performers' lives, legal status, health, rights, and working conditions. Absence at the decision-making table and in the design lab puts porn performers at greater risk—of worse public policy, of additional criminalization, of retracted rights. And yet the costs of engagement are high. The risk is that in constantly reacting—to parliamentary inquiries, to media headlines, to corporate blunders, to discriminatory laws, to surveillance regimes—the energy of sex worker rights movements is directed primarily to responsive, reactionary work (effectively as unpaid consultants to diagnose the problems of big tech) or to urgent survival and mobilization work (circumventing algorithms, inventing new spellings, lexicons, and grammars that escape detection, finding legislative loopholes, improving digital privacy, avoiding detection). It is diverted from our long-term goals, such as community building, liberatory dreaming, and world-making: the generative, joyful, and imaginative work that allows sex workers to thrive. This diversion is perhaps one of the greatest travesties in that it invites exhaustion and burnout, siphons off vital resources and energies, and interrupts our momentum.

We saw in chapter 7 that inevitable pitfalls result from engaging in law reform processes, including the narrow range of voices, the personal and political risks of engagement (from dilution of goals to self-incrimination), and the respectability politics that divides communities. Some organizations are allocating substantial time and resources responding to one anti-porn bill after another. Performer groups that are fighting back often comprise performers who are stretched to capacity and already volunteer their time and expertise. This chapter demonstrates that similar pitfalls await when engaging with big tech and academia. When they diagnose the problem as pornography, tech companies rely on problematic built-in assumptions: that pornography does not belong in cultural life, that participating in pornography strips one of their right to privacy, that identity verification amounts to safety, and that simply removing sexual content will somehow solve sexual exploitation, assault, or abuse.

In addition to rejecting the terms of reference that frame public consultations and law reform processes, we need to also reject the unspoken presumptions that frame pornography debates in tech spaces. By abandoning these starting points, we can create different trajectories for sexually explicit media. The answer to many of these problems is not simply better algorithms or more diverse data sets. What's missing in so many conversations are questions about the *design* and *deployment* of technology. How is it being used and toward what ends? Whom is it serving, and how are the burdens and benefits distributed? As Sasha Costanza-Chock (2020) writes, "There are many cases where a design justice analysis asks us not to make systems more inclusive, but to refuse to design them at all" (19). Around the world, sex workers are at the forefront of imagining new ways to reenvision technologies to make them work not against us, but for us.

Birth Preparation

I WANT YOU TO OVERCOME YOUR WHOREPHOBIA! An artwork by Jacq the Stripper looms above us. Sex worker art, indie porn magazines, and erotic books adorn the shelves. The wall is meticulously lined with ball gags, paddles, collars, blindfolds, ear muffs, carabiners, safety scissors, nipple clamps, floggers, and gas masks. We are in the KinkBnB Hedon House preparing for a saucy threesome. Canes are stashed in the corner like an umbrella stand. Upcycled furniture is equipped with Tarot decks and dried flowers. We are surrounded by a full beat of nitrile gloves, assorted condoms, lubes, hand sanitizer, dental dams, a sharps (used needles) bin, and alcohol wipes. In case we need it, there's a spanking horse, bondage chair, suspension ring, and pallet wrap.

I cradle my belly. We are shooting a film called *MotherFuckers*, an explicit documentary about porn star parents. I trace the sleeping bump inside my uterus—I am six months pregnant. Although the space is garnished with a dimly lit stainless steel aesthetic, it is a queer whore family vibe. A group of us are snacking on vegan treats, rifling through our suitcases, and chatting with the handsome resident house boi. I am shooting with Helen, who had her daughter at nineteen and is about to become a grandmother, and Friedrich Kreuz, whose rainbow kids I have had the pleasure of babysitting. It's a family affair.

For me, this scene is a form of birth prep. It's a chance to stop, honor, and enjoy this precious, once-in-a-lifetime moment. I have been approaching labor like a marathon, treating my body like an endurance athlete. While pregnant I have done life drawing modeling and erotic photo shoots and have seen a sexological bodyworker to prime my body for this epic event. I have been watching active births on YouTube, reading about orgasmic birth, and dreaming of a waterbirth. What better way to prepare, I thought, than some wholesome pregnancy porn with my friends?

We sit in the courtyard, among the peeling paint and sprawling succulents, discussing our varied journeys through pregnancy, birth, mother-fucking, and queer parenting. What, who, and how we craved; the changes to our bodies, sensations, desires. "There's something about pregnant bodies that just makes me want to worship," says Helen. "The swollen, engorged, fecund body; there's just something sublime in it. I just want to get on my knees!" "Just go easy on my nipples," I say. "My mammary glands are out of control."

I am nervous about birth but invested in tapping into my best power bottom headspace. If you can have sex at a play party and orgasm on cue in front of a camera crew, my burlesque-performing osteopath friend tells me, you have the skills to tune in for a vaginal birth. I have a series of toys lined up ready for perineum stretching and birth preparation, ranging from silicone cocks to an epi-no, a vaginal dilator designed to prevent the need for an episiotomy, gifted to me by my stripper friend. Friedrich is musing about how BDSM is an excellent preparation for birth. "Getting into that rhythm, building up slowly," he says, in his pink ACT UP T-shirt, "it mirrors the practice of birth anyway. You start up with small contractions that get bigger and bigger, breathing your way into them." I wriggle into the sling, sliding my feet into stirrups, announcing that I can't lie on my back for too long as the supine position can block oxygen to the baby.

As we talk, Helen and Friedrich massage my feet and belly. We trace my *linea nigra* all the way from my pubic bone, up my stomach, and up each breast. They are breathing love down to my baby, releasing oxytocin and endorphins. It's impossible not to think about what the future holds for our kids, our future generations of activists. How will our brave little babes manage to move through this world trusting their bodies, knowing themselves, working together?

I am proud to be a sex working mama who can equip my children with non-judgmental, shame-free information and nuanced communication skills that cover bodies, boundaries, touch, desires, health, safety, pleasure, and care. Pornography, says Helen, put her in touch with her own sexuality and helped her heal the hatred she had toward her own body. Known as the "porno mum" at her kid's school, she reflects: "For me it was quite transformative, being able to pass on that love of my body that I did not have before sex work to my daughter."

It's a tender moment—our apprehension for the future is tempered by the trust we have in our inner whore wisdom, and our faith in our incredible kids. Helen smiles at me: "I just don't think I would have been as good a mum without sex work."

Conclusion

Indie Provocations

As a category, *pornography* makes just as little sense as it did when it was first deployed as a regulatory construct in the eighteenth century. With the proliferation of sexual media in the twenty-first century (from camming and direct-to-consumer sites, virtual reality content to deepfakes and generative material), what counts as pornography is just as blurry, contested, and politicized as it always was. The boundary work undertaken to differentiate these forms of media can offer a nuanced vocabulary for understanding sexual media, but the project of ascertaining what is or isn't pornography is ultimately a vexed one. Instead, the deliberate haziness of the category permits it to serve as a justification for extensions of state, tech, and administrative power and control.

Studying indie porn illuminates how populations and our sexualities come to be governed through disciplinary practices. The ongoing war on pornography is used to rationalize and defend increased surveillance, widespread criminalization, racialized policing, military occupations, colonial violence, anti-immigration, biased technologies, abstinence education, financial discrimination, and the prison industrial complex. The preoccupation with defining, identifying, detecting, and reducing the circulation of pornography then acts to obscure the multifaceted meanings of sexual expression and to obfuscate the problematic history of its regulation. An increasing technological investment in porn detection exposes the political alliances driving anti-porn agendas, governments' deputization of big tech, and the limitations of regulatory approaches based on obscenity, offensiveness, copyright, and individual privacy. While the technologies may be new, the debates are old, and they call for collective responses that redistribute power, wealth, and resources.

Porn both produces and reflects culture, discoursing with the social preoccupations of the time. If governments want better porn, therefore, they need to build more equitable and just societies, offline and online. Instead, governments tend to scapegoat and exceptionalize porn, criminalizing the economies available to marginalized folks as a means of survival, increasing their labor precarity and then demanding that porn be consensual, authentic, diverse, and ethical. Identity verification and algorithmic surveillance are pitched as the panacea, incentivizing an upscale in automation and tech solutionism. And yet ethical pornography requires more than documenting, recording, and filing consent paperwork. With more people producing erotic media in a time of rental crisis, labor cuts, and food shortages, when performers have material needs to be taken care of (childcare, hospital bills, prescription medicines), platforms cannot seriously sustain the delusion that consent under capitalism can simply be identified by screening software.

Indie pornographies—as they have done throughout the twentieth century—offer us ways to think about sex, work, and media beyond frameworks of explicitness, profit, and risk. But as a deeply stigmatized industry, indie porn is susceptible to respectability politics that seek recognition, visibility, and legalization. As an intersectional movement, our resistance strategies need to dismantle the current regulatory landscape in ways that curb rather than expand state mechanisms of oppression. This involves being led by the most marginalized and working to abolish the carceral state, to refuse work, and to ensure that all people have access to housing and health care. Like other social movements, the challenge for indie porn lies in how to resist state and tech violence without dividing communities, creating hierarchies, and reproducing stigma.

Indie Porn as Relational

This book demonstrates that indie porn—like the people who produce it—is never completely independent. Rather, indie porn is relational. It is imbricated in multiple systems—it relies upon production and distribution networks, it sits in dialogue with media and culture, and it is deeply rooted in interpersonal relationships. The values of indie producers, while they may be espoused by individuals, have long legacies in community movements: Black feminist care ethics, queer liberation, trans bodily autonomy, disability justice, sex worker rights. In this way, indie porn is more about interdependence and relationality than independence and individualism. Its focus on skill sharing, collaborative decision-making, and nonhierarchical organizing depends on building and sustaining long-term relationships that allow it to be produced outside of corporate studios and distributed via community channels. Because, as I discussed in chapter 1, independence arises from a relationship (demarcation from a dominant benchmark), and because that benchmark consistently changes, what constitutes independence continually shifts. Therefore, indie porn is perpetually in dialogue with power. It strives for independence from dominant values, systems, practices, and conventions. It stands for the possibility of a different way of doing things, an alternative route, a departure point. But it does this *through* relationships—seeing whole people, valuing their contributions, honoring their lives, and tending to them with an ethic of care.

These relationships can become strained as indie porn enters the marketplace and embarks on processes of labor extraction and monetization. As producers make compromises for commerciality, visibility, and respectability—around search engine optimization, marketing, cost-cutting—they produce their own hierarchies of benefit and disadvantage. Relational systems are still employed here: White performers achieve visibility at the expense of racialized performers, producers attract income because of performers' authenticity labor, vanilla sex acts are accepted while kink activities remain derided, performers working legally receive social capital while those who cannot afford to comply are criminalized, and so on. It is a tactic of governments to divide communities by driving competition, hoarding wealth, and gatekeeping opportunities. In response, indie porn could easily be swallowed up into this system to resemble big tech's business model of individualized, outsourced labor, with further entrenched inequities. But because relationships are the bedrock of indie porn, performers and producers are finding ways to share that wealth, whether it be through collective ownership, mutual aid, or solidarity projects. Such initiatives acknowledge that it is communities—rather than individuals—that make indie porn both possible and valuable.

Indie Porn's Promises

What kinds of promises does indie porn make? It depends. In their more commercial and conservative iterations, indie pornographies can present an appeal for diversity and inclusion toward a pluralistic vision of participation. But in their more radical iterations, they issue fundamental challenges to the regulation of pornography: to its positioning as a distinct subject outside of society and culture, to its interpretation according to pathological frameworks, to its governance by actors who are detached from its production and consumption, and to the value afforded to sexual labor. First, they challenge the sequestering of sexually explicit materials into a separate regulatory category altogether that ought to be kept out of public space. Following Walter Kendrick's description of pornography not as a "thing," but as a "concept"—one with boundaries that are constantly being redrawn by regulators, producers, and performers—they challenge how pornography has been situated in modernity as something that ought to be kept out of the hands of innocent minds. Rather than situate sex as exceptional, these movements challenge presumptions that sexually explicit material is without value: of only prurient interest, as "dirt for dirt's sake," or lacking in serious literary, artistic, scientific, or political value. Rather than position pornography as something that requires redeeming, my participants attest to the value of sexually explicit materials, including their importance in recording sexual subcultures, their contributions to critical social conversations, their use as educative tools, their community-building functions, and their capacity to resonate with and *move* viewers.

With regulators seeking new ways to control, contain, and restrict access to pornographies, indie porn provocateurs critique the assumption that sex on screen should be treated as more dangerous or corruptive than nonexplicit media content or that it needs to be sequestered in any case. In line with Lauren Berlant and Michael Warner's writing on sex in public (1998), queer and feminist pornographers critique how pornography regulation acts to maintain institutions of cisgender, heterosexual privilege. The act of designating representations of sex to the private, personal realm outside the public or political sphere obscures the fact that heterosexual intimacies permeate public culture. When heterosexual intimacies are depoliticized, normalized, and institutionalized, it becomes increasingly difficult to recognize more fragile and temporal queer intimacies, values, ethics, and world-making projects apparent in porn subcultures.

Second, indie pornographies challenge the categorization, organization, and hierarchization of sexual practices into what Gayle Rubin ([1984] 2011) calls regimes of "sexual stratification and erotic persecution" (159). They resist the stigmatization, pathologization, and criminalization of fetish practices, kink intimacies, and body fluids and their readings as abject, risky, or extreme. They challenge the erasure of practices like squirting, anal sex, fisting, piercing, golden showers, stumping, muffing, and other nonprocreative, gender-fluid practices and critique how blood, urine, and ejaculate operate to threaten the stable boundaries of the intact, cisgender, hetero, able body. In doing so, they issue a broader interrogation of and wider exposé of the cis-heteronormativity and phallocentrism of law and the ways in which historical taxonomies of perversions from psychiatry and medicine continue to manifest in content moderation.

Third, indie pornographies challenge decision-making structures that govern sexual content. They contest the criteria, transparency, processes, and accountability mechanisms of bodies who are empowered to arbitrate and mediate community standards. They challenge the makeup of classification boards (questioning their representativeness), the qualifications of platform "trust and safety" councils (to assess sexual material), the law enforcement practices of police (their carceral agendas), the decision-making of customs officials (their misunderstandings of sexual anatomy), the interests of politicians (their electoral investments), and the practices of payment processers (their aversion to reputational risk). They reveal that these investments are largely concerned with the maintenance of a sexist, white supremacist, queerphobic, whorephobic, and ableist order of power and wealth.

Fourth, indie porn asserts the value of sexual labor. As more and more pornography is self- or collectively produced, pornography regulation falls short of providing protections for workers concerned with industrial rights, workplace safety, and digital privacy. And yet indie porn performers tell us that if platforms and governments valued what it takes to actually sex work, at both an occupational and personal level, then they would urgently divert resources into decentralizing internet infrastructure, supporting the emergence of new cooperatives, and facilitating the equitable distribution of wealth and power among laborers rather than internet intermediaries.

Regulatory Challenges

If these are the provocations, then what are the regulatory fantasies? Regulators fantasize that pornography is inherently dangerous, corruptive, and harmful and use this rationale to justify greater regulatory intervention, regulation, and surveillance. But underlying this logic is a fear that the democratization of culture threatens to undermine the normative social order and subsequently their authority. To combat this, regulators create an economic, technological, and regulatory environment that deters indie porn production. A tangled web of regulations ensures that diverse sexual representations are deliberately kept out of public space. Classification, broadcasting, criminal, content, and customs legislation leave few opportunities for the sharing of critical ideas, images, and conversations about sexual cultures. Practices that would diversify content are explicitly prohibited, becoming criminal intimacies, or are otherwise suppressed, demoted, and demonetized. Administrative decisions employ wide interpretations of what constitutes offensive or prohibited material, resulting in the ripping, cutting, destruction, or confiscation of artworks and cultural materials. Enforcement is selective and targeted, often driven by media, complaints, or electoral campaigns. This landscape is designed to deter indie production, leaving producers in a state of uncertainty, vulnerability, and anxiety at the whim of individual complaints. It is designed to deflect responsibility from governments onto the industry itself.

Through their efforts, regulators work to make indie porn production unviable. They contribute to an online landscape where distribution is largely centralized, limiting opportunities for equitable participation. As payment intermediaries determine who can sell content online, their discriminatory requirements push out small producers. In turn, they make space for the flourishing of tube sites to dominate the market by pirating content and streaming it for free. This fosters an unwillingness among consumers to pay for porn and threatens the viability of producing independent pornography altogether. Ownership of the "means of production" has not led to self-sufficiency; instead, the privatization of online space has led to significant wealth disparities between producers and platforms.

Regulators tolerate pornography when it benefits them, and when it doesn't, they treat it as expendable. Despite adult businesses being integral to the commercial development of new technologies and platforms, regulators treat their demise as collateral damage. The outcome is the instant deletion of cultural archives without oversight or justification; the broad capture of adjacent content; and a facade of participation that actually resembles new regimes of power through which bodies are produced (likeability, clickability, popularity). Business decisions to remove sex (images, discussions, transactions) from online spaces reinforce the reality that platforms are responsible not to their userbase, but to their shareholders. The persuasive, deep-seated nature of sex work stigma renders sex a liability. The compulsion to avoid sex scandals or reputational risks is so great that it surpasses the commercial incentives of permitting sex-related businesses to operate.

Despite these efforts, pornography persists. The state may be unlikely to subsidize sex-radical porn, but in the meantime, it provokes and produces it by eliciting workarounds and circumventions by savvy, creative hustlers. Through its vocality and virality, pornography is an embarrassing reminder of regulators' own redundancy, their lack of qualifications to make decisions about sex, and their lack of authority to govern. Porn remains a fleshy reminder of the corporeal materiality of regulators' bodies and their capacity to be physically moved by destabilizing desires. Through this self-fulfilling prophecy, regulators manifest the very thing they are afraid of.

Creative Strategies

How can indie porn folk and allies resist the tyranny of platforms whose primary motives are profit and reputation while relying on them for income? How can they resist the authority of governments who seek to expand their power and control, as subjects within them? How can indie producers work against porn stigma within the industry, to undo rather than benefit from it? In their conflict with the regulatory framework, indie producers offer lessons about how to practice resistance politics in an era of neoliberalism and capitalist co-optation.

Indie pornographies have proved to be adaptable, flexible, and creative. They have built campaigns, partnerships, and alliances to ensure their own survival and find new means to reach their audiences. They have initiated campaigns to compel users to "pay for your porn" and "support your local pornographer," and pursued copyright violations to hold tube sites to account. They have pitched their products as niche and specialty, promoted their content as artisanal and fair trade, and built a base of ethical consumers. They have diversified their income streams, found revenue sources in patronage and affiliates, created alternative platforms, and developed voluntary industry codes.

In addition to these strategies for economic survival, producers employ three key generative strategies: opting out of existing systems, prefiguring their own ethical standards, and developing systems for self-governance and community regulation. First, the distrust and disillusionment many producers feel with the legal framework means that they simply opt out of compliance altogether. Many view the current laws as unjust and outdated, lagging behind both technological developments and cultural shifts. Combined with a lack of transparent and consistent enforcement, this leads to a disrespect for the law. As a matter of practicality, producing porn often requires disregarding the law or circumventing it. As a matter of civil disobedience, producing feminist, queer, or kink pornography can necessitate willfully disobeying the law.

Second, performer-producers practice a prefigurative politics (which aims to reflect the societies they aspire to create) by practicing alternative systems of ethics. In the absence of formal legal protections or industry standards around workplace health and safety or industrial rights, producers and performers are pioneering their own standards. Referencing international trends but grounded in local politics, they demonstrate an ethics of care and a devolution of power that recognizes the value of performers; centers on collaboration; promotes access to health, safety, and digital rights; remunerates gendered labor; prioritizes transparency; emphasizes consent; and demonstrates care for one another beyond the confines of the product itself.

Third, queer and feminist producers are developing their own community standards and accountability mechanisms. Through the processes of self-reflection, feedback mechanisms, and ongoing community engagement, producers respond dynamically to changing community standards around production, marketing, and advocacy. Many indie producers are signposting content for consumers, encouraging performers to choose their own tags and descriptors, engaging in industry discussions about power and privilege, and diverting financial resources to those in need. Indie producers are engaged in mutual aid and solidarity work. Government attempts at regulation fall short of these existing self-regulatory practices and demonstrates the importance of engaging local partners in cultivating ethical codes.

Resistance, Not Respectability

These strategies have not been without their consequences. While indie porn tells us about the importance of resistance, it also warns us about the trap of respectability politics. In their very definition, indie pornographies distinguish themselves as something different from mainstream pornographies. The concepts of *feminist* porn, *ethical* porn, and *alternative* porn represent generative, world-making projects but can also perform a *compensatory* function that can buy into the stigma surrounding sexual labor. Where these become marketable aspects of business, indie pornographers make income by (advertently or inadvertently) reproducing porn stigma. Where they distance themselves from mainstream content and marginalized workers (such as those who are migrant, bareback, drug users, working unlawfully, or "just there for the money") and where they appeal to media and government for approval or endorsement, these projects can both capitalize on and perpetuate stigma associated with pornography more generally. Some approaches attempt to make porn more palatable instead of challenging the regulatory fantasies that criminalize it.

There thus remains the risk that indie porn becomes a self-congratulatory fantasy of democratic participation while operating as a market intervention that fuels, rather than disrupts, a capitalist system. When social capital accrues from declarations of inclusive practice, there is less incentive to redistribute power among communities. There remains stratification in who is represented, and some cases, claims of democratization look more like outsourcing of content creation.

While laws regulating pornography are urgently in need of change, attempts to engage with law reform are fraught with risk. Performers, producers, and retailers adopt different engagement strategies depending on their politics and outlaw status. Law reform processes lack meaningful consultation methods; they frame pornography debates in terms of freedom of speech or protection from harm and represent political compromise rather than evidence-based policy. Because law reform processes are stalled or accelerated by politicians' own investments in electoral success, law reform efforts are stymied. Historically, incremental changes that have been identified as wins on some fronts (predominantly for retailers) have resembled losses on others (especially for performers).

Placing too much faith in legal recognition has led to movement demands being articulated as bids for respectability. Internalized, anticipated, and experienced stigma shapes how indie pornographies look and how our advocacy goals emerge. In the bid to distance themselves from mainstream pornography and seek certified recognition as ethical, these movements can conflate ethics with aesthetics and act to defer stigma onto more marginalized groups at the expense of structural change. As Dinesh Wadiwel said in our interview, "Any practice can be co-opted or subsumed within the value system of an economy or become valorized in a particular way where those who are seeking to make this sort of radical intervention actually will lose control of this process." There's no doubt that including more diverse bodies, ethnicities, genders, and sexualities in porn can have an important affirmative role for porn consumers, but if visibility is the sole political strategy, marginalized folks will simply be commodified and subsumed into larger capitalistic structures. Performers are actively challenging the hubris over diversity and inclusion and, where they have become producers themselves, are emphasizing the importance of joint ownership and material benefits.

This is not to say that DIY projects will always be subsumed by capital or that they lack value, but we need to remain attuned to shifting power dynamics and committed to foregrounding *collective* benefit, during both production *and* distribution. If indie pornographies want to change not only sexual representation but also race and class inequalities, if they want to serve, empower, and benefit our vibrant communities and use porn as a medium to do so, it requires the democratization of both the process and the profits.

Revolution Not Reform

If we welcome the diverse content prompted by the decentralization of production, then we must be prepared for what confronts us there. In people's bedrooms we don't find neatly packaged individuals with singular, marketable identities; we find whole, messy humans with bills to pay, caregiver responsibilities, health conditions, traumas, desires, dreams, and complex lives. If producers, distributors, and regulators care about the material conditions of performers, they ought to care about the intersecting oppressions that impact their lives. A political agenda for indie porn therefore demands widespread change across multiple areas rather than a narrow focus on recognition and certification. As Dean Spade (2013) notes, "Resistance conceived through single axis frameworks can never transform conditions of intersectional violence and harm" (1050). Because of this interconnected web, indie porn producers—who may be both part of and share affinities with other marginalized folk, informal economy workers, and criminalized industries—are in a distinct position to build coalitions for longer lasting social change.

The relational qualities of indie porn present opportunities for solidarity. In our lives as hustlers, hackers, and scrappers, we are well equipped to pool energies, resources, learnings, and aid toward interconnected struggles. There are places where those shared interests are obvious—bodily autonomy, reproductive justice, labor exploitation. But because almost everyone is impacted by porn stigma, these connections may also be found in unexpected places. From the young people searching for affirming content to the parents with inadequate vocabulary to broach it; from the politicians who watch porn in secret to the partners who feel threatened by it; from the people whose family albums are periodically scanned for child abuse material to those whose nude selfies are maliciously leaked, scraped, or made into deepfakes—porn stigma bears an unacceptable cost upon our lives and relationships. And yet, whether you know it or not, someone you love is a sex worker.

Many precarious laborers share aspects in common with porn performers that could be leveraged for political action. Shifts away from fixed employment toward sharing, gig, and hustle economies affect mobile workers across creative industries—from musicians to beauty influencers to food delivery drivers. The "Pay for Your Porn" movement (much like the wages-for-housework campaign in the 1970s) calls for invisible, underpaid, and sexualized labor to be valued, an appeal that may resonate with those who use their bodies for work—janitors, dancers, or caregivers. With outsourced laborers imbricated in the process of porn regulation—including the underpaid, offshore moderators tasked with classifying sexually explicit content—there is growing resentment at the inequity in labor supply chains whereby US and European tech companies overwhelmingly own the infrastructures and media production is geographically dispersed. Indie porn does not solve the broader problem with work that disability activists have long identified—the reification of wage labor under capitalism, the positioning of productivity as a prerequisite to dignity, housing, and health care or as a status symbol that divides who is deserving and who is unworthy. However, the acts of making precarious labor visible and asserting its value are steps toward resisting work as we know it and calling for its redistribution.

The demands of indie pornographers share values with environmental campaigns for sustainability, resource distribution, and climate justice. The movement for fair trade products to improve labor conditions and reduce income disparities between wealthy and low-income nations (especially those recovering from colonization, war, invasion, imperialism, climate crisis, famine, and resource exploitation) is relevant to industries of coffee, chocolate, and fashion as well as pornography. The movement for "slow porn," like slow food, slow fashion, and slow tech, is an international call to reduce mass consumption and environmental damage in favor of local, sustainable processes. The popularity of green pornography and eco-sexuality demonstrates an interest in earth care and animal liberation, which require international action to curb the climate crisis and rely upon giving land and land care back to First Nations peoples. There are opportunities here for indie producers and performers—especially those with white, class, and nationality privilege—to support local and global movements for earth justice, Indigenous sovereignty, and decolonization.

There are further avenues for porn workers to organize alongside communities impacted by techniques of biopolitical surveillance. As algorithms are deployed as part of hiring practices, predictive policing, and service eligibility, they make it difficult to control one's intimate data. The turn to digital identity verification and facial recognition has impacts for porn performers, whose work histories become inescapable fixed points of data. Payment intermediaries' control of financial infrastructure impacts not only porn workers but also undocumented people, political organizers, and mutual aid fundraisers. Ending financial discrimination therefore requires abolishing the system of racial capitalism that underpins both banking industries and sexual economies.

There is plenty to do in an indie porn agenda. If producers are concerned with exploitation, they could agitate to cancel student debt and demand free education, given that many students create content to pay off their college loans. Instead of using forced/voluntary binaries in their marketing, producers can support calls from racialized migrant sex workers to establish safe migration pathways, ending the border industrial complex that leads to Asian sex workers facing immigration scrutiny for carrying condoms or lingerie. Where they market MILF porn (featuring older women or mothers), producers could support childcare collectives supporting working mothers and unpack the archetype of the bad parent in family policing and welfare systems. Producers of trans pornography ought to be active in combatting the escalating anti-trans legislation that prevents access to medical care, bans classroom discussions of LGBTQ+ content, and restricts safe access to bathrooms. Producers could work to repeal criminal laws around sex work and HIV and support depictions of serodiscordant and HIV-positive intimacies. To assist performer decision-making, we could advocate for universal health care, support initiatives for food security, or campaign for housing as a human right. To end raids, targeting, and prosecution of queer porn businesses, we could decriminalize pornography and defund the police. If regulators accept that prisons are criminogenic and unlikely to produce more ethical sexual communicators, we could move away from carceral responses and take transformative justice approaches to sexual violence. Instead of only fighting for accurate labor classification, we could be organizing against the ubiquity of work itself.

In looking toward the future, indie pornographies offer us lessons, processes, and tools: visions for something more than recognition, something beyond better porn. Resistance is not only about struggle but also about the dreaming of speculative, imaginative, liberatory, supposedly impossible futures. If the power of indie pornographies is in their capacity to *imagine* alternative realities, they implore us to keep imagining (beyond rubber stamps, codified standards, and legal recognition). It is within these collective projects and community-building processes that we are prompted to generate new worlds with different ways in which we might relate to sex, work, media, and each other.

References

ACON. 2014. "What Is Safer Sex? Position Statement." Sydney: ACON. https://www.acon
.org.au/wp content/uploads/2015/04/What-is-Safe-Sex-Position-2014.pdf.

Adams, M., and J. Raisborough. 2008. "What Can Sociology Say about Fair Trade? Class,
Reflexivity and Ethical Consumption." *Sociology* 42 (6): 1165–82.

Adler, L. 2018. *Gay Priori: A Queer Critical Legal Studies Approach to Law Reform*. Durham,
NC: Duke University Press.

Adult Performer Advocacy Committee (APAC). n.d.a. "APAC Stamp, California." Captured December 3, 2018; accessed March 3, 2024. https://web.archive.org/web
/20181203153947/www.apac-usa.com/apac-stamp.

Adult Performer Advocacy Committee (APAC). n.d.b. "Performer Bill of Rights, California."
Accessed August 23, 2018. https://apacommittee.org/performer-bill-of-rights/.

Ahmed, S. 2012. *On Being Included: Racism and Diversity in Institutional Life*. Durham, NC:
Duke University Press.

Ahmed, S. 2017. *Living a Feminist Life*. Durham, NC: Duke University Press.

Albert, K. 2022. "Five Reflections from Four Years of FOSTA/SESTA." Posted May 14. *Car-
dozo Arts & Entertainment Law Journal*.

Albury, K. 2004. "The Ethics of Porn on the Net." In *Remote Control: New Media, New
Ethics*, edited by C. Lumby and E. Probyn, 196–211. Cambridge: Cambridge University
Press.

Albury, K. 2015. "Iloveclaude.com: Pornographic Vernacular in Sexual Health Promotion
for Women." *Porn Studies* 2 (2–3): 222–36.

Alois, JD. 2014. "Crowdfunding Site Shuts Down Porn Stars Medical Crowdfunding Campaign." *Crowd Fund Insider*, May 17. http://www.crowdfundinsider.com/2014/05/38854
-crowdfunding-site-shuts-porn-stars-medical-crowdfunding-campaign.

Alptraum, L. 2014. "Is Porn Really So 'High Risk' That Porn Stars Shouldn't Have Bank Accounts?" *Guardian*, April 29. http://www.theguardian.com/commentisfree/2014/apr/29
/porn-stars-high-risk-bank-accounts.

Anonymous. 2010. "Shade Grown Organic Porn?" Ask MetaFilter, May 3. https://ask
.metafilter.com/154669/Shade-grown-organic-porn.

Antoniou, A. K., and D. Akrivos. 2017. *The Rise of Extreme Porn: Legal and Criminological Perspectives on Extreme Pornography in England and Wales.* London: Palgrave Macmillan.

A. O. Movement Collective. 2019. "(W/HOLE)." Accessed March 22, 2024. https://www .theaomc.org/whole.

Are, C., and S. Paasonen. 2021. "Sex in the Shadows of Celebrity." *Porn Studies* 8 (4): 411–19.

Ashford, C. 2011. "(Homo) Normative Legal Discourses and the Queer Challenge." *Durham Law Review* 1:77–99.

Ashforth, B. E., and G. E. Kreiner. 2014. "Dirty Work and Dirtier Work: Differences in Countering Physical, Social, and Moral Stigma." *Management and Organization Review* 10 (1): 81–108.

Ashley, V. 2016. "Porn—Artifice—Performance—and the Problem of Authenticity." *Porn Studies* 3 (2): 187–90.

Attwood, F. 2007. "No Money Shot? Commerce, Pornography and New Sex Taste Cultures." *Sexualities* 10 (4): 441–56.

Attwood, F. 2010a. "Dirty Work: Researching Women and Sexual Representation." In *Secrecy and Silence in the Research Process: Feminist Reflections*, edited by R. Gill and R. Flood, 177–87. Abingdon, UK: Routledge.

Attwood, F., ed. 2010b. *Porn.com: Making Sense of Online Pornography.* New York: Peter Lang.

Attwood, F. 2012. "Art School Sluts: Authenticity and the Aesthetics of Altporn." In *Hard to Swallow: Hard-Core Pornography on Screen*, edited by C. Hines and D. Kerr, 42–56. New York: Columbia University Press.

Attwood, F., and I. Q. Hunter. 2009. "Not Safe for Work? Teaching and Researching the Sexually Explicit." *Sexualities* 12 (5): 547–57.

Attwood, F., and C. Smith. 2010. "Extreme Concern: Regulating 'Dangerous Pictures' in the United Kingdom." *Journal of Law and Society* 37 (1): 171–88.

Australian Broadcasting Corporation. 2010. "Hungry Beast. The Labiaplasty Fad." YouTube. https://www.youtube.com/v/pK9GtT-khb0.

Australian Government. 2005. *Guidelines for the Classification of Films and Computer Games.*

Barakat, H., and E. M. Redmiles. 2022. "Community under Surveillance: Impacts of Marginalization on an Online Labor Forum." *Proceedings of the International AAAI Conference on Web and Social Media* 16 (1): 12–21.

Barcan, R. 2000. "Home on the Rage: Nudity, Celebrity, and Ordinariness in the Home Girls/Blokes Pages." *Continuum: Journal of Media and Cultural Studies* 14 (2): 145–58.

Barnett, D. 2010. "A Return to Wowserism in the Name of Politics." *The Drum*, June 15. http://www.abc.net.au/unleashed/34994.html.

Barrett-Ibarria, S. 2018. "Sex Workers Pioneered the Early Internet—and It Screwed Them Over." *Vice*, October 3. https://motherboard.vice.com/en_us/article/qvazy7/sex-workers -pioneered-the-early-internet.

Barwulor, C., A. McDonald, E. Hargittai, and E. M. Redmiles. 2021. "'Disadvantaged in the American-Dominated Internet': Sex, Work, and Technology." In *Proceedings of the 2021 CHI Conference on Human Factors in Computing Systems*, 1–16. New York: Association for Computing Machinery.

Baudrillard, J. 1983. *Simulations*. Translated by P. Foss, P. Patton, and P. Beitchman. Los Angeles: Semiotext(e).

Baudrillard, J. 1994. *Simulacra and Simulation*. Ann Arbor: University of Michigan Press.

Bauer, R. 2014. *Queer BDSM Intimacies: Critical Consent and Pushing Boundaries*. London: Palgrave Macmillan.

Baym, N. K. 2015a. "Connect with Your Audience! The Relational Labor of Connection." *Communication Review* 18 (1): 14–22.

Baym, N. K. 2015b. "Social Media and the Struggle for Society." *Social Media + Society* 1 (1). https://doi.org/10.1177/2056305115580477.

Baym, N. K. 2018. *Playing to the Crowd: Musicians, Audiences, and the Intimate Work of Connection*. New York: NYU Press.

BBC Radio 4. 2015. "Can Porn Be Ethical?" September 28. https://www.bbc.co.uk/programmes/b06d2g5d.

Beebe, B. 2022. "'Shut Up and Take My Money!': Revenue Chokepoints, Platform Governance, and Sex Workers' Financial Exclusion." *International Journal of Gender, Sexuality and Law* 2 (1): 140–70.

Bennett, T. 2013. "Just Plain Dirt and Nothing Else? Sexually Explicit Films and Australian Classification Law." *Alternative Law Journal* 38 (2): 87–91.

Bennett Moses, L. 2013. "How to Think about Law, Regulation and Technology: Problems with 'Technology' as a Regulatory Target." *Law Innovation and Technology* 5:1–20.

Berg, H. 2014. "Working for Love, Loving for Work: Discourses of Labor in Feminist Sex-Work Activism." *Feminist Studies* 40 (3): 693–721.

Berg, H. 2015a. "Business as Usual." *Jacobin*, February 15. https://www.jacobinmag.com/2015/02/porn-industry-labor-adult-expo.

Berg, H. 2015b. "Sex, Work, Queerly: Identity, Authenticity and Laboured Performance." In *Queer Sex Work*, edited by M. W. Laing, K. Pilcher, and N. Smith, 23–31. Abingdon, UK: Routledge.

Berg, H. 2016. "'A Scene Is Just a Marketing Tool': Alternative Income Streams in Porn's Gig Economy." *Porn Studies* 3 (2): 160–74.

Berg, H. 2017. "Porn Work, Feminist Critique, and the Market for Authenticity." *Signs: Journal of Women in Culture and Society* 42 (3): 669–92.

Berg, H. 2021. *Porn Work: Sex, Labor, and Late Capitalism*. Chapel Hill: University of North Carolina Press.

Berlant, L., and M. Warner. 1998. "Sex in Public." *Critical inquiry* 24 (2): 547–66.

Bernstein, E. 2007. "The Sexual Politics of the New Abolitionism." *differences* 18 (3): 128–51.

Bernstein, E. 2010. "Militarized Humanitarianism Meets Carceral Feminism: The Politics of Sex, Rights and Freedom in Contemporary Antitrafficking Campaigns." *Signs: Journal of Women in Culture and Society* 36 (1): 45–71.

Biasin, E., G. Maina, and F. Zecca, eds. 2014. *Porn after Porn: Contemporary Alternative Pornographies*. Milan: Mimesis International.

BIPOC Adult Industry Collective. 2021. "June 2020–July 2021 Impact Report." https://www.bipoc-collective.org/_files/ugd/2ca6df_cb529baa286d4381973de4c802ff115f.pdf.

Blake, P. 2019. "Age Verification for Online Porn: More Harm Than Good?" *Porn Studies* 6 (2): 1–10.

Blinne, K. C. 2012. "Auto (Erotic) Ethnography." *Sexualities* 15 (8): 953–77.

Blue, V. 2006. *The Smart Girl's Guide to Porn.* Jersey City, NJ: Cleis.

Blue, V. 2015. "PayPal, Square and Big Banking's War on the Sex Industry." *Engadget*, December 2. http://www.engadget.com/2015/12/02/paypal-square-and-big-bankings-war-on-the-sex-industry.

Blue, V. 2019. "Sex, Lies and Surveillance: Something's Wrong with the War on Sex Trafficking." *Engadget*, May 31. https://www.engadget.com/2019-05-31-sex-lies-and-surveillance-fosta-privacy.html.

Blunt, D., and Z. Stardust. 2021. "Automating Whorephobia: Sex, Technology and the Violence of Deplatforming." *Porn Studies* 8 (4): 350–66.

Blunt, D., and A. Wolf. 2020. "Erased: The Impact of FOSTA-SESTA and the Removal of Backpage on Sex Workers." *Anti-trafficking Review* (14): 117–21.

Bonner, F. 2013. "Recording Reality: Documentary Film and Television." In *Representation: Cultural Representations and Signifying Practices*, 2nd ed., edited by S. Hall, J. Evans, and S. Nixon, 60–119. London: Sage.

boyd, d., K. Levy, and A. Marwick. 2014. "The Networked Nature of Algorithmic Discrimination." In *Data and Discrimination: Collected Essays*, edited by S. Peña Gangadharan and V. Eubanks, 43–57. Washington, DC: Open Technology Institute.

Breslaw, A. 2013. "So What *Is* Feminist Porn? Find Out from a Woman Who Makes It." *Cosmopolitan*, November 7. https://www.cosmopolitan.com/sex-love/news/a16343/tristan-taormino-feminist-porn-interview.

Brooks, S. 2010. *Unequal Desires: Race and Erotic Capital in the Stripping Industry.* Albany, NY: SUNY Press.

Buolamwini, J., and T. Gebru. 2018. "Gender Shades: Intersectional Accuracy Disparities in Commercial Gender Classification." In *Proceedings of Machine Learning Research* (Conference on Fairness, Accountability, and Transparency) 81:77–91.

Bussel, R. K. 2013. "Organic, Fair Trade Porn: On the Hunt for Ethical Smut." *Daily Beast*, April 13. https://www.thedailybeast.com/organic-fair-trade-porn-on-the-hunt-for-ethical-smut.

Butler, J. 1996. "Imitation and Gender Insubordination." In *Women, Knowledge, and Reality: Explorations in Feminist Philosophy*, 2nd ed., edited by A. Garry and M. Pearsall, 371–88. New York: Routledge.

Butler, J. 2004. *Undoing Gender.* New York: Routledge.

Butler, J. 2011. *Bodies That Matter: On the Discursive Limits of Sex.* London: Routledge.

Butterfly Asian and Migrant Sex Workers Support Network. 2018. "Behind the Rescue: How Anti-trafficking Investigations and Policies Harm Migrant Sex Workers." NWSP—Global Network of Sex Work Projects, June 4. http://www.nswp.org/resource/behind-the-rescue-how-anti-trafficking-investigations-and-policies-harm-migrant-sex-workers.

Calder, B. 2016. *Pink Ink: The Golden Era for Gay and Lesbian Magazines.* Newcastle upon Tyne, UK: Cambridge Scholars Publishing.

Calvert, C. 2017. "The Only Worker Prop 60 Helps Is Michael Weinstein." *Huffington Post*, December 6.

Cárdenas, M. 2014. "#QUEER #FISTING #PORN: Queer Porn as Postcapitalist Virus." In *Porn after Porn: Contemporary Alternative Pornographies*, edited by E. Biasin, G. Maina, and F. Zecca, 107–16. Milan: Mimesis International.

Cauvin, J.-L., dir. 2016. *Organic Porn: A New Adult Film Company Offers Porn with Porn Stars Who Were Raised in a Trauma Free Environment*. YouTube, April 13. https://www.youtube.com/watch?v=QtnXTihGqB4.

Chateauvert, M. 2014. *Sex Workers Unite: A History of the Movement from Stonewall to Slut-Walk*. Boston: Beacon.

Chen, L. n.d. "OnlyBans." Accessed January 16, 2023. https://www.lenachen.com/onlybans.

Christian, N. 2018. "Grinder Slammed for Exposing Users' HIV Status." SBS News, April 3. https://www.sbs.com.au/news/grindr-slammed-for-exposing-users-hiv-status.

Clark-Florey, T. 2019. "Does 'Cunt' Break the Rules? Twitter Finds It Hard to Decide." *Jezebel*, July 16. https://jezebel.com/does-cunt-break-the-rules-twitter-finds-it-hard-to-dec-1836225738.

Cloud Salon. 2021. "Veil Machine." The New School. Accessed March 22, 2024. https://event.newschool.edu/cloudsalonveilmachine.

Comella, L. 2008. "It's Sexy. It's Big Business. And It's Not Just for Men." *Contexts* 7 (3): 61–63.

Comella, L. 2015. "Navigating Campus Controversy: An Interview with Adult Performer Conner Habib." *Porn Studies* 2 (2–3): 283–85.

Comella, L. 2016. "Remembering a Legend: Candida Royalle, 1950–2015." *Porn Studies* 3 (1): 96–98.

Comella, L. 2017. *Vibrator Nation: How Feminist Sex-Toy Stores Changed the Business of Pleasure*. Durham, NC: Duke University Press.

Comella, L., and S. Tarrant, eds. 2015. *New Views on Pornography: Sexuality, Politics, and the Law*. London: Bloomsbury.

Committee on Women's Rights and Gender Equality, European Parliament. 2012. "Motion for a European Parliament Resolution on Eliminating Gender Stereotypes in the EU." Report 2012/2116(INI). Brussels: European Union.

Constable, A., and S. May. 2012. "Their Playground, Their Rules: Interactive Social Media and Health Promotion for Sub-population Groups." Poster presented at the First National Sexual and Reproductive Health Conference, Melbourne.

Coombes, E., A. Wolf, D. Blunt, and K. Sparks. 2022. "Disabled Sex Workers' Fight for Digital Rights, Platform Accessibility, and Design Justice." *Disability Studies Quarterly* 42 (2). https://doi.org/10.18061/dsq.v42i2.9097.

Coopersmith, J. 1998. "Pornography, Technology and Progress." *Icon*, no. 4, 94–125.

Coopersmith, J. 2008. "Do It Yourself Pornography: The Democratization of Pornography." In *Pronnovation? Pornography and Technological Innovation*, edited by J. Grenzfurthner, G. Friesinger, and D. Fabry, 48–55. San Francisco: RE/Search Publications.

Cossman, B. 2013. "Censor, Resist, Repeat: A History of Censorship of Gay and Lesbian Sexual Representation in Canada." *Duke Journal of Gender Law and Policy* 21:45–66.

Cossman, B., S. Bell, L. Gotell, and B. L. Ross. 1997. *Bad Attitude/s on Trial: Pornography, Feminism, and the Butler Decision*. Toronto: University of Toronto Press.

Costanza-Chock, S. 2020. *Design Justice: Community-Led Practices to Build the Worlds We Need*. Cambridge, MA: MIT Press.

Coté, M., and J. Pybus. 2007. "Learning to Immaterial Labour 2.0: MySpace and Social Networks." *Ephemera* 7 (1): 88–106.

Crawford, K., and T. Gillespie. 2016. "What Is a Flag For? Social Media Reporting Tools and the Vocabulary of Complaint." *New Media and Society* 18 (3): 410–28.

Crowley, V. 2008. "Body, Gender, Gurlesque, Intersex." In *Cultural Theory in Everyday Practice*, edited by N. Anderson and K. Schlunke. New York: Oxford University Press.

Crozier, I. 2012. "(De-)Constructing Sexual Kinds since 1750." In *Routledge History of Sex and the Body, 1500 to the Present*, edited by S. Toulalan and K. Fisher, 142–60. London: Routledge.

Crutcher, E. E. 2015. "'She's Totally Faking It!': The Politics of Authentic Female Pleasure in Pornography." In *New Views on Pornography: Sexuality, Politics, and the Law*, edited by L. Comella and S. Tarrant, 319–34. London: Bloomsbury.

Cruz, A. 2016. *The Color of Kink: Black Women, BDSM, and Pornography*. New York: New York University Press.

Curtis, Sophie. 2015. "Google Bans 'Explicit' Images and Videos from Blogger." *Telegraph*, February 24. http://www.telegraph.co.uk/technology/google/11431413/Google-bans -explicit-images-and-videos-from-Blogger.html.

Cuthbertson, A. 2016. "Porn Stars and Sex Workers Targeted with Facial Recognition App." *Newsweek*, April 29. http://www.newsweek.com/porn-actress-facial-recognition-findface -sex-worker-453357.

Daring, C. B., J. Rogue, D. Shannon, and A. Volcano. 2012. *Queering Anarchism*. Oakland, CA: AK Press.

Darling, K. 2013. "IP without IP: A Study of the Online Adult Entertainment Industry." *Stanford Technology Law Review* 17 (2): 655–717.

Davis, A., and the BSE Collective, eds. 2019. *Black Sexual Economies: Race and Sex in a Culture of Capital*. Urbana: University of Illinois Press.

Day, R. J. F. 2005. *Gramsci Is Dead: Anarchist Currents in the Newest Social Movements*. London: Pluto.

Dean, J. 2005. "Communicative Capitalism: Circulation and the Foreclosure of Politics." *Cultural Politics* 1 (1): 51–74.

Dean, T. 2009. *Unlimited Intimacy: Reflections on the Subculture of Barebacking*. Chicago: University of Chicago Press.

Dean, T. 2011. "The Erotics of Transgression." In *The Cambridge Companion to Gay and Lesbian Writing*, edited by H. Stevens, 65–80. Cambridge: Cambridge University Press.

Dean, T. 2015. "Mediated Intimacies: Raw Sex, Truvada, and the Biopolitics of Chemoprophylaxis." *Sexualities* 18 (1–2): 224–46.

Dean, T., S. Ruszczycky, and D. Squires, eds. 2014. *Porn Archives*. Durham, NC: Duke University Press.

Decoding Stigma. n.d. A Working Group Affiliated with Hacking//Hustling. Accessed March 22, 2024. https://decodingstigma.tech.

DeGenevieve, B. 2014. "The Emergence of Non-standard Bodies and Sexualities." *Porn Studies* 1 (1–2): 193–96.

Dennis, K. 2009. *Art/Porn: A History of Seeing and Touching*. Oxford, UK: Berg.

Díaz, A., and L. Hecht-Felella. 2021. "Double Standards in Social Media Content Moderation." New York: Brennan Centre for Justice, NYU School of Law.

Dickson, E. J. 2014. "Amazon Is Deleting Sex Workers' Wish Lists without Warning." Daily Dot, May 2. https://www.dailydot.com/irl/amazon-sex-worker-wish-lists.

Douglas, M. 1966. *Purity and Danger*. Abingdon, UK: Routledge.

Drysdale, K. 2019. *Intimate Investments in Drag King Cultures: The Rise and Fall of a Lesbian Social Scene*. Cham, Switzerland: Springer.

Duffy, B. E. 2017. *(Not) Getting Paid to Do What You Love: Gender, Social Media, and Aspirational Work*. New Haven, CT: Yale University Press.

Duggan, L., and N. D. Hunter. 2006. *Sex Wars: Sexual Dissent and Political Culture*. New York: Routledge.

Duguay, S., J. Burgess, and N. Suzor. 2018. "Queer Women's Experiences of Patchwork Platform Governance on Tinder, Instagram, and Vine." *Convergence* 26 (2): 237–52.

Easterbrook-Smith, G. 2022. "OnlyFans as Gig-Economy Work: A Nexus of Precarity and Stigma." *Porn Studies* 10 (3): 252–67.

Economist. 2015. "Naked Capitalism." September 26.

Egwuatu, C., Z. Stardust, M. Miller-Young, and D. Ducati. 2024. "Curating Desire: The White Supremacist Grammar of Tagging on Pornhub." In *Sexual Racism and Social Justice: Reckoning with White Supremacy and Desire*, edited by D. Callander, P. Farvid, A. Baradaran, and T. Vance. New York: Oxford University Press.

Elwes, J. 2016. *Machine Learning Porn*. Digital video. https://www.jakeelwes.com/project-MLPorn.html.

Ergen, F. 2018. "An Analysis on the Impact of Ethical Porn Discourse on the Communication of Pornographic Content Online." Master's thesis, Uppsala University.

Erickson, L. 2015. "Unbreaking Our Hearts: Cultures of Undesirability and the Transformative Potential of Queercrip Porn." PhD diss., York University, Toronto, Ontario.

Erickson, L., 2020a. "Flaunting towards Otherwise: Queercrip Porn, Access Intimacy and Leaving Evidence." In *The Routledge Handbook of Disability and Sexuality*, edited by Russell Shuttleworth and Linda Mona, 275–89. Abingdon, UK: Routledge.

Erickson, L. 2020b. "Loree Erickson on Queercrip Porn: Interview with Sophia de Guzman." *The EyeOpener* (Toronto Metropolitan University student newspaper), February 11.

Eros Association. 2018. "New Eros Association Study Says Aussie Porn Is Female-Led, Queer." XBIZ, January 23. http://www.xbiz.com/news/233146/new-eros-association-study-says-aussie-porn-is-female-led-queer.

Ethical Porn Partnership. 2015. "What Is the Ethical Porn Partnership?" November 15. https://web.archive.org/web/20151115213734/http:/ethicalporn.org/.

Fabbri, T. 2019. "Why Is Instagram Deleting the Accounts of Hundreds of Porn Stars?" BBC News, November 23. https://www.bbc.com/news/blogs-trending-50222380.

Flew, T. 2015. "Porn, Censorship, Classification and Free Speech: Global Paradoxes in the Governance of Media Content." Invited public lecture to Faculty of Law, Humanities and the Arts, University of Wollongong, October 1.

Foldes, L. n.d. *NSFW Venus*. Accessed December 26, 2023. https://nsfw-venus.livia-foldes.com.

Ford, A. 2016. "Transliteracy and the Trans New Wave: Developing a New Canon of Cinematic Representations of Gender Diversity and Sexuality." *Journal of Communication and Media Studies* 1 (2): 1–19.

Foucault, M. 1991. "The Repressive Hypothesis." In *The History of Sexuality*, vol. 1; reprinted in *The Foucault Reader*, edited by Paul Rabinow, 301–29. London: Penguin.

Foucault, M. 1998. "The Will to Knowledge." In *The History of Sexuality*, vol. 1. Translated by Robert Hurley. London: Penguin.

Friedman, G. 2021. "Jobless, Selling Nudes Online and Still Struggling." *New York Times*, January 31. https://www.nytimes.com/search?query=Jobless%2C+Selling+Nudes+Online+and+Still+Struggling.

Frith, H. 2015. "Visualising the 'Real' and the 'Fake': Emotion Work and the Representation of Orgasm in Pornography and Everyday Sexual Interactions." *Journal of Gender Studies* 24 (4): 386–98.

Furry Girl. n.d. VegPorn: Sex Positive Indie Porn Made by Vegetarians and Vegans. Inactive website. http://www.vegporn.com.

Gallant, C. 2017. "Why I Started the Feminist Porn Awards 10 Years Ago (And What I Got Wrong)." *Huffington Post*, January 10. https://www.huffingtonpost.com/entry/why-i-started-the-feminist-porn-awards-ten-years-ago_us_587559afe4b0f8a725448343.

Gallop, C. 2013. "David Cameron, Don't Block Porn, Disrupt It." *Wired*, August 14.

Gamson, J. 2000. "Sexualities, Queer Theory, and Qualitative Research." In *Handbook of Qualitative Research*, 2nd ed., edited by N. K. Denzin and Y. S. Lincoln, 347–65. Thousand Oaks, CA: Sage.

Garcia, G. 2020. "SHIFT+CONTROL+END+DELETE: Encoded Stigma." Interactive Telecommunications Program (ITP) thesis paper, NYU Tisch School for the Arts.

Garcia, G. 2021. "The Cybernetic Sex Worker." Decoding Stigma Substack, December 16. Originally published as "You Have Fallen in Love with a Whore," *Dirty Furniture Magazine*, no. 5/6: "Phone," Summer 2021.

Gebilagin, L. n.d. "100% Organic Porn." Lizzagebilagin.com. Accessed December 6, 2018. https://www.lizzagebilagin.com/portfolio-item/100-ethical-porn. (Originally published in *Cleo* magazine, Australia.)

Gerrard, Y., and H. Thornham. 2020. "Content Moderation: Social Media's Sexist Assemblages." *New Media and Society* 22 (7): 1266–86.

Gibson, P. C., and R. Gibson, eds. 1993. *Dirty Looks: Women, Pornography, Power*. London: British Film Institute.

Gillespie, T. 2010. "The Politics of 'Platforms.'" *New Media and Society* 12 (3): 347–64.

Global Alliance against Trafficking in Women (GAATW). 2007. *Collateral Damage: The Impact of Anti-trafficking Measures on Human Rights around the World*. GAATW report, December 18. https://gaatw.org/resources/publications/908-collateral-damage-the-impact-of-anti-trafficking-measures-on-human-rights-around-the-world.

Graeber, D. 2018. *Bullshit Jobs: A Theory*. New York: Simon and Schuster.

Green, L., C. Lumby, and J. Hartley. 2010. "Refused Classification and the Proposed Australian Internet Filter: An Assault on the Open Society." *Australian Journal of Communication* 37 (3): 1–14.

Gregory, T. 2017. "The Maintenance of White Heteronormativity in Porn Films That Use Australia as an Exotic Location." *Porn Studies* 4 (1): 88–104.

Gregory, T., and A. Lorange. 2018. "Teaching Post-pornography." *Cultural Studies Review* 24 (1): 137–49.

Groeneveld, E. 2018. "Remediating Pornography: The *On Our Backs* Digitization Debate." *Continuum* 32 (1): 73–83.

Hacking//Hustling. 2020. "Posting into the Void." Accessed March 22, 2024. https://hackinghustling.org/wp-content/uploads/2020/09/Posting-Into-the-Void.pdf.

Haimson, O. L., D. Delmonaco, P. Nie, and A. Wegner. 2021. "Disproportionate Removals and Differing Content Moderation Experiences for Conservative, Transgender, and Black Social Media Users: Marginalization and Moderation Gray Areas." *Proceedings of the ACM on Human-Computer Interaction* 5, no. CSCW2, art. 466, 1–35.

Hall, S. 2013. "The Spectacle of the 'Other.'" In *Representation: Cultural Representations and Signifying Practices*, 2nd ed., edited by S. Hall, J. Evans, and S. Nixon, 215–66. Thousand Oaks, CA: Sage.

Halperin, D. M. 1995. *Saint Foucault: Toward a Gay Hagiography*. New York: Oxford University Press.

Hamilton, V., H. Barakat, and E. M. Redmiles. 2022. "Risk, Resilience and Reward: Impacts of Shifting to Digital Sex Work." Preprint, arXivLabs, Cornell University, May 4. https://arxiv.org/pdf/2203.12728.pdf.

Hamilton, V., A. Soneji, A. McDonald, and E. M. Redmiles. 2022. "'Nudes? Shouldn't I Charge for These?': Motivations of New Sexual Content Creators on OnlyFans." Preprint, arXivLabs, Cornell University, October 7. https://arxiv.org/pdf/2205.10425.pdf.

Haraway, D. 2003. "Situated Knowledges: The Science Question in Feminism and the Privilege of Partial Perspective." In *Turning Points in Qualitative Research: Tying Knots in a Handkerchief*, edited by Y. S. Lincoln and N. K. Denzin, 21–46. Walnut Creek, CA: AltaMira.

Harradine, B. 1989. "Export of Pornographic Videos." Press release, October 15.

Harris, M., B. Carlson, and E. Poata-Smith. 2013. "Indigenous Identities and the Politics of Authenticity." In *The Politics of Identity: Emerging Indigeneity*, edited by M. Harris, M. Nakata, and B. Carlson, 1–9. Sydney: University of Technology Sydney E-Press.

Heineman, J. 2016. "Schoolgirls: Embodiment Practices among Current and Former Sex Workers in Academia." PhD diss., University of Las Vegas. https://digitalscholarship.unlv.edu/thesesdissertations/2866.

Held, V. 2018. *Justice and Care: Essential Readings in Feminist Ethics*. New York: Routledge.

Henderson, M. 2013. "Pornography in the Service of Lesbians: The Case of Wicked Women and Slit Magazines." *Australasian Journal of Popular Culture* 2 (2): 159–82.

Hennessy, R. 2000. *Profit and Pleasure: Sexual Identities in Late Capitalism*. New York: Routledge.

Hester, H., and Z. Stardust. 2019. "Sex Work in a Postwork Imaginary: On Abolitionism, Careerism and Respectability." In *New Feminist Studies: Twenty-First Century Critical Interventions*, edited by J. Cooke, 69–82. Cambridge: Cambridge University Press.

Higginbotham, E. B. 1993. *Righteous Discontent: The Women's Movement in the Black Baptist Church, 1880–1920*. Cambridge, MA: Harvard University Press.

Hill, K. 2022. "A Dad Took Photos of His Naked Toddler for the Doctor: Google Flagged Him as a Criminal." *New York Times*, August 21. https://www.nytimes.com/2022/08/21/technology/google-surveillance-toddler-photo.html.

Hillis, K., M. Petit, and K. Jarrett. 2012. *Google and the Culture of Search*. New York: Routledge.

Hill-Meyer, T. 2013. "Where the Trans Women Aren't: The Slow Inclusion of Trans Women in Feminist and Queer Porn." In *The Feminist Porn Book: The Politics of Producing*

Pleasure, edited by T. Taormino, C. Penley, C. Parreñas Shimizu, and M. Miller-Young, 155–63. New York: Feminist Press.

Hochschild, A. R. (1983) 2012. *The Managed Heart: Commercialization of Human Feeling.* Berkeley: University of California Press.

Holtzman, B., C. Hughes, and K. Van Meter. 2007. "'Do It Yourself' and the Movement beyond Capitalism." In *Constituent Imagination: Militant Investigation//Collective Theorization,* edited by S. Shukaitis, D. Graeber, and E. Biddle, 44–61. Chico, CA: AK Press.

hooks, b. 2001. *All about Love: New Visions.* New York: HarperCollins.

Horn, T. 2014. "How the Financial Sector Is Making Life Miserable for Sex Workers." *Vice,* July 14.

Houston, S. L. 2015. "Mighty Real: Shine Louise Houston Reveals It All." PinkLabel.tv. https://pinklabel.tv/on-demand/mighty-real-shine-louise-houston-reveals-it-all.

Howell, K. 2016. "Porn Makers Use Airbnb, Rental Houses for Filming without Telling Home Owners." *Washington Times,* February 27. http://www.washingtontimes.com/news/2016/feb/27/porn-makers-use-airbnb-rental-houses-filming-witho/?page=all.

Hunt, L., ed. 1993. *The Invention of Pornography: Obscenity and the Origins of Modernity, 1500–1800.* New York: Zone Books.

Huntley, R. 1995. "Queer Cuts: Censorship and Community Standards." *Media International Australia,* no. 78 (November).

Jacobs, K. 2004. "Pornography in Small Places and Other Spaces." *Cultural Studies* 18 (1): 67–83.

Jacobs, K. 2007. *Netporn: DIY Web Culture and Sexual Politics.* Lanham, MD: Rowman and Littlefield.

Jacobs, K. 2014. "The Promise of Radical Obscenities." In *Porn after Porn,* edited by E. Biasin, G. Maina, and F. Zecca, 121–40. Milan: Mimesis International.

Jaggar, A. M. 1991. "Feminist Ethics: Projects, Problems, Prospects." In *Feminist Ethics,* edited by C. Card, 78–98. Lawrence: University Press of Kansas.

Jaggar, A. M. 2013. "Feminist Ethics." In *The Blackwell Guide to Ethical Theory,* edited by H. LaFollette and I. Persson, 433–60. Hoboken, NJ: Wiley.

Jagose, A. 2013. *Orgasmology.* Durham, NC: Duke University Press.

Jamgochian, A., and S. L. Houston. 2014. "The History, Politics, and Ethics of Pornographic Authenticity (Theory/Practice)." Presented at the Feminist Porn Conference, University of Toronto, April.

Janssen, S. 2016. "Sensate Vision: From Maximum Visibility to Haptic Erotics." *feminists@law* 5 (2): 1–26.

Jeffreys, E. 2007. "Street-Based Sex Workers." *proVision Magazine* (Scarlet Alliance), no. 2, "Stigma," 28.

Johnston, J. 2008. "The Citizen-Consumer Hybrid: Ideological Tensions and the Case of Whole Foods Market." *Theory and Society* 37 (3): 229–70.

Jones, A. 2015. "For Black Models, Scroll Down: Webcam Modeling and the Racialization of Erotic Labor." *Sexuality and Culture* 19 (4): 776–99.

Jones, A. 2021. "Cumming to a Screen Near You: Transmasculine and Non-binary People in the Camming Industry." *Porn Studies* 8 (2): 239–54.

Kahn, U. 2014. *Vicarious Kinks: S/M in the Socio-legal Imaginary.* Toronto: University of Toronto Press.

Karaian, L. 2009. "The Troubled Relationship of Feminist and Queer Legal Theory to Strategic Essentialism: Theory/Praxis, Queer Porn, and Canadian Anti-Discrimination Law." In *Feminist and Queer Legal Theory: Intimate Encounters, Uncomfortable Conversations*, edited by M. A. Fineman, J. E. Jackson, and A. P. Romero, 375–94. Brookfield, VT: Ashgate.

Katz, S. 2016. "Disability Inclusive DIY Porn Tips." In *The DIY Porn Handbook: Documenting Our Own Sexual Revolution*, by M. Young, 155–59. Emeryville, CA: Greenery.

Keller, D. 2019. "Who Do You Sue? State and Platform Hybrid Power over Online Speech." Aegis Series Papers No. 1902. Stanford, CA: Hoover Institution.

Kempadoo, K., and J. Doezema, eds. 1998. *Global Sex Workers: Rights, Resistance, and Redefinition*. London: Routledge.

Kendrick, W. M. 1996. *The Secret Museum: Pornography in Modern Culture*. Berkeley: University of California Press.

Kim, J., and E. Jeffreys. 2013. "Migrant Sex Workers and Trafficking—Insider Research for and by Migrant Sex Workers." ALAR: *Action Learning and Action Research Journal* 19 (1): 62.

Kincaid, H. 1998. "Which Is More of a Threat—Pornography or Its Censorship?" *Alternative Law Journal* 23 (1): 6–18.

Kingkade, T. 2020. "California Bill to Force Porn Actors to Get Fingerprinted Outrages the Adult Industry." NBC News, February 22. https://www.nbcnews.com/news/us-news /california-bill-force-porn-actors-get-fingerprinted-outrages-adult-industry-n1140401.

Kipnis, L. 1992. "(Male) Desire, (Female) Disgust: Reading *Hustler*." In *Cultural Studies*, edited by L. Grossberg, C. Nelson, and P. Treichler, chap. 21. Abingdon, UK: Routledge.

Kipnis, L. 1996. *Bound and Gagged: Pornography and the Politics of Fantasy in America*. Durham, NC: Duke University Press.

Klein, N. 2010. "*No Logo* at Ten." In *No Logo*, 10th anniversary ed. London: Fourth Estate.

Knight, T. 2016. *Burn My Shadow: A Selective Memory of an X-Rated Life*. Los Angeles: Rare Bird Books.

Knox. B. 2014. "Tearing Down the Whorearchy from the Inside." *Jezebel*, July 2. https:// jezebel.com/tearing-down-the-whorearchy-from-the-inside.

Kristeva, J. 1982. *Powers of Horror: An Essay on Abjection*. Translated by L. S. Roudiez. New York: Columbia University Press.

Kuo, R., and L. Lee. 2021. "Dis/Organizing Toolkit: How We Build Collectives beyond Institutions." Hacking//Hustling. Accessed March 22, 2024. https://hackinghustling.org /disorganizing-toolkit.

Kurylo, B. 2017. "Pornography and Power in Michel Foucault's Thought." *Journal of Political Power* 10 (1): 71–84.

Ladder, S. 2022. "Site Restrictions." Google spreadsheet. Accessed July 21, 2024. https://docs .google.com/spreadsheets/d/1vuwKN-yuOJDlLiOa8CyCVA8BMpXg7knCZxS8YgFE98Y /edit#gid=0

Langdridge, D. 2006. "Voices from the Margins: Sadomasochism and Sexual Citizenship." *Citizenship Studies* 10 (4): 373–89.

Langdridge, D., and M. Barker. 2013. *Safe, Sane, and Consensual: Contemporary Perspectives on Sadomasochism*. London: Palgrave Macmillan.

Laurin, D. 2019. "Subscription Intimacy: Amateurism, Authenticity and Emotional Labour in Direct-to-Consumer Gay Pornography." AG *about Gender* 8 (16): 61–79.

Lawson, K. 2000. "Police Inquiry into MP's Porn Show." *Canberra Times*, May 30.

Lee, J. 2015a. "Click 'I Agree': Consent and Feminism in Commercial Pornography." Global Information Society Watch. Accessed March 22, 2024. https://www.giswatch.org/en/sexual-rights/click-i-agree-consent-and-feminism-commercial-pornography.

Lee, J., ed. 2015b. *Coming Out Like a Porn Star: Essays on Pornography, Protection, and Privacy*. Berkeley, CA: ThreeL Media.

Lee, J. 2015c. "Ethical Porn Starts When We Pay for It." *Medium*, January 21. https://medium.com/@jizlee/ethical-porn-starts-when-we-pay-for-it-8a6f266ab473.

Lee, J. 2015d. "They Came to See the [Queer] Porn Star Talk." *Porn Studies* 2 (2–3): 272–74.

Lee, J. 2016. "Tricks of the Trade." In *DIY Porn Handbook: A How-to Guide to Documenting Our Own Sexual Revolution*, by M. Young, 63–74. Emeryville, CA: Greenery.

Lee, J., and R. Sullivan. 2016. "Porn and Labour: The Labour of Porn Studies." *Porn Studies* 3 (2): 104–6.

Leonard, W., and A. Mitchell. 2000. "The Use of Sexually Explicit Materials in HIV/AIDS Initiatives Targeted at Gay Men: A Guide for Educators." Report prepared for the Australian National Council on AIDS Hepatitis C and Related Diseases, July.

Levin Russo, J. 2007. "'The Real Thing': Reframing Queer Pornography for Virtual Spaces." In *C'lickme: A Netporn Studies Reader*, edited by K. Jacobs, M. Janssen, and M. Pasquinelli, 239–52. Amsterdam: Institute of Network Cultures.

Levy, A. 2010. *Female Chauvinist Pigs: Women and the Rise of Raunch Culture*. New York: Free Press.

Ley, D., N. Prause, and P. Finn. 2014. "The Emperor Has No Clothes: A Review of the 'Pornography Addiction' Model." *Current Sexual Health Reports* 6:94–105.

Liberman, R. 2015. "'It's a Really Great Tool': Feminist Pornography and the Promotion of Sexual Subjectivity." *Porn Studies* 2 (2–3): 174–91.

Lingel, J. 2021. *The Gentrification of the Internet: How to Reclaim Our Digital Freedom*. Berkeley: University of California Press.

Lipton, S. 2012. "Trouble Ahead: Pleasure, Possibility and the Future of Queer Porn." *New Cinemas: Journal of Contemporary Film* 10 (2–3): 197–207.

Liu, H. 2007. "Social Network Profiles as Taste Performances." *Journal of Computer-Mediated Communication* 13 (1): 252–75.

Lorde, A. (1978) 1997. "Uses of the Erotic: The Erotic as Power." In *Sista Outsider: Essays and Speeches by Audre Lorde*. Berkeley: Crossing Press.

Lubove, S. 2003. "Visa's Porn Crackdown." *Forbes*, May 1. https://www.forbes.com/2003/05/01/cz_sl_0501porn.html#6edf7c90162a.

Lust, L. 2010. *Good Porn: A Woman's Guide*. Translated by X. P. Callahan. Berkeley, CA: Seal.

Mac, J., and M. Smith. 2018. *Revolting Prostitutes: The Fight for Sex Workers' Rights*. London: Verso.

Mackay, J., and P. Mackay. 2020. "NDNGirls and Pocahotties: Native American and First Nations Representation in Settler Colonial Pornography and Erotica." *Porn Studies* 7 (2): 168–86.

Maginn P., and C. Steinmetz. 2011. "Sex in the City: The Changing Face of Adult Retailing." *The Conversation*, September 4. https://theconversation.com/sex-in-the-city-the-changing-face-of-adult-retailing-3083.

Magnet, S. 2007. "Feminist Sexualities, Race and the Internet: An Investigation of Suicidegirls.com." *New Media and Society* 9 (4): 577–602.

Maina, G. 2014. "After *The Feminist Porn Book*: Further Questions about Feminist Porn." *Porn Studies* 1 (1–2): 182–85.

Mǎntescu, L. 2016. "Ecoporn, Irrationalities and Radical Environmentalism." THESys Discussion Paper No. 2016-3. Berlin: Research Institute on Transformations of Human-Environment Systems, Humboldt-University.

Marks, L. H. 2013. "Period Porn: Bodily Fluids On/Scene and Off/Scene Bodily Fluids." June 7. New York: Society for Menstrual Cycle Research, Marymount Manhattan College.

Marston, M. 2020. "OnlyEmployees: Ending the Misclassification of Digital Sex Workers in the Shared and Gig Economy." *American University Journal of Gender, Social Policy and the Law* 29 (1): 89–122.

Martin, M. 2012. "The *Rumpus* Interview with Madison Young." *The Rumpus*, May 3. https://therumpus.net/2012/05/the-rumpus-interview-with-madison-young.

Marwick, A. E. 2007. "The People's Republic of YouTube? Interrogating Rhetorics of Internet Democracy." October 1. Vancouver: Association of Internet Researchers 8.0.

Marwick, A. E. 2013. *Status Update: Celebrity, Publicity, and Branding in the Social Media Age.* New Haven, CT: Yale University Press.

Maxxine, C., and D. A. Hidalgo. 2015. "A Performer and a Professor: Two Friends and Colleagues Talk Porn . . . in College." *Porn Studies* 2 (2–3): 279–82.

McGlotten, S. 2014. "Zombie Porn: Necropolitics, Sex, and Queer Socialities." *Porn Studies* 1 (4): 360–77.

McGlotten, S., and S. Vangundy. 2013. "Zombie Porn 1.0: Or, Some Queer Things Zombie Sex Can Teach Us." *Qui Parle: Critical Humanities and Social Sciences* 21 (2): 101–25.

McGowan, E. 2020. "Daisy Ducati Thinks the Interracial Porn Tag Is Racist, Period." *The Bustle*, June 24. https://www.bustle.com/wellness/daisy-ducati-opens-up-about-racism-in-the-porn-industry-22993400.

McGuire, A. *Black Witness: The Power of Indigenous Media.* St Lucia: University of Queensland Press.

McKee, A. 2005. "The Need to Bring the Voices of Pornography Consumers into Public Debates about the Genre and Its Effects." *Australian Journal of Communication* 32 (2): 71–94.

McKee, A. 2016. "Pornography as a Creative Industry: Challenging the Exceptionalist Approach to Pornography." *Porn Studies* 3 (2): 107–19.

McKee, A. 2017. "The Pornography Consumer as Other." In *Routledge Companion to Media, Sex and Sexuality*, edited by C. Smith, F. Attwood, and B. McNair, 383–93. Abingdon, UK: Routledge.

McKee, A., K. Albury, M. Dunne, S. Grieshaber, J. Hartley, C. Lumby, and B. Mathews. 2010. "Healthy Sexual Development: A Multidisciplinary Framework for Research." *International Journal of Sexual Health* 22 (1): 14–19.

McKee, A., K. Albury, and C. Lumby. 2008. *The Porn Report.* Carlton: Melbourne University Press.

McKee, A., A. Dawson, and M. Kang. 2023. "The Criteria to Identify Pornography That Can Support Healthy Sexual Development for Young Adults: Results of an International Delphi Panel." *International Journal of Sexual Health* 35 (1): 1–12.

McKee, A., K. Litsou, P. Byron, and R. Ingham. 2022. *What Do We Know about the Effects of Pornography after Fifty Years of Academic Research?* Abingdon, UK: Routledge.

McKee, A., and C. Lumby. 2022. "Pornhub, Child Sexual Abuse Materials and Anti-pornography Campaigning." *Porn Studies* 9 (4): 464–76.

McKee, A., B. McNair, and A. F. Watson. 2014. "Sex and the Virtual Suburbs: The Pornosphere and Community Standards." In *(Sub)Urban Sexscapes: Geographies and Regulation of the Sex Industry*, edited by P. J. Maginn and C. Steinmetz, 159–74. Abingdon, UK: Routledge.

McLelland, M. 2018. "Art as Activism in Japan: The Case of a Good-for-Nothing Kid and Her Pussy." In *Routledge Companion to Media and Activism*, edited by G. Meikle, 162–70. Abingdon, UK: Routledge.

McLelland, M., and S. Yoo. 2007. "The International Yaoi Boys' Love Fandom and the Regulation of Virtual Child Pornography: The Implications of Current Legislation." *Sexuality Research and Social Policy* 4 (1): 93–104.

McNair, B. 2009. "Teaching Porn." *Sexualities* 12 (5): 558–67.

McNair, B. 2013. *Porno? Chic! How Pornography Changed the World and Made It a Better Place.* Abingdon, UK: Routledge.

Meier, A. 2015. "Pornography into Bright Daylight: A Review of the Berlin Porn Film Festival, 23–27 October 2013." *Porn Studies* 2 (2–3): 290–92.

Middleton, A. 2014. "*Archer* Magazine Pulled from Newsagent Shelves." *Archer*, June 18. http://archermagazine.com.au/2014/06/archer-magazine-pulled-from-newsagent-shelves.

Midwinter-Pitt, V., dir. 2007. *Rampant: How a City Stopped a Plague.* New Petersham, NSW: Chapman Pictures Pty Ltd., Australia.

Miller-Young, M. 2014. *A Taste for Brown Sugar: Black Women in Pornography.* Durham, NC: Duke University Press.

Mingus, M. 2011. *Access Intimacy: The Missing Link.* Leaving Evidence, May 5. https://leavingevidence.wordpress.com/2011/05/05/access-intimacy-the-missing-link/.

Mollow, A., and R. McRuer. 2012. "Introduction." In *Sex and Disability*, edited by R. McRuer and A. Mollow, 1–34. Durham, NC: Duke University Press.

Mondin, A. 2014. "Fair-Trade Porn + Niche Markets + Feminist Audience." *Porn Studies* 1 (1–2): 189–92.

Monea, A. 2022. *The Digital Closet: How the Internet Became Straight.* Cambridge, MA: MIT Press.

moon, m. 2021. "Symposium Introduction: Sex Workers' Rights, Advocacy, and Organizing." *Columbia Human Rights Law Review* 52 (3): 1062–83.

Morgans, J. 2015. "Australia's Thriving Art-Porn Industry Is Run By Women." *Vice*, May 8. https://www.vice.com/en_au/article/zngea5/australia-has-a-thriving-art-porn-industry-run-by-women.

Mortimer-Sandilands, C., and B. Erickson, eds. 2010. *Queer Ecologies: Sex, Nature, Politics, Desire.* Bloomington: Indiana University Press.

Mowlabocus, S. 2010. "Porn 2.0? Technology, Social Practice, and the New Online Porn Industry." In *Porn.Com: Making Sense of Online Pornography*, edited by F. Attwood, 69–87. New York: Peter Lang.

Moynihan, C. 2016. "Men Struggle with Porn Addiction, Some Women Want to Feed It: Good News and Bad News about One of the Greatest Evils of the 21st Century." *Merca-*

tonet: *Navigating Modern Complexities*, March 10. https://www.mercatornet.com/men
-struggle-with-porn-addiction-some-women-want-to-feed-it.

Ms Naughty. 2013. "What Happened When I Asked Vimeo to Define 'Pornography.'"
Ms Naughty's Porn for Women, June 28. http://msnaughty.com/blog/2013/06/28/what
-happened-when-i-asked-vimeo-to-define-pornography.

Mulvey, L. 1975. "Visual Pleasure and Narrative Cinema." *Screen* 16 (3): 6–18.

MyFreeCams Wiki. n.d. "Rules for Models." MyFreeCams.com. Accessed December 29,
2023. https://wiki.myfreecams.com/wiki/Rules_for_Models.

Nagle, J., ed. 1997. *Whores and Other Feminists*. New York: Routledge.

Nagy, T. 2013. "Artisanal, Locally Grown, Free Range Porn for Women." *Huffington Post*,
March 4; updated May 4. https://www.huffingtonpost.com/toni-nagy/porn-for-women
_b_2783342.html.

Nash, J. C. 2014. *The Black Body in Ecstasy: Reading Race, Reading Pornography*. Durham,
NC: Duke University Press.

Neville, L. 2018. *Girls Who Like Boys Who Like Boys: Women and Gay Male Pornography and
Erotica*. New York: Springer.

Nichols, B. 2017. *Introduction to Documentary*. Bloomington: Indiana University Press.

Noble, S. U. 2018. *Algorithms of Oppression: How Search Engines Reinforce Racism*. New
York: NYU Press.

Oliva, T. D., D. M. Antonialli, and A. Gomes. 2021. "Fighting Hate Speech, Silencing Drag
Queens? Artificial Intelligence in Content Moderation and Risks to LGBTQ Voices Online." *Sexuality and Culture* 25:700–732.

Osgerby, B. 2014. "Porn to Be Wild: Identity and the Aesthetics of 'Otherness' in Subcultural Erotica." In *Porn after Porn*, edited by E. Biasin, G. Maina, and F. Zecca, 37–55.
Milan: Mimesis International.

Ovidie, dir. 2017. *Pornocracy: The New Sex Multinationals*. Paris: Canal+ / Centre National
du Cinéma et de L'image Animée (CNC) / Fatalitas Productions and Magneto Presse.

Paasonen, S. 2010. "Labors of Love: Netporn, Web 2.0 and the Meanings of Amateurism."
New Media and Society 12 (8): 1297–1312.

Paasonen, S. 2011. *Carnal Resonance: Affect and Online Pornography*. Cambridge, MA: MIT
Press.

Paasonen, S., K. Jarrett, and B. Light. 2019. *#NSFW: Sex, Humor, and Risk*. Cambridge, MA:
MIT Press.

Penley, C. 2004. "Crackers and Whackers: The White Trashing of Porn." In *Porn Studies*,
edited by L. Williams, 309–34. Durham, NC: Duke University Press.

Penley, C. 2015a. "Collision in a Courtroom." In *Images, Ethics, Technology*, edited by S.
Pearl and B. Zelizer, 70–100. New York: Routledge.

Penley, C. 2015b. Keynote presentation at Trans/Forming Feminisms: Media,
Technology, Identity Conference, University of Otago, Dunedin, New Zealand,
November 25–27.

Peters, J. 2020. "Sexual Content and Social Media Moderation." *Washburn Law Journal*
59:469–88.

Petley, J. 2009. "Pornography, Panopticism and the Criminal Justice and Immigration Act
2008." *Sociology Compass* 3 (3): 417–32.

Petley, J. 2014. "The Regulation of Pornography on Video-on-Demand in the United Kingdom." *Porn Studies* 1 (3): 260–84.

Pezzutto, S. 2019. "From Porn Performer to Porntrepreneur: Online Entrepreneurship, Social Media Branding, and Selfhood in Contemporary Trans Pornography." *AG about Gender* 8 (16): 30–60.

Pezzutto, S. 2020. "The Rise of the 'Porntrepreneur': Even Hustlers Need Side Hustles in the Gig Economy." *The Conversation*, January 21. https://theconversation.com/the-rise-of-the-porntrepreneur-even-hustlers-need-side-hustles-in-the-gig-economy-129067.

Pezzutto, S. 2023. "Sex Influencers: An Ethnographic Study of Transgender Pornography Workers." PhD diss., Australian National University.

Piepzna-Samarasinha, L. L. 2018. *Care Work: Dreaming Disability Justice*. Vancouver: Arsenal Pulp Press.

PiggyBankGirls. n.d. "The Fair Trade Porn Concept." Accessed December 27, 2018. https://web.archive.org/web/20180128193212/https:/www.piggybankgirls.com/about-us.

Pilipets, E., and S. Paasonen. 2020. "Nipples, Memes, and Algorithmic Failure: NSFW Critique of Tumblr Censorship." *New Media and Society* 24 (6): 1459–80.

Pink Label. 2014. "iPornography: An Interview with iPhone Pornographer The Madame." Accessed March 22, 2024. https://pinklabel.tv/on-demand/ipornography-an-interview-with-iphone-pornographer-the-madame/#.

Pinkser, J. 2016. "The Hidden Economics of Porn." *Atlantic*, April 4. https://www.theatlantic.com/business/archive/2016/04/pornography-industry-economics-tarrant/476580/.

Platzer, C., M. Stuetz, and M. Lindorfer. 2014. "Skin Sheriff: A Machine Learning Solution for Detecting Explicit Images." In *Proceedings of the 2nd International Workshop on Security and Forensics in Communication Systems*, 45–56. New York: Association for Computing Machinery.

Plummer, K. 1995. *Telling Sexual Stories: Power, Change and Social Worlds*. Abingdon, UK: Routledge.

Poe, C., dir. n.d. *Fucking against Fascism*. Trouble Films. Chelsea Submits.com. Accessed January 7, 2024. https://chelseasubmits.com/product/fucking-against-fascism.

Pornhub Insights. 2022. "The 2022 Year in Review." December 8. https://www.pornhub.com/insights/2022-year-in-review.

Preciado, P. B. 2013. *Testo Junkie: Sex, Drugs, and Biopolitics in the Pharmacopornographic Era*. New York: Feminist Press.

Press Association. 2014. "Face-Sitting Protest outside Parliament against New Porn Rules." *Guardian*, December 12.

Prostasia Foundation. 2019. "Best Practice Principles for Sexual Content Moderation and Child Protection." November 26. https://prostasia.org/project/sexual-content-moderation-principles.

Puar, J. 2007. *Terrorist Assemblages: Homonationalism in Queer Times*. Durham, NC: Duke University Press.

Qin, L., V. Hamilton, Y. Ayadin, M. Scarlett, S. Wang, and E. M. Redmiles. 2023. "Toward Safer Intimate Futures: Recommendations for Tech Platforms to Reduce Image Based Sexual Abuse." Report by the European Sex Workers Rights Alliance, Max Planck Institute for Software Systems, Brown University, and University of Washington. Accessed

January 3, 2024. https://assets.nationbuilder.com/eswa/pages/329/attachments/original/1695279661/ESWA_NDII_publication_full3.pdf?1695279661.

Reece, R. L. 2015. "The Plight of the Black Belle Knox: Race and Webcam Modelling." *Porn Studies* 2 (2–3): 269–71.

Rehberg, P. 2017. "APAC Extends Stamp Approval to Directors, Producers." Venus Adult News. Accessed February 27, 2024. https://www.venus-adult-news.com/en/regions/world/apac-extends-stamp-approval-directors-producers.

Renov, M., ed. 2012. *Theorizing Documentary*. New York: Routledge.

Richards, S. J. 2016. *The Queer Film Festival: Popcorn and Politics*. London: Palgrave Macmillan.

Rissel, C., J. Richters, R. O. de Visser, A. McKee, A. Yeung, and T. Caruana. 2017. "A Profile of Pornography Users in Australia: Findings from the Second Australian Study of Health and Relationships." *Journal of Sex Research* 54 (2): 227–40.

Rosenbloom, A. L. 2013. "Inaccuracy of Age Assessment from Images of Postpubescent Subjects in Cases of Alleged Child Pornography." *International Journal of Legal Medicine* 127 (2): 467–71.

Rosewarne, L. 2012. *Periods in Pop Culture: Menstruation in Film and Television*. Lanham, MD: Lexington Books.

Roth, Y. 2015. "'No Overly Suggestive Photos of Any Kind': Content Management and the Policing of Self in Gay Digital Communities." *Communication, Culture and Critique* 8 (3): 414–32.

Rothwell, J., dir. 2015. *How to Change the World: The Revolution Will Not Be Organised*. London: Met Film Production.

Ruberg, B. 2016. "Doing It for Free: Digital Labour and the Fantasy of Amateur Online Pornography." *Porn Studies* 3 (2): 147–59.

Rubin, G. S. (1984) 2011. "Thinking Sex: Notes for a Radical Theory of the Politics of Sexuality." In *Deviations: A Gayle Rubin Reader*, 137–81. Durham, NC: Duke University Press.

Rubin, G. S. (1991) 2011. "The Catacombs: A Temple of the Butthole." In *Deviations: A Gayle Rubin Reader*, 224–40. Durham, NC: Duke University Press.

Rubin, G. 2009. "A Little Humility." In *Gay Shame*, edited by D. M. Halperin and V. Traub, 369–74. Chicago: University of Chicago Press.

Ryan, D. 2013. "Fucking Feminism." In *The Feminist Porn Book: The Politics of Producing Pleasure*, edited by T. Taormino, C. Penley, C. P. Shimizu, and M. Miller-Young, 121–29. New York: Feminist Press.

Ryan, P. 2019. "Netporn and the Amateur Turn on OnlyFans." In *Male Sex Work in the Digital Age*, 119–36. London: Palgrave Macmillan.

Ryberg, I. 2008. "Maximizing Visibility." *Film International* 6 (6): 72–79.

Ryberg, I. 2015. "Carnal Fantasizing: Embodied Spectatorship of Queer, Feminist and Lesbian Pornography." *Porn Studies* 2 (2–3): 161–73.

Sabo, A. G. 2012. *After Pornified: How Women Are Transforming Pornography and Why It Really Matters*. Winchester, UK: Zero Books.

Sanchez, S. 2022. "The World's Oldest Profession Gets a Makeover: Sex Work, OnlyFans, and Celebrity Participation." *Women Leading Change: Case Studies on Women, Gender, and Feminism* 6 (1): 4–17.

Sargeant, J. 2015. "First Notes on Contemporary Independent Pornography and Possibil- ity: Function, Form and Philosophy." *Runway Journal*, no. 9. http://runway.org.au/first -notes-on-contemporary-independent-pornography-and-possibility-function-form-and -philosophy.

Saunders, R. 2020. "Interventionalist Pornography." In *Bodies of Work: The Labour of Sex in the Digital Age*, 251–90. London: Palgrave Macmillan.

Scott, K. L. 2016. "Performing Labour: Ethical Spectatorship and the Communication of Labour Conditions in Pornography." *Porn Studies* 3 (2): 120–32.

Scott, L. M. 2005. *Fresh Lipstick: Redressing Fashion and Feminism*. New York: Palgrave Macmillan.

Scott, S. 2015. "The Condomlessness of Bareback Sex: Responses to the Unrepresentabil- ity of HIV in Treasure Island Media's *Plantin' Seed* and *Slammed*." *Sexualities* 18 (1–2): 210–23.

Seise, C. 2010. "Fucking Utopia: Queer Porn and Queer Liberation." *Sprinkle: A Journal of Sexual Diversity Studies* 3:19–29.

Senate Legal and Constitutional Legislation Committee. 2000. Inquiry into the Provi- sions of the Classification (Publications, Films and Computer Games) Amendment Bill (No. 2) 1999.

Senate Standing Committees on Environment and Communications, Parliament of Australia. 2016. *Harm Being Done to Australian Children through Access to Pornography on the Internet*. November 23. https://www.aph.gov.au/parliamentary_business/committees /senate/environment_and_communications/onlineaccesstoporn45/report.

Senft, T. M. 2008. *Camgirls: Celebrity and Community in the Age of Social Networks*. New York: Peter Lang.

Senft, T. M., and N. K. Baym 2015. "What Does the Selfie Say? Investigating a Global Phe- nomenon: Introduction." *International Journal of Communication* 9:1588–606.

Shakespeare, T., K. Gillespie-Sells, and D. Davies. 1996. *The Sexual Politics of Disability: Untold Desires*. London: Cassell.

Sharkey, G. 2018. "Seeing Yourself on Screen: Queer Pornography, Queer Theory." PhD diss., University of Sydney.

Shih, E. 2023. *Manufacturing Freedom: Sex Work, Anti-trafficking Rehab, and the Racial Wages of Rescue*. Berkeley: University of California Press.

Shimizu, C. P., and H. Lee. 2004. "Sex Acts: Two Meditations on Race and Sexuality." *Signs: Journal of Women in Culture and Society* 30 (1): 1385–402.

Skeggs, B. 2002. *Formations of Class and Gender: Becoming Respectable*. Los Angeles: Sage.

Slit magazine. 2012. "Simulacra." *Slit*, no. 15.

Smith, C. 2007. *One for the Girls! The Pleasures and Practices of Reading Women's Porn*. Bristol, UK: Intellect.

Smith, C., and F. Attwood. 2014. "Anti/Pro/Critical Porn Studies." *Porn Studies* 1 (1–2): 7–23.

Smith, C., F. Attwood, and M. Barker. 2015. "Queering Porn Audiences." In *Queer Sex Work*, edited by M. Laing, K. Pilcher, and N. Smith, 177–88. Abingdon, UK: Routledge.

Smith, C., M. Barker, and F. Attwood. 2015. "Why Do People Watch Porn? Results from PornResearch.org." In *New Views on Pornography: Sexuality, Politics, and the Law*, edited by L. Comella and S. Tarrant, 267–86. London: Bloomsbury.

Spade, D. 2013. "Intersectional Resistance and Law Reform." *Signs: Journal of Women in Culture and Society* 38 (4): 1031–55.

Spade, D. 2015. *Normal Life: Administrative Violence, Critical Trans Politics, and the Limits of Law.* Durham, NC: Duke University Press.

Sparrow, J. 2012. *Money Shot: A Journey into Porn and Censorship.* Melbourne: Scribe.

Sperring, S., and Z. Stardust. 2019. "Engorged—Fucking with the Maternal: An Analysis of Anti-normativity, Cultural Legitimacy, and Queer Authenticity." In *Mothers, Sex and Sexuality,* edited by H. Zwalf, M. Walks, and J. Mortenson, chap. 11. Bradford, Ontario: Demeter.

Spivak, G. 1990. *The Postcolonial Critic: Interviews, Strategies, Dialogues.* Edited by S. Harasym. New York: Routledge.

Sprinkle, A. 1991. *Post-porn Modernist.* Amsterdam: Torch Books.

Sprinkle, A., and C. Leigh (Harlot), dirs. 2002. *Herstory of Porn: Reel to Real.* San Francisco: Annie Sprinkle.

Srnicek, N. 2017. *Platform Capitalism.* Hoboken, NJ: Wiley.

Stardust, Z. 2020. "Sex in the Academy/Sex in the Field: Bodies of Ethics in Activist Research." In *Navigating Fieldwork in the Social Sciences: Stories of Danger, Risk and Reward,* edited by P. Wadds, N. Apoifis, S. Schmeidl, and K. Spurway, 13–37. London: Palgrave Macmillan.

Stardust, Z., D. Blunt, G. Garcia, L. Lee, K. D'Adamo, and R. Kuo. 2023. "High Risk Hustling: Payment Processors, Sexual Proxies and Discrimination by Design." *City University of New York Law Review* 26 (1): 57–138.

Stardust, Z., A. Obeid, A. McKee, and D. Angus. 2024. "Mandatory Age Verification for Pornography Access: Why It Can't and Won't 'Save the Children.'" *Big Data and Society* 11 (2). https://doi.org/10.1177/20539517241252129.

Stegeman, H. M. 2021. "Regulating and Representing Camming: Strict Limits on Acceptable Content on Webcam Sex Platforms." *New Media and Society,* OnlineFirst, November 27.

Steinbock, E. 2014. "Pornography." *Transgender Studies Quarterly* 1 (1–2): 156–58.

Steinem, G. 1980. "Erotica and Pornography: A Clear and Present Difference." In *Take Back the Night: Women on Pornography,* edited by L. Lederer, 35–39. New York: William Morrow.

Stephens, B., and A. Sprinkle, prods. 2013. *Goodbye Gauley Mountain: An Ecosexual Love Story.* Fecund Arts.

Strub, W. 2015. "Queer Smut, Queer Rights." In *New Views on Pornography: Sexuality, Politics, and the Law,* edited by L. Comella and S. Tarrant, 147–64. London: Bloomsbury.

Strub, W. 2019. "Sanitizing the Seventies: Pornography, Home Video, and the Editing of Sexual Memory." *Feminist Media Histories* 5 (2): 19–48.

Stryker, K. 2018. "The Soapbox: How PayPal and WePay Discriminate against the Adult Industry." *The Frisky,* September 23. https://thefrisky.com/the-soapbox-how-paypal-wepay-discriminate-against-the-adult-industry.

Stüttgen, T. 2009. *Post Porn Politics: Queer-Feminist Perspectives on the Politics of Porn Performance and Sex Work as Culture Production.* Berlin: b_books.

Stychin, C. 1995. *Law's Desire: Sexuality and the Limits of Justice.* London: Routledge.

SuicideGirls. n.d. "What Should My Photoset Be Like?" and "What Kind of Things Should I Avoid in My Photoset?" SuicideGirls.com, Frequently Asked Questions. Accessed December 30, 2023. http://suicidegirls.com/girlsfaq.

Sullivan, C. 2022. "Workin' It Online: Indigenous Sex Workers Navigating the Digital Environment." Digital Intimacies Conference, Centre for Indigenous Global Futures, Macquarie University, Sydney, December 1–2.

Sullivan, R., and A. McKee. 2015. *Pornography: Structures, Agency and Performance.* Hoboken, NJ: Wiley.

Survivors Against SESTA. 2018. "Documenting Tech Actions." Accessed July 21, 2024. https://survivorsagainstsesta.org/documentation/.

Suzor, N. P. 2009. "On the (Partially) Inalienable Rights of Participants in Virtual Communities." *Media International Australia Incorporating Culture and Policy* 130 (1): 90–101.

Suzor, N. 2010. "The Role of the Rule of Law in Virtual Communities." *Berkeley Technology Law Journal* 25 (4): 1818–86.

Taormino, T. 2006. "The Danger of Protecting Our Children: Government Porn Regulation Threatens Alternative Representations and Doesn't Save Kids." *Yale Journal of Law and Feminism* 18:277–81.

Taormino, T., C. Penley, C. P. Shimizu, and M. Miller-Young. 2013. *The Feminist Porn Book: The Politics of Producing Pleasure.* New York: Feminist Press.

Tarrant, S. 2016. *The Pornography Industry: What Everyone Needs to Know.* New York: Oxford University Press.

Taylor, A. 2014. *The People's Platform: Taking Back Power and Culture in the Digital Age.* New York: Metropolitan.

Taylor, P. L. 2005. "In the Market but Not of It: Fair Trade Coffee and Forest Stewardship Council Certification as Market-Based Social Change." *World Development* 33 (1): 129–47.

Tedmanson, D., and D. Wadiwel. 2010. "Neoptolemus: The Governmentality of New Race/Pleasure Wars?" *Culture and Organization* 16 (1): 7–22.

Theorizing the Web. 2014. "Sex Work and the Web." https://www.youtube.com/watch?v=YzJnLCKw93c.

Thompson, J. D. 2015. "Invisible and Everywhere: Heterosexuality in Anti-pornography Feminism." *Sexualities* 18 (5/6): 750–64.

Thorneycroft, R. 2020. "If Not a Fist, Then What about a Stump? Ableism and Heteronormativity within Australia's Porn Regulations." *Porn Studies* 7 (2): 162–67.

Tiidenberg, K., and E. van der Nagel. 2020. *Sex and Social Media.* Leeds, UK: Emerald.

Tronto, J. C. 1993. *Moral Boundaries: A Political Argument for an Ethic of Care.* New York: Routledge.

United Nations General Assembly. 2021. *Report of the Special Rapporteur on the Promotion and Protection of the Right to Freedom of Opinion and Expression. Seventy-Sixth Session.*

van der Nagel, E. 2013. "Faceless Bodies: Negotiating Technological and Cultural Codes on Reddit Gonewild." *Scan: Journal of Media Arts Culture* 10 (2): 1–10.

van der Nagel, E. 2021. "Competing Platform Imaginaries of NSFW Content Creation on OnlyFans." *Porn Studies* 8 (4): 394–410.

Van Doorn, N. 2010. "Keeping It Real: User-Generated Pornography, Gender Reification, and Visual Pleasure." *Convergence* 16 (4): 411–30.

Vanting, G. 2014. "Manufacturing Realness." Presented at the Second Annual Feminist Porn Conference, University of Toronto, April 5–6.

Vanting, G. 2015a. "On Casting the Rainbow." POV Paper 2: Quarterly Mindfuck. http://essence.sgv.ch/project/pov-paper-quarterly-mindfuck.

Vanting, G. 2015b. "On Coming In." In Coming Out Like a Porn Star: Essays on Pornography, Protection, and Privacy. Berkeley, CA: ThreeL Media.

Vörös, F. 2015. "Troubling Complicity: Audience Ethnography, Male Porn Viewers and Feminist Critique." Porn Studies 2 (2–3): 137–49.

Voss, G. 2015. Stigma and the Shaping of the Pornography Industry. London: Routledge.

Wadiwel, D. 2009. "Sex and Lubricative Ethic." In The Ashgate Research Companion to Queer Theory, edited by N. Giffney and M. O'Rourke, 491–506. London: Routledge.

Walker, L. M. 1993. "How to Recognize a Lesbian: The Cultural Politics of Looking Like What You Are." Signs: Journal of Women in Culture and Society 18 (4): 866–90.

Walter, N. 2011. Living Dolls: The Return of Sexism. London: Virago.

Warner, M., ed. 1993. Fear of a Queer Planet: Queer Politics and Social Theory. Minneapolis: University of Minnesota Press.

Warner, M. 2000. The Trouble with Normal: Sex, Politics, and the Ethics of Queer Life. Cambridge, MA: Harvard University Press.

Way, M. 2015. "Fuck Your Feminist Porn." Tits and Sass, September 18. https://titsandsass.com/fuck-your-feminist-porn.

Webber, V. 2022. "The Impact of Mastercard's Adult Content Policy on Adult Content Creators: Survey Results and Analysis." February 9. https://www.academia.edu/70941554/The_Impact_of_Mastercards_Adult_Content_Policy_on_Adult_Content_Creators.

Webber, V., and R. Sullivan. 2018. "Constructing a Crisis: Porn Panics and Public Health." Porn Studies 5 (2): 192–96.

Weiss, M. 2011. Techniques of Pleasure: BDSM and the Circuits of Sexuality. Durham, NC: Duke University Press.

Weitzer, R. 2011. "Review Essay: Pornography's Effects: The Need for Solid Evidence: A Review Essay of Everyday Pornography, edited by Karen Boyle (New York: Routledge, 2010) and Pornland: How Porn Has Hijacked Our Sexuality, by Gail Dines (Boston: Beacon, 2010)." Violence against Women 17 (5): 666–75.

Wilkinson, E. 2017. "The Diverse Economies of Online Pornography: From Paranoid Readings to Post-capitalist Futures." Sexualities 20 (8): 981–98.

Williams, L. (1989) 1999. Hard Core: Power, Pleasure, and the "Frenzy of the Visible." Berkeley: University of California Press.

Williams, L., ed. 2004a. Porn Studies. Durham, NC: Duke University Press.

Williams, L. 2004b. "Second Thoughts on Hard Core: American Obscenity Law and the Scapegoating of Deviance." In More Dirty Looks: Gender, Pornography and Power, edited by P. C. Church, 165–75. London: British Film Institute.

Williams, Z. 2014. "Is There Such a Thing as Ethical Porn?" Guardian, November 1. https://www.theguardian.com/culture/2014/nov/01/ethical-porn-fair-trade-sex.

Witt, A., N. Suzor, and A. Huggins. 2019. "The Rule of Law on Instagram: An Evaluation of the Moderation of Images Depicting Women's Bodies." University of New South Wales Law Journal 42 (2): 557–96.

Wurster, J. D. 2012. "The Logics of Good Exposure: Empowerment, Whore Stigma, and Free Labor in SuicideGirls' Social Network Porn." PhD diss., McGill University.

Young, M. 2014a. "Authenticity and Its Role within Feminist Pornography." *Porn Studies* 1 (1–2): 186–88.

Young, M. 2014b. "Reel Love: Navigating Relationships On Camera and Off—Challenges, Failures and Successes in Documenting Your Sex Life." Presentation at the Second Annual Feminist Porn Conference, University of Toronto, April 5–6.

Young, M. 2016. DIY *Porn Handbook: A How-to Guide to Documenting Our Own Sexual Revolution.* Emeryville, CA: Greenery.

Zecca, F. 2014. "Porn Sweet Home: A Survey of Amateur Pornography." In *Porn after Porn: Contemporary Alternative Pornographies*, edited by E. Biasin, G. Maina, and F. Zecca, 321–38. Milan: Mimesis International.

Zeischegg, C. (aka Danny Wylde). 2018. *Body to Job.* Los Angeles: Rare Bird Books.

Index

ButchBoi.com, 43
Butler, Judith, 163–64

California Senate, 94
camming, 33, 36, 50, 135–36, 144, 199, 239–40, 253, 263
Canadian Supreme Court, 102, 227
capitalism, 7, 34, 17–18, 109, 150–51, 175, 194, 201, 203, 216, 243; and big tech, 153; and Black feminist ethics of care, 72, 265; and consent, 264; and DIY culture, 44, 179–80; and emotional labor, 176; extractive, 255; and fast porn, 9; and indie porn, 12–13, 53, 56–57, 269, 271, 273; platform, 129; and Pornhub, 123–24; and porn marketing, 145–46; and porn stigma, 242; racial, 14, 128, 273. *See also* anti-capitalism; neoliberalism
Carlson, Bronwyn, 164
Cat O'Nine Tails, 82, 104, 130, 132, 150, 221, 225–26; Shot with Desire, 47, 74
censorship, 2, 103–4, 107–8, 146, 152, 235, 257; anti-censorship campaigns, 58; and feminism, 17; Freedom of Speech Legislation Amendment (Censorship) Bill, 118; gendered, 138, 141–43; and health promotion, 59; online, 244, 251–52; racist/fatphobic, 134; self-censorship, 91–92, 115, 128, 143. *See also* classification; content removal; indecency; obscenity law; refused classification (RC) status
Centeno, Antonio: *Yes, We Fuck!*, 4, 60
charmed circle, 221
Chen, Lena: OnlyBans, 252, 254
child protection legislation, 80, 248
child sexual abuse material (CSAM), 80, 99, 109, 201, 247
chronic illness, 20, 35. *See also* disability
ciscentrism, 50, 95, 127
cisnormativity, 19–20, 62, 136, 138
cissexism, 20, 50, 236
classification, 14, 17, 22–24, 111, 140–41, 188, 215, 221, 235–36, 240, 267–68, 273; and age, 115, 250; and category blurring, 55, 62; criminalizing porn, 10, 15; on digital platforms, 127, 138, 244–47, 259; genre differentiation, 98; inconsistencies in, 106, 137; and legal reform, 118–19; and nudity policies, 11, 244–47; and preemptive editing, 91–92,

142; and risk, 7, 21, 242; sexual norms in, 2, 96–97, 102–3, 109, 121, 138, 229; unclassified content, 5, 93, 113–14, 230. *See also* Australian Classification Board; censorship; Non Violent Erotica (NVE) category; refused classification (RC) status
clip sites, 10–11, 32, 36, 44, 132, 136
coalitional strategies, 153, 243, 258–59, 265, 272–74
Coding Rights, 254
Cohen, Darryl, 114
collective ownership, 21, 56–58, 265
colonialism/imperialism, 9, 17, 101, 141, 164, 198, 200, 226, 242, 245, 247, 263, 273
Comella, Lynn, 190
coming in, 212
coming out, 211–12
Communications Decency Act (1934, US), Section 230, 146
community porn, 24, 39, 265
community standards, 11, 99, 102–4, 119–22, 128, 138–39, 201, 255, 267, 270
compliance, 70, 83–86, 122, 136, 231, 240, 269; costs of, 115–16
Comstock Act (1873, US), 101
condoms, 32, 69–70, 75–76, 91, 94, 220–21, 261, 274. *See also* Measure B (2012, Los Angeles, CA)
consent, 141, 111–12, 136, 165, 177, 247, 249, 251, 262, 264, 270; classification of, 141–42; consent cultures, 9, 68, 73–75; and good porn, 215, 220–21; in indie porn, 58, 61–62, 68, 70, 73–75, 78, 80, 84–85, 120, 187, 188, 196, 201
Consent Labs, 142
content moderation, 21, 24, 221, 267, 273; automated, 141; failures of, 138–41, 151–52, 244, 252; retro moderating, 82–83. *See also* flagging (on digital platforms)
content removal, 138–41, 249; preemptive, 33, 91, 142–43
contracts, 39–40, 68–69, 73, 78, 85, 124, 150, 179, 204, 215, 219, 235, 241. *See also* model releases; 2257 Form
Coombes, Emily, 243
co-optation, 13, 16, 40, 124, 129, 195, 236, 254, 269, 271
copyright, 31, 81, 123, 191, 241, 264, 269

feminist ethics of care, 71, 79, 82–83, 85, 220, 270

feminist porn, 2–3, 8, 25, 32, 39, 51, 103, 212, 266, 269; archiving of, 48, 78; authenticity in, 160, 163, 164, 166–67, 171–72, 175, 177; challenges of, 46, 117, 119, 131, 136, 143, 179–80; and consumer vs. performer values, 196; and ethical porn, 185, 187, 189, 192–98, 204, 208, 232; and good porn, 219, 221–22, 224–27; history of, 8, 42–43; production politics of, 51, 73, 120–21, 124–26, 129, 214, 270; trans women in, 19, 22

Feminist Porn Awards, 1–2, 41, 53

Feminist Porn Conference, 2, 162

Femme Productions, 8

femmes, 1, 20, 25, 37, 63, 86, 161, 256

fetishism, 3, 38, 81, 91, 93, 95, 104–5, 108–12, 144, 118, 121, 135, 214, 229–30, 267. See also kink

fetishization: of disability, 20, 223; of race, 37, 199

fetish porn, 3, 93, 132

Filmhuis Cavia, 5

financial discrimination, 130–34, 252

First Nations Peoples, 273. See also Aboriginal Peoples; Indigenous Peoples

fisting, 3, 120, 195, 267; pleasures of, 63–66, 105, 110–11, 122, 175; prohibitions on, 11, 93, 95, 104, 109, 153

flagging (on digital platforms), 11, 78, 134, 136, 138, 141–42, 240, 244, 252

flagging (queer hanky code), 3

Flew, Terry, 118–20, 135

Flinders University, 24; Eros Foundation archives, 24, 92

Flores, April, 1; Voluptuous Cyberskin Pussy, 191

Flux, Niko: E-Viction, 253, 257, 258

Flynn, Michelle, 45, 54, 72–73, 81, 83, 142

Foldes, Livia, 245; NSFW Venus, 246, 247

Food Not Bombs, 207

Ford, Accadia, 106

Foucault, Michel, 96, 163, 175

Four Chambered Heart, A, 191

Foxxx, Ana, 55

freedom of speech, 101, 117, 146, 271

Freedom of Speech Legislation Amendment (Censorship) Bill, 118

free porn, 11, 13, 18, 44, 107, 123, 126, 128, 130, 133, 176, 193, 268

Free Speech Coalition, 80; INSPIRE program, 71; Performer Availability Screening Service (PASS), 75–76

Frey, Aven, 46–47, 197, 197. See also Sensate Films

Frith, Hannah, 174

Fuck for Forests, 43, 185

Fuck Me in the Ass 'Cause I Love Jesus, 3

fundraising, 14, 43, 57–58, 132, 136, 185, 238, 259, 273

Furry Girl, 43, 135

Fury, Sybil: E-Viction, 253, 257, 258

Gadigal Country, 1, 157

Gallant, Chanelle, 53

Gallop, Cindy: Make Love Not Porn, 121, 167, 251

Gamson, Joshua, 180

Garcia, Gabriella, 243, 248, 254

Garnellen, KAy, 64

gay and lesbian liberation movements, 72; rights movements, 216, 233

gay for pay performances, 163

gay porn, 3, 18, 42–43, 48, 59, 147

Gay USA, 42

GayVN, 133

Gebru, Tinmit, 250

generative content, 97, 191, 264

gentrification, 5, 11, 25, 107, 148–51, 189

Gerrard, Ysabel, 152

gig economy, 10, 12, 24, 40, 44, 150–51, 161, 178

Gillespie, Tarleton, 140–41

GitHub, 246, 247

Glitta Supernova, 225. See also Gurlesque

gloves, 61, 64, 76, 91

G Media, 68–69, 114, 130, 193

Goddess Ixchel, 75

golden era of porn, 2, 35, 43, 217

golden showers, 32, 91, 93, 104–5, 109–10, 116, 267

good porn, 13–14, 21, 167, 209, 213–36

Google, 11, 79, 129, 184, 195, 247–49, 257; Cloud Vision, 245; Google Drive, 147; Google Play, 147; Safe Search, 244

Graeber, David, 35

Grandmothers against Removals, 58

stigma, 7, 10, 13, 24, 206, 223, 233, 235, 249, 252, 267; HIV, 111, 228; and methodology of book, 23–24; porn, 68, 74, 79, 85, 125, 150, 167, 175, 192, 202, 211–12, 214–20, 231, 242, 264, 269–72; preventing labor organizing, 41; queer, 120; sex work, 16, 84, 236, 243–44, 254, 259, 268. See also destigmatization; slut shaming; whorephobia

Stop Enabling Sex Traffickers Act (SESTA)/ Allow States and Victims to Fight Online Sex Trafficking Act (FOSTA) (HR 1865, 2018, US), 146–48, 255, 257

Strano, Jack, 43

stunt sex, 181

Stüttgen, Tim, 183

Su, May Ling: OnMyPeriod.com, 135

subscription intimacy, 18

SuicideGirls, 37, 144, 157–59, 168, 179, 223

Sullivan, Corrinne, 37

Sullivan, Rebecca, 199

Sundahl, Deborah, 42–43, 63

Survivors Against SESTA, 147

Suzor, Nicolas, 143

Swan, Robbie, 69, 114, 229–30

Swedish Film Institute, 121

Switter, 255–57

Syjuco, Stephanie, 247

tagging, 11, 50, 195–96, 198, 227, 249, 270

Taormino, Tristan, 8, 63, 80, 187, 219

taste performances, 171

Taylor, Astra, 129

tech companies, 11, 40, 129, 148, 152–53, 199, 242, 244, 253, 260, 273. See also big tech; and individual companies

techno-utopianism, 20, 127, 129

Thornham, Helen, 152, 248

Tilde, the Melbourne Trans and Gender Diverse Film Festival, 23, 50

Tits and Sass, 172

tokenism, 223

Toytool Committee, "Support Your Local Pornographers" campaign, 3, 41, 42, 269

trade relationships, 197–200, 203, 205

trafficking, 99, 132, 146, 148, 202–3, 233, 242, 247–48, 257

Trans Lifeline, 8, 105

trans men, 22, 42, 58

trans people, 19, 22, 58; censorship of, 137–38; as performers, 12, 18, 20, 42–43, 45, 50, 53, 58, 174, 223, 226; as site owners, 22

transphobia, 131, 139, 153, 170, 201, 219, 223, 236, 274

trans porn, 3, 18, 20, 37, 43, 53, 59, 93, 106, 223, 274

trans women, 19, 50, 57, 170, 174, 226

Trash, Luna, 69, 79, 231, 233; Trash Dolls, 37, 82; Trash Vixens, 130, 144

Treasure Island Media, 48; Teenage Truvada Whore, 111; Viral Loads, 111

treatment as prevention (TASP), 75

Trouble, Courtney, 1, 43, 219; Indie Porn Revolution, 8, 31, 43, 194; Lesbian Curves, 46

tube sites, 13, 32, 73, 128, 130, 132, 145, 205, 235, 248; diversity washing by, 123–25; and ethical porn, 201; impact on porn revenue, 44; pirating content, 11, 123, 133, 268, 269; regulation on, 136; tagging on, 196. See also individual sites

Tumblr, 97, 151–52; nudity policy, 137

Twitter/X, 126, 136–38, 151, 208, 211, 248, 255–56

2257 Form, 80, 201, 216

Uber, 18, 40, 180

US Congress, 148

US Department of Homeland Security, 78

user-generated porn, 10, 38, 127–29, 145–46

US Supreme Court, 101, 140

US v. Stagliano (2010), 15

van der Nagel, Emily, 144

Van Meter, Kevin, 207

Vanniall, 165

Vanting, Gala, 5, 46, 56, 58, 116–17, 119–20, 143, 150; on authenticity, 168, 173–74, 182; Chrysalis, 4; on classification categories, 55; on diversity, 222; on documentary porn, 47; on ethical porn, 193, 198, 203–4, 206; Gonzo, 60; privacy protection work, 80; production ethics of, 51, 53, 58, 72, 76, 79; on representing diverse sexual practices, 104–5; sex education work, 63, 65, 66; on slow porn, 197; on stigma, 211–12. See also Sensate Films

Varon, Joana, 254